In Good Faith:

the UK's Constitution, Governments and Parliaments

In Good Faith:

the UK's Constitution, Governments and Parliaments

by Paul Grant

© Paul Grant

paul@grant5.co.uk

Any content in this book that originally appeared in 'Understanding British Government', written by Paul Grant and Christopher Jary, and published by the National School of Government (NSG) 2008-2011, was released from Crown Copyright upon the closure of the NSG in March 2012.

Contents

Preface 1

1. The British Constitution 5

2. The Prime Minister and Cabinet 87

3. Ministers, Civil Servants and Departments 137

4. The House of Commons 155

5. The House of Lords 191

6. The Functions of Parliament 219

7. The 2017-19 Parliament 293

8. Devolution 307

Concluding Thoughts 333

About the Author 343

Preface

So much has happened in British government and politics since 2008 when my former colleague and good friend Christopher Jary and I wrote the first edition of a book entitled 'Understanding British Government' on which this book draws. The UK has left the European Union. It has also experienced a period of coalition government (a rarity in peacetime) and a period of minority government. And now, in the aftermath of Brexit and during the Covid pandemic, the very future of the United Kingdom seems to be in question. I am old enough to remember many of the key political events of the 1960s, such as the devaluation of sterling in 1967. This was an event of huge political significance but I'm not sure that it, or any subsequent event in British government and politics, had quite the seismic impact of the Brexit referendum result of June 2016. That result led to the most turbulent years in living memory as far as the British body politic is concerned, with two more Conservative Prime Ministers having to resign over 'Europe'. Events in the House of Commons between the 2017 and 2019 general elections were like nothing that had been seen for decades. The 1974-79 period perhaps comes the closest - and some of the events of that period are referenced in this book – but in my view, for sheer drama, they fall short of those of 2017-2019.

Although the British system of government has often frustrated me more than it has impressed, I would accept that during the majority of my lifetime it has essentially worked, often almost in spite of itself. Whether this is still the case though is, in my view, a matter for debate. As we shall see in the coming chapters, having a system of government that operates without any proper written rulebook relies on those working within it to behave as what Lord (Professor Peter) Hennessy describes as 'good chaps' (of both sexes). Peter is someone who is quoted on a number of occasions in this book. This is not only because he is, in my view, the foremost expert on the British Constitution but also because it's him, more than anyone, who inspired me to take a greater interest in how the United Kingdom is governed. For many years he would appear as a guest speaker on my 'Parliament, Government and the Civil Service' training course which I ran at the Civil Service College (later the National School of Government) for new graduate entrants to the Civil Service Fast Stream. It was not just his knowledge that so impressed me, but also his method of delivery, with humour a regular feature of his talks. So I was very fortunate to hear him speak on many occasions in the 1990s.

During the 25 years that I worked as a civil servant, the key people in government did, in my view, largely play by the rules, whether those rules were written or unwritten. In other words, they usually behaved like 'good chaps'. Whatever my personal views, I was comfortable as a civil servant working for the British Government whether it was being led by Margaret Thatcher, John Major, Tony Blair, Gordon Brown or David Cameron. (I left the Civil Service before Theresa May became Prime Minister.) Recent events, however, might have made working as a civil servant rather more difficult for me. This reliance on the Prime Minister and other senior political figures behaving properly has been considerably tested recently, I believe, and when Peter Hennessy himself expresses concerns about whether those currently in power are behaving like 'good chaps', I begin to worry. This is something to which I will return in my closing remarks at the end of the book.

Preface

What prompted Christopher Jary and me to write 'Understanding British Government' was that, with around 50 years' experience between us of working in the British Civil Service, much of it spent teaching our fellow civil servants about how the system works, we felt that an account by two insiders might be of interest. As it's now over nine years since I left the Civil Service, this book is not an insider's view. That may have its disadvantages, but I am pleased that it has removed some of the constraints imposed on me when I was writing as a civil servant. So this book doesn't offer the view of someone currently working in government. What it might do however is, I hope, provide an interesting and rather more detached view of the way the British system of government operates, for good and for bad.

Some of Christopher's contributions to 'Understanding British Government' are reflected in this book and appear with his permission. However, the book offers my perspective alone and any views and errors contained in it should be attributed solely to me.

Paul Grant
September 2021

1

The British Constitution

Put yourself in the shoes of a newly-elected Prime Minister. During a rare quiet moment in your first few hours in Downing Street you might stop for a moment and think: 'So what now? Here I am as the new head of the British Government but what do I actually have the power to do?' Like anyone who has just been appointed the boss of a big organisation, the new Prime Minister will want to understand the rules of the game. Where does the power in this organisation really lie? What are the constraints on my power as the boss? What sort of relationship do I have with other very senior people? What scope do those who work for me or to whom I am accountable have to make my life difficult? If you thought that someone was going to give you a ready-made handbook that answers these questions, you'd be sorely disappointed.

In other countries the British Prime Minister's counterpart – the American President, the German Chancellor or the French President – would be able to find out the answers to these questions in a relatively straightforward way. Each of these countries has a 'rule book', that is, a written 'codified' constitution that sets out how the system of government operates, how the various institutions of government interact with each other and the rights and responsibilities of its citizens. And a new Head of Government in these countries will also have an army of lawyers to advise them what these rules mean in practice.

This is not how things work in the United Kingdom. There is no single document that can be described as the 'British Constitution'.[1] Some might question whether Britain has a constitution at all or, if it does, that it's not worth the paper it's not written on, as some might say. But this is to misunderstand the nature of the British Constitution. It is wrong to think either that there is no British Constitution or that it is wholly unwritten. Although one can't buy a copy of the British Constitution in a bookshop or download it from the internet, that doesn't mean that it doesn't exist. A considerable proportion of Britain's constitutional arrangements are in fact written down - most often (although not always) in the form of Acts of Parliament. Below we discuss some of the more important features of the British Constitution that are formally written down.

The Written Constitution

The precise proportion of the British Constitution that is written down is impossible to calculate because there will always be varying definitions as to what forms part of the constitution and what doesn't. Some aspects of the written constitution go back hundreds of years, two particularly important parts of which are Magna Carta and the Bill of Rights.

Magna Carta

For many centuries after its signing in 1215, Magna Carta was regarded as the oldest part of the written constitution.[2] Indeed, those parts of it that are still in existence continue to be regarded as such.[3] It was constitutional for two reasons: first because it defined the Monarch's relationship with an institution which over the following centuries developed into

---

[1] Israel and New Zealand are the two other countries in the world that, like the UK, do not have formal codified constitutions.

[2] Technically Magna Carta was part of the English, rather than the British, Constitution.

[3] These are the paragraphs concerning the freedom of the English Church, the "ancient liberties" of the City of London and the right to due process.

what we would now recognise as Parliament, and, second, because it set down some fundamental rights of some, if not all, of the Monarch's subjects. Paragraph 12, for example, gave 'Parliament' the right to agree or not to any new taxes:

> No scutage nor aid shall be imposed in our kingdom, unless by the common council of our kingdom.

Habeas Corpus – the right not to be held without trial – appears at paragraphs 39 and 40:

> No freeman shall be seized, or imprisoned, or dispossessed, or outlawed, or in any way destroyed; nor will we condemn him, nor will we commit him to prison, excepting by the legal judgment of his peers, or by the laws of the land. To none will we sell, to none will we deny, to none will we delay right or justice.

Although most of Magna Carta has been superseded by subsequent legislation,[4] many of the basic principles set out in it, such as the two mentioned above, are part of modern British law. They are also reflected in the constitutions of many other countries.

The Bill of Rights

The Bill of Rights, passed in the late 17th century, also defines the relationship between Monarch and Parliament and is another cornerstone of written constitutional law. The Bill of Rights was the 'deal' agreed between the English Parliament and William of Orange and his wife Mary that allowed them to accede to the English throne. Placing certain restrictions on the power of the Monarchy, it effectively ended the concept of the 'divine right of kings'. In particular the Bill of Rights states:

> That the pretended power of suspending the laws or the

---

[4] In particular by the Statute Law Revision Act of 1863

> *execution of laws by regal authority without consent of Parliament is illegal....*
>
> *That levying money for or to the use of the Crown by pretence of prerogative, without grant of Parliament...is illegal....*
>
> *That the raising or keeping a standing army within the kingdom in time of peace, unless it be with consent of Parliament, is against law....*
>
> *That the freedom of speech and debates or proceedings in Parliament ought not to be impeached or questioned in any court or place out of Parliament.*

Magna Carta and the Bill of Rights are not dust-covered ancient documents with no relevance to 21st century Britain; they are still relevant to the governance of the country today. The last of these extracts from the Bill of Rights concerns the principle of parliamentary privilege. Although the meaning of 'impeach' is not clear – it could perhaps mean hinder, challenge or censure – this article is taken to mean that nothing said or done in Parliament can be used in a court of law. This includes anything said in parliamentary committees, not just by parliamentarians but also by members of the public who may be appearing as witnesses. When, in March 2010, four parliamentarians were charged with offences under the Theft Act, they attempted to use this principle to demand that their case be heard in Parliament rather than in a normal court of law.[5] This principle of parliamentary privilege allows comments to be made in Parliament without fear of prosecution. This was relevant in 2011 when the Liberal Democrat MP John Hemmings used the cover of parliamentary privilege to raise the issue of the super-injunction granted to the footballer Ryan Giggs regarding media reports about his private life. Hemmings faced some criticism for using this ancient principle in this way but there is no doubt that it protected him

---

[5] Although the parliamentarians' case was rejected by the Supreme Court in November 2010, parliamentary privilege was once again an issue when Denis MacShane was forced to step down as an MP in November 2012. (See www.bbc.co.uk/news/uk-politics-20196877)

from any action in the courts.[6]

More recently, in March 2021 David Davis MP invoked parliamentary privilege when speaking in the Commons about what might be described as the 'Alex Salmond Affair'. In his speech he specifically mentioned how:

> *Scottish parliamentarians were not given the same powers and privileges that Members of this House enjoy. That means that evidence relevant to the Holyrood inquiry can be freely discussed here today using parliamentary privilege, but if an MSP in Holyrood were to do the same, they would likely find themselves facing down prosecution.* [7]

Davis was making an interesting point about a key difference between the Westminster and Scottish Parliaments, something that we explore further in the chapter on devolution.

A final example of the use of parliamentary privilege occurred in July 2021 when the SDLP MP, Colom Eastwood, used it to name a British soldier who was facing two murder charges relating to the events of 'Bloody Sunday' in Derry in 1972. Eastwood named the soldier, despite the latter having been granted anonymity by the judge who was hearing the case.[8] Eastwood received some criticism for this but he was given a degree of support for his action by the Speaker, Sir Lindsay

---

[6] In particular, Speaker Bercow rebuked John Hemmings in the following terms: "Let me just say to the honourable gentleman, I know he's already done it, but occasions such as this are occasions for raising the issues of principle involved, not seeking to flout orders for whatever purpose." https://publications.parliament.uk/pa/cm201011/cmhansrd/cm110523/debtext/110523-0001.htm

[7] https://hansard.parliament.uk/Commons/2021-03-16/debates/03E5E1D7-13F3-4AB3-85F2-214EA9179324/ScotlandAct1998ScottishCivilService An MSP is a 'Member of the Scottish Parliament'. For more on this and other aspects of devolved government in the UK, see chapter 8.

[8] https://hansard.parliament.uk/Commons/2021-07-13/debates/CDF9AFDF-4BFA-4FA1-8481-B68CAF2DDB5F/ArmedForcesBill

Hoyle, who said:

> *A Member may state whatever they think fit in debate and...the member is protected by parliamentary privilege from any action for defamation, as well as from any other question or molestation. This freedom extends to statements which, if made out of Parliament, would breach injunctions....*
>
> *Freedom of speech must, however, be used responsibly. It is a grave step to use privilege to breach a court order. As the Joint Committee on Privacy and Injunctions made clear: 'privilege places a significant responsibility on parliamentarians to exercise it in the public interest. The presumption should be that court orders are respected in Parliament and that when a Member does not comply with one he or she can demonstrate that it is in the public interest.' It is for others to judge whether the action of the hon. Member for Foyle (Colum Eastwood) was indeed in the public interest. However, the hon. Member broke no rules of order....*[9]

The Parliament Acts

In 1911 and 1949, two Acts of Parliament were passed which redefined the balance of power within Parliament between the House of Lords and the House of Commons. These are the 'Parliament Acts' and they form another important part of the written British Constitution. Since a resolution of 1671 which stated "that in all aids given to the King by the Commons, the rate of tax ought not to be altered by the Lords" and a further resolution of 1678 which restated

---

[9] https://hansard.parliament.uk/Commons/2021-07-14/debates/DAD888A0-ED03-4052-8C36-AB90644BAB8B/LegacyOfNorthernIreland%E2%80%99SPast. In the first paragraph of Sir Lindsay's words he is quoting from 'Erskine May'. This is the so-called 'Bible of Parliament' which is discussed further in the section on Constitutional Reform below.

the "undoubted and sole right of the Commons" to deal with all bills of "aids and supplies", the Lords had traditionally recognised the supremacy of the Commons in financial matters. (This is the principle of 'financial privilege' which is discussed further in the section on legislation in chapter six.) In 1909, however, the Lords refused to pass Liberal Chancellor Lloyd-George's 'People's Budget'. The resulting constitutional crisis was resolved only after two general elections were fought on the issue. The Lords, faced with the threat of the creation of a large number of Liberal peers, were forced to pass the 1911 Parliament Act, restricting their power in two ways.

First, their powers over 'money bills' (i.e. legislation that exclusively concerns the raising or spending of money) were removed. Since 1911, any bill deemed by the Speaker of the House of Commons to be a money bill cannot be rejected or amended by the Lords or even delayed for more than a month.[10] (One might assume that annual Finance Bills, which follow the Budget, are money bills. In fact, because the scope of Finance Bills usually extends some way beyond purely financial matters, they often aren't. However, legislation like Finance Bills and Consolidated Fund Bills which, respectively, concern the raising of taxation and the spending of public money, do fall within the scope of the principle of financial privilege. It can therefore be expected that such bills will not be rejected or amended by the Lords.)

Second, if the Lords rejected legislation that wasn't a money bill three times over a period of two years, the Commons could use the powers set out in the 1911 Act to override the Lords' veto. In 1949 a second Parliament Act was passed to reduce this to two rejections over a period of

---

[10] Strictly speaking the Lords can make amendments to money bills. What's important is that if Commons don't accept those amendments then after a month the bill can be sent to the Queen for Royal Assent. Thus money bills have occasionally been amended in the Lords with the amendments agreed by the Commons.

one year. Interestingly the 1911 Act had to be invoked to overcome the Lords' opposition to the 1949 legislation. Since 1949 this has in practice meant that, if the Lords reject a bill that has been passed by the Commons in any particular year and do the same again the following year, then the Commons can invoke the terms of the Parliament Acts to override the Lords and send the bill to the Monarch for Royal Assent.[11] There is one exception to the otherwise universal rule that the Commons ultimately can override the Lords on any matter using the Parliament Acts: the extension of a Parliament beyond the maximum of five years. The last time this was relevant was in 1940 when the Lords gave their consent, because of wartime circumstances, to suspending the election that was due in that year. Interestingly though, the Fixed-term Parliaments Bill (see below), which became an act in September 2011, would also have been subject to the absolute veto of the Lords since it contained a clause allowing the Prime Minister, by order, to delay the date of a general election for up to two months beyond the five year maximum.[12]

In most other countries, information on the balance of power between the two Houses of Parliament, for example the National Assembly and Senate in France, the Bundestag and Bundesrat in Germany or the House of Representatives and Senate in America, can be found in that country's constitution. In the UK however it is found in a couple of relatively simple Acts of Parliament: the Parliament Acts of 1911 and 1949.[13]

---

[11] The bill in year two must be exactly the same as the previous year's bill, except for any Lords' amendments from year one which the Commons have accepted. There must also have been a 12 month period between the second reading of the bill in the Commons in year one and its third reading in year two. The bill must also be presented to the Lords in year two at least one month before the end of the parliamentary session.

[12] Fixed-term Parliaments Act 2011 Section 1(5):
www.legislation.gov.uk/ukpga/2011/14/section/1/enacted

[13] For more information of how an Act of Parliament is made, see the section on Legislation in Chapter 6.

Given the frequent disagreements between the two Houses of Parliament (especially during more radical Labour governments) one might think that the Parliament Acts would have been used frequently since 1911, but this is not the case. Since 1911 the Parliament Acts have been used only seven times. One reason for their sparse use may be that simply to ignore the views of the House of Lords, which invoking the act implies, is a constitutional 'nuclear option'. More pressing though is the wish of any government not to have to go through the process of putting a bill through Parliament twice (or three times prior to 1949) before the Parliament Acts can be invoked. One of the main constraints on any government is the lack of legislative time in Parliament. There is therefore pressure on all governments to do deals with the Lords rather than resort to the Parliament Acts. From time to time, however, the Parliament Acts *are* used. They were used most often – three times – by the Labour Governments after 1997. Most noteworthy was their use to bypass opposition in the Lords to the legislation banning fox hunting. The bill was never passed by the House of Lords. The Lords failed to agree it in 2003 and it was finally passed only when the government invoked the Parliament Acts the following year. This triple use of the Parliament Acts points up the difficult relationship these governments had with the House of Lords, which stemmed partly from the Lords' opposition to the governments' proposals for reforming their Lordships' House. (For more on this see chapter five.)

Other Parts of the Written Constitution

Other ancient constitutional acts concern the succession to the English throne (the Act of Settlement 1701), the union between England and Scotland (the Act of Union 1707) and the various acts that extended the right to vote. In 2011, the Heads of Government of the 16 countries where the Queen is the Head of State agreed that the rule of primogeniture, whereby male children of the Monarch take precedence over their female siblings in terms of inheriting the throne, should be ended. To give effect to this, a Succession to the Crown Act was passed by Westminster in

2013, followed by similar legislation in the other 15 countries of the realm. This act, which also removed the ban on the Monarch marrying a Roman Catholic (but not the ban on the Monarch him- or herself being a Roman Catholic) required both the Act of Settlement and the Bill of Rights, as well as the Acts of Union with Scotland and with Ireland, to be amended.

The years since 1997 have seen some major changes to Britain's constitutional arrangements. In particular we have seen:

- legislatures with substantial powers set up in Scotland, Wales and Northern Ireland with smaller amounts of power devolved to city-wide authorities in England
- the passing of the Human Rights Act, enshrining in British law the rights that are set out in the European Convention on Human Rights
- important changes to the separation of power between the executive, legislature and judiciary
- significant changes to the composition and functions of the House of Lords
- a move to fixed-term Parliaments at Westminster. (Expected to be reversed during the 2021-22 parliamentary session.)
- the UK's departure from the European Union

All of these changes have been made by Acts of Parliament which now form part of Britain's written constitution. Most of these are discussed in more detail later in this book.

The Unwritten Constitution

If there are two posts in British government whose job descriptions many people would like to see, they would probably be the Queen's and the Prime Minister's. Yet the powers that go with both offices flow almost entirely from precedent and convention. We will consider the powers and functions of the

Prime Minister later, but let's look first at the Head of State, the Queen.

The Monarch

In centuries gone by, as is generally understood, the British Monarch exercised real power. But in the 21st century the prevalent view is that, in a sophisticated modern democracy like that of the United Kingdom, the Queen can have very little power. Certainly, most of the powers once exercised by the Monarch are now exercised by ministers on her behalf and those ministers' powers in turn are often limited by what Acts of Parliament allow them to do. In 1834, William IV was able to sack his Prime Minister, Lord Melbourne, whereas today the idea of the Monarch removing the Head of Government would be unthinkable. (Even William's successor Queen Victoria was unable to dismiss her Prime Minister William Gladstone whom she detested.) But whilst it is correct that in 'normal' circumstances the Monarch nowadays exercises little power, circumstances aren't always normal and, even when they are, the Queen still exercises some functions that are central to the constitution. For example, she appoints the Prime Minister, prorogues and dissolves Parliament and gives Royal Assent to bills passed by Parliament. What is key though is whether she exercises any real power in doing so.

Appointing the Prime Minister

When a government is defeated at a general election, the incumbent Prime Minister normally tenders her resignation to the Queen the day after the election. A matter of minutes later, the leader of the party which now controls the majority of the seats in the House of Commons travels to Buckingham Palace to be invited by the Monarch to form a government. (If the party that wins the majority is the same as that which was in government prior to the election, there is no need for the incumbent Prime Minister to be invited by the Monarch to form a government – she just stays in office.) The process is usually very straightforward. In May 1997 it could not have been clearer which party had won the election nor who was its leader. There was therefore no doubt that the Queen would invite Tony Blair to become the new Prime Minister immediately following the resignation of John Major. This has been the usual pattern of British elections because the 'first past the post' electoral system usually disproportionately skews the result in favour of the winning party. Traditionally one party has therefore usually won a clear majority of the seats in the House of Commons (i.e. more seats than are won by all the other parties combined). But this is not always the case, as is apparent from the results of the general elections of May 2010 and June 2017. Of these two, the former is the more interesting as, not only did it lead to a change of government, the government that ensued was a coalition.

At the May 2010 election, the Conservative Party won the most seats in the House of Commons but they were without a majority. This was the first time since February 1974 that no single party had won a majority of the seats. So who should the Queen invite to form the government? In almost any other country, the constitution would set out the procedure to be followed in such circumstances by the Head of State. But in the UK this situation fell into the uncharted territory of the unwritten constitution.

According to convention, a Prime Minister and her government can remain in power after an inconclusive election result until Parliament reassembles after the election. The government would then put its programme before the Commons in the Queen's Speech. If the Commons voted down the government's programme, the government would then be obliged to resign.

In the case of the February 1974 hung Parliament, the incumbent Prime Minister Edward Heath remained as Prime Minister for a short time while he negotiated unsuccessfully with the Liberal leader Jeremy Thorpe to form a coalition government. There are a number of reasons why those negotiations ultimately failed. Particularly important was the fact that even if the seats the Liberals had won were added to those of the Conservatives, the coalition still wouldn't have had a majority in the Commons and could therefore have been thrown out of office almost as soon as it had taken power. (The Liberals had only won 14 seats despite gaining over six million votes.) Thorpe also faced the problem that many in his own party were against the idea of going into coalition with the Conservatives. Some suggest that a further problem was that one of Thorpe's demands was that he become Home Secretary in any coalition government. With any other Liberal leader, that might have been acceptable to Heath. But given that Heath, as Prime Minister, would probably by then have known about the shocking story that would soon engulf Jeremy Thorpe, forcing his resignation as party leader and leading to him being charged with conspiracy to murder, it would have been impossible to put Thorpe in that very sensitive ministerial position. Thus Heath's attempts to form a coalition failed and on the Monday after the election he tendered his resignation. The Queen then turned to Harold Wilson to form a government.

In May 2010 however, things took a little longer to be resolved.

Cabinet Manual

The process to be followed in the event of a hung Parliament wasn't, by the time of the 2010 election, quite as unwritten as it had been in 1974. Anticipating the possibility of such an election result, in the months running up to the 2010 election, senior officials in the Cabinet Office began to prepare for what should be done in the event of the election producing a hung Parliament. They looked at what happened in 1974, in particular drawing on the written record kept by the then Prime Minister's Principal Private Secretary Robert Armstrong, and they consulted constitutional experts. They role-played coalition negotiations, with senior officials playing the parts of senior politicians from the main parties. And, perhaps most importantly of all, they drew up some guidance concerning 'the dissolution and summoning of Parliament, parliamentary general elections, government formation, hung parliaments, restrictions on government and other activity during the electoral period'. Significantly this guidance for the first time formally authorised civil servants, in the event of a hung Parliament, to help not only the incumbent government with its coalition negotiations but the opposition parties too, subject to the approval of the Prime Minister. Thus senior civil servants were allowed to facilitate the discussions between the Conservative and Liberal Democrat parties which eventually led to the creation of the Coalition Government.

This guidance appeared prior to the 2010 election as a draft chapter on 'Elections and Government Formation' of a 'Cabinet Manual'. The whole manual itself was published the following year. The full version includes chapters on the following:[14]

- The Sovereign
- Elections and government formation
- The Executive – the Prime Minister, ministers and the structure of government
- Collective Cabinet decision-making
- The Executive and Parliament
- The Executive and the law
- Ministers and the Civil Service
- Relations with the Devolved Administrations and local government
- Relations with the European Union and other international institutions
- Government finance and expenditure
- Official information

This draft chapter was of particular constitutional interest as

---

[14] The Cabinet Manual
www.cabinetoffice.gov.uk/sites/default/files/resources/cabinet-manual.pdf

it offered, for the first time, official, written guidance to politicians and civil servants about what should happen in the event of a general election producing an unclear result. Paragraph 2.12 of the full document says:

> *Where an election does not result in an overall majority for a single party, the incumbent government remains in office unless and until the Prime Minister tenders his or her resignation and the government's resignation to the Sovereign. An incumbent government is entitled to wait until the new Parliament has met to see if it can command the confidence of the House of Commons, but is expected to resign if it becomes clear that it is unlikely to be able to command that confidence and there is a clear alternative.*

Thus for the first time the convention that an incumbent Prime Minister may remain in office while trying to form a government had been written down in a formal document, albeit one with no legal underpinning. This is important in terms of the role played by the Monarch in a hung Parliament. But the guidance offered by the Cabinet Manual still left some important questions unanswered. For example, the incumbent Prime Minister may be allowed to stay in office while trying to form a government, but what should the Queen do if the incumbent resigns? Is she obliged to accept her resignation, particularly if it's not clear who she should appoint in her place? And if, at the resignation audience, the outgoing Prime Minister advises the Queen who she should invite to form the next government (as Gordon Brown is presumed to have advised the Queen to appoint David Cameron as Prime Minister), is the Queen obliged to accept her advice?

And what if the party leader invited to form a new government felt unable to do so? By his own account David Cameron didn't feel quite ready to form a government when Gordon Brown went to Buckingham Palace on 11 May 2010 to resign.[15] This is a view confirmed by David Laws MP, a member of the Liberal Democrats' negotiating team, when he says in his book on the creation of the Coalition Government that

> *(David Cameron) arrived at (Buckingham Palace) just after 8pm, less than half an hour after Gordon Brown's departure....Mr Cameron accepted the offer from the Queen to establish a new government. But, as yet, neither he nor we could be sure that this government would be a coalition.*[16]

But what if Cameron had felt unable to form a government? Would the UK have then been without a government for a few days? For this reason, some have suggested that the Cabinet Manual ought to express clearly not only the right of an incumbent Prime Minister to remain in office in such circumstances but the duty to do so.[17] Had there been a clear expression of this duty in May 2010, Gordon Brown might have avoided some of the more lurid headlines in the tabloid newspapers in the days following the election, for example *The Sun's* "Squatter, 59, holed up in No 10"![18]

Another omission in the Cabinet Manual is the procedure to be adopted when a Prime Minister ceases office at a time other than at a general election i.e. through resignation or death. The former is not at all uncommon - Tony Blair, Margaret Thatcher, Harold Wilson, David Cameron and Theresa May are all examples. In each of these cases, the procedure was reasonably straightforward: the incumbent Prime Minister announced their

---

[15] Speaking on the BBC's 'Five Days That Changed Britain'. 29 July 2010.

[16] David Laws '22 Days in May' p.192 Biteback Publishing Ltd, 2010

[17] See for example the House of Lords Constitution Committee's 2014 report on 'The Constitutional Implications of Coalition Government, paragraph 31. http://www.publications.parliament.uk/pa/ld201314/ldselect/ldconst/130/13005.htm

[18] https://www.reddit.com/r/ukpolitics/comments/6gmzec/the_suns_headline_may_8th_2010_squatter_holed_up/

intention to resign as Prime Minister and leader of their party. This triggered an internal party election to choose a new leader who, once elected, was then appointed by the Queen to replace the outgoing Prime Minister.

Death in office might be rare (it hasn't actually happened since Lord Palmerston's death in 1865) but given how close Margaret Thatcher was to being assassinated in the Brighton bombing of 1984 and, perhaps, Boris Johnson to dying of Covid in April 2020, one might expect to find some reference to it in the manual. In most countries, the order of succession in the event of the Head of Government's death would be clear. In the USA it's known who is the 18th person in line to the Presidency. But in the UK we're not even clear who is the first in line. Robert Armstrong, who had become Cabinet Secretary by the time of the Brighton bombing, described the events of that night in evidence to the Lords Constitution Committee's inquiry into the Cabinet Manual. It makes interesting reading:

> *I was very much involved at the time of the bombing of the Grand Hotel. There was about half an hour in the middle of the night when news had come through about the bomb but I didn't know whether Mrs Thatcher was still alive until Lord (Robin) Butler rang me up at about half-past three to tell me. During that half hour, I thought rather hard about the situation and came to the conclusion that the Queen's Private Secretary, possibly aided and assisted by the Cabinet Secretary or someone else, would have consultations with leading members of the Cabinet, from which would emerge a recommendation to the Queen as to whom she should send for as an interim Prime Minister until a successor was elected. We can all speculate about who that might have been in 1984. One can see that two or three people might have been consulted.*[19]

Some might argue that the Cabinet Manual could have set out the procedure more clearly but that wasn't a view shared by Robert

---

[19] www.publications.parliament.uk/pa/ld201011/ldselect/ldconst/107/11020202.htm

Armstrong:

> *I don't think that it is for this document to do that, as I think that it goes beyond its range. For this document, the right stopping point is that the Prime Minister is expected not to resign until a successor can confidently be recommended.... In the case of the demise of a Prime Minister, you can't describe what happens....* [20]

The lack of any clear procedure to follow in the event of the death of a Prime Minister in office was again exposed when Boris Johnson was in intensive care suffering from Covid in April 2020. A BBC podcast first broadcast in March 2021 gives us an interesting insight as to how fearful those at the centre of government were that the Prime Minister might die and how unsure they were about what to do should that happen. On the podcast, the BBC's Political Editor Laura Kuenssberg and her producer Paul Twinn spoke as follows:

> LK: *There was a serious risk, and everyone knew it, that Boris Johnson was so sick he might die. That afternoon, that knowledge was shared by a tiny group of people inside No 10. Meetings with fewer than a dozen staff, the then Cabinet Secretary Mark Sedwill, Dominic Raab the Foreign Secretary, whose job it was to fill in, and only a few others. The Prime Minister's communications Chief Lee Cain, just out of his own self isolation, had made his way into Downing Street too. And there were genuine discussions about what would happen if the Prime Minister lost his life to the virus.*

> *The possibility that ministers might even gather in the Cabinet Room with the doors closed until they chose a successor was talked about, but there was no fixed protocol, and no conclusion was reached, I'm told. The Tory party had even started to consider how to transfer the leadership without a contest, fearing that the country would have thought 'we were venal' one said, if there were a competition after the Prime Minister's death. Cabinet ministers were*

---

[20] Ibid.

summoned urgently for a conference call. One said, 'all of a sudden we were asked to join, not knowing if he was alive'. Number 10 then prepared to make the news public. The Downing Street voice on the other end of the phone that night cracked with fear, as I was called to get to the Foreign Office as quickly as possible with a camera to talk to Dominic Raab, sent out to try to reassure the country. The feeling in the room, didn't feel very reassuring....

PT: *I think we've covered a lot of things over the last few years that felt like a big national moment, but this was just beyond actually, the idea that the prime minister could die. We'd never considered how we would cover that. We didn't know what the protocols were. We might know how to cover the death of a Monarch or members of the royal family but it's just unfathomable.*

LK: *And as we discovered there was no fixed protocol.... The country was spiralling into a crisis, and for a moment, could have lost its Prime Minister. And the government machine discovered there was no firm plan for what would have happened if he'd died....*[21]

In April 2021, when the Cabinet Secretary, Simon Case, was asked about this specific circumstance of Boris Johnson's hospitalisation and what would have happened had he died, he commented as follows:

What is very clear is that, in the event of a Prime Minister dying suddenly, the conventional party processes for identifying a leader and therefore it being clear who the sovereign should call on would not work. I think the assumptions would be that what you would end up having to do is to separate out the strict processes of party leadership and the job of Prime Minister and, in effect, have an interim

---

[21] The podcast is available for download here: https://www.bbc.co.uk/sounds/search?q=Covid%20Confidential&suggid=urn%3Abbc%3Aprogrammes%3Ap08dqbpn

> *Prime Minister. Of course, constitutionally, there is no such thing, but it would likely have to be a decision for Cabinet to nominate somebody who could step into the role of Prime Minister in the belief that they could fulfil that requirement and command a majority in the House. The sovereign would need to be given a rapid and clear recommendation by the Government on who to call on. By our estimation, and given the pressures of the job, we do not think you would want to leave it for more than 48 hours before identifying such a person.*
>
> *[I] would be encouraging Cabinet to meet as soon as possible to take those decisions to ensure that the gap is as short as possible. Obviously, as part of the historical convention, the Principal Private Secretary to the Prime Minister and the Private Secretary to the Queen work together to make sure there is good order in the constitution. The assumption is also that Cabinet would need to identify an honest broker in the room to facilitate the Cabinet discussion. One assumes that would be, for example, the Chief Whip. Therefore, the Cabinet Secretary would be working with the Chief Whip to ensure that that conversation happened in such a way that a conclusion was drawn, so that the sovereign had clear advice and, above all else, we made sure that there was a Prime Minister who protected the sovereign from getting involved in any political controversy.[22]*

The Cabinet Secretary makes an interesting comment about the potential role of the Chief Whip – not the most senior of ministers in the government – during such a crisis. He also refers to the important role that would be played by two key officials: the Principal Private Secretary to the Prime Minister and the Private Secretary to the Queen. Perhaps it was modesty that stopped him mentioning the third key person in this process – himself. These three have sometimes been

---

[22] https://committees.parliament.uk/oralevidence/2084/default/

described by historians as the 'golden triangle'.[23]

One might assume that following the death of a Prime Minister in office, the Deputy Prime Minister would take over as Head of Government, even if only on an interim basis. However, most of the time no such person exists and, even when they do, would we really expect John Prescott to have taken over if Tony Blair had died in office or Nick Clegg if the same had happened to David Cameron? Almost certainly not. In the former case, Gordon Brown was the clear number two in the Blair Government, not Prescott, and it would have been Brown, almost certainly, who would have been invited to take over as Prime Minister. In the case of Clegg, he only had the title Deputy Prime Minister because he was the leader of the junior coalition partner. If David Cameron had died in office, he would have had to be replaced by a Conservative.

In the September 2021 reshuffle, Boris Johnson gave Dominic Raab the title of Deputy Prime Minister. On one level Raab seemed to have been promoted, given that he had hitherto held the title 'First Secretary of State' (see below). The reality however was the opposite, given that Raab was actually at the same time demoted from the job of Foreign Secretary to that of Justice Secretary. Being given the formal title of Deputy Prime Minister by Boris Johnson was widely seen at the time as being a sop to soothe Raab's anger at his demotion and certainly didn't suggest in any way that Raab was Johnson's natural successor.

As the Cabinet Manual makes clear, being Deputy Prime Minister means nothing in terms of succession: *the fact that a person has the title of Deputy Prime Minister does not constrain the Sovereign's power to appoint a successor to a Prime Minister.*[24]

In more recent times, Prime Ministers have often given the title

---

[23] See Peter Hennessy's reference to the 'golden triangle' in evidence to the House of Lords Constitution Committee in 2011:
https://publications.parliament.uk/pa/ld201011/ldselect/ldconst/107/11020204.htm

[24] Ibid. Paragraph 3.11

'First Secretary of State' to a minister in their cabinet. Gordon Brown gave this title to Peter Mandelson. William Hague received the title from David Cameron as did, later, George Osborne. Theresa May made Damian Green First Secretary of State when she became Prime Minister and when she was replaced by Boris Johnson the title moved to Dominic Raab. What does having this title mean in practice? It has certainly meant that the holder of this title would stand in for the Prime Minister if he was, for example, unable to attend Prime Minister's Questions in the House of Commons. And when Boris Johnson was hospitalised in April 2020, Dominic Raab temporarily replaced him in virtually all of his functions. If Johnson had died, would Raab therefore have become Prime Minister? The extract from the BBC podcast quoted above suggests possibly not, unless he was the agreed choice of the Cabinet. But in the immediate term someone has to be appointed as the new Prime Minister (to be responsible for crucially important decisions such as the launching of Britain's nuclear deterrent) even if that person is soon replaced by a newly elected leader of the governing party.

When the Cabinet Manual was published, some commentators suggested that it was, in effect, a written constitution for the UK. But while the document has great importance, this is an exaggeration. In the words of Peter Hennessy and Andrew Blick, it *provide(d) the broadest description of the constitutional landscape to be found in any official document yet published in the UK,*[25] but that doesn't make it anywhere close to being a written constitution. Apart from anything else it says little about the workings of Parliament: it is very much a document written by government, about government, for government. And were the document really that important, would it remain largely unamended since 2011, still containing a chapter, as it currently does, on the UK's membership of the European Union?[26]

---

[25] Andrew Blick and Peter Hennessy 'The Hidden Wiring Emerges' Published by the Institute for Public Policy Research August 2011

[26] The Cabinet Secretary, Simon Case, in evidence to the Public Administration and Constitution Affairs Committee of the House of Commons did, in April 2021, accept that the Cabinet Manual would need to be updated if the Fixed-term Parliaments Act were repealed, as Boris Johnson's government has committed to do. And he confirmed to the

Could it perhaps be the "starting point" for a written constitution? Possibly. But perhaps rather it is simply an attempt to write down some existing – albeit extremely important – conventions.

When he appeared before the House of Lords Constitution Committee in April 2021, the former Cabinet Secretary Lord Sedwill described the Cabinet Manual thus:

> *It is a codification of the conventions and laws regulating Cabinet government. It is not the source of them....In that sense, it is rather like the Highway Code: a plain English version of a panoply of road traffic legislation. The way that road traffic legislation is enforced is a pretty good analogy for the way we think of the Cabinet Manual. It is useful in Cabinet government, as the Highway Code is a useful and accessible means of working out how to keep ourselves safe on the roads.*[27]

Perhaps it's best though to leave it to Peter Hennessy to describe the manual:

> *The Cabinet Office sent us shortly before Christmas [2010] 148 pages of an entirely new constitutional document: the draft Cabinet Manual, as minted by officials, defined by the Cabinet's Home Affairs Committee and approved at full Cabinet level.... It is, in my judgment, an artefact of considerable constitutional significance, although it is not, nor is it intended to be, the core of a written constitution. Essentially, it is the executive's operating manual, describing those moving parts of the constitution and associated procedures that the executive, both Ministers and officials, believe impinge currently on their work.... I warmly welcome its publication, not merely because of the*

House of Lords Constitution Committee in the following month that revising the manual was on the agenda, acknowledging that the UK's departure from the EU, amongst other governmental changes, required the manual to be updated.

[27] https://committees.parliament.uk/oralevidence/2099/pdf/

clarity that it adds to the delicate matter of the Sovereign's remaining personal prerogative of appointing a Prime Minister, but generally as a substantial step towards greater transparency in the engine room of central government.... The draft Cabinet Manual lacks poetry. Not one of its phrases is likely to cling to the Velcro of memory. It is a very British document: a bundle of laws, conventions and procedures, just like the constitution itself. [28]

It is generally felt that the main characters in the 2010 election, political and official, played to the rules of the unwritten constitution extremely well, so that although the process was quite drawn out, with David Cameron not becoming Prime Minister until almost a week after the election, the Monarch was at no time seen to have entered into the political fray.[29] But, ultimately, the Queen still has to decide who to appoint as Prime Minister - albeit on the advice of very senior and experienced officials - because there is no one else to do so. Constitutional experts mostly agree, therefore, that appointing a Prime Minister is one of the remaining prerogatives of the Monarch where, in very specific and occasional circumstances, real power may have to be exercised.

Dissolving and Proroguing Parliament

'Dissolution' marks the end of 'a Parliament' (that is, the period between two general elections) and therefore takes place in advance of

---

[28] https://hansard.parliament.uk/lords/2011-01-20/debates/f4a5b0bf-5355-451c-ae2a-33fa97dec8bb/LordsChamber

[29] The role played the Cabinet Secretary in the aftermath of the 2010 general election is one that came under scrutiny from a number of political commentators and constitutional experts. The Political and Constitutional Reform Select Committee launched an inquiry after the election "to explore constitutional and practical issues relating to government and coalition formation that emerged following the general election in May 2010". One of the key witnesses to give evidence to the committee was the then Cabinet Secretary himself, Sir Gus O'Donnell. His evidence to the committee can be found here:
www.publications.parliament.uk/pa/cm201011/cmselect/cmpolcon/c528-iv/c52801.htm

an election. A Parliament will be divided up into a number of sessions, each of which begins with the State Opening of Parliament and ends when Parliament is 'prorogued'. Typically a parliamentary session might last a year (it's not uncommon to hear people referring to a 'parliamentary year') but, as we shall see, this isn't always the case.

Dissolution of Parliament

This is an area of the constitution that was considerably changed by the passing of the 2011 Fixed-term Parliaments Act. Under the Parliament Act 1911, a Parliament cannot sit for more than five years before an election must take place. (Until 1911 the limit had been seven years.) But political history shows that general elections have often occurred more frequently – perhaps at four yearly intervals, rather than five. Before 2011 the Prime Minister had been able to ask the Monarch at any time if she would dissolve Parliament to allow a general election to take place. This was one of a number of powers which Gordon Brown, on his accession to the premiership, had suggested might be taken away from the Prime Minister and given to Parliament to vote on its own dissolution. It was therefore ironic that the issue that most damaged Gordon Brown in the early months of his premiership was whether to call an election in the autumn of 2007. But it was the creation of the Coalition Government in May 2010 that heralded real changes in this area.

Where in the past a Parliament lasted the full five years, it generally suggested that the incumbent government had been hanging on by its fingertips hoping for public opinion to shift. This was certainly true in 1997 and 2010. And even in 1992 it was by no means clear that John Major's Government would be re-elected. In contrast, Margaret Thatcher's elections of 1983 and 1987 and Tony Blair's of 2001 and 2005, each called four years after the previous election, were ones where the government could be fairly sure of winning. A confident Prime Minister would usually 'go to the country' after four years or so.

Sometimes Parliaments had been somewhat shorter. The

election of February 1974 took place less than four years after the previous one because the Prime Minister, Edward Heath, chose to hold an election on the specific issue of 'Who governs Britain?' There was serious unrest in the coal mining industry and the Prime Minister felt that the only way of resolving the issue was to hold an election. Unfortunately for Mr Heath, the electorate's response to his 'Who governs?' question was: 'Not you!' The next election followed just eight months later. After scraping victory in the February 1974 election, Harold Wilson headed a minority government until deciding to fight another election in October, when he won a tiny majority.

The constitutional question for the Queen traditionally had been: when a Prime Minister asks for a dissolution of Parliament, was she obliged to grant one? Usually the answer to this had been yes. There was no question that she would grant a dissolution in 2001 and 2005. Nor would there have been any issue about granting a dissolution prior to the October 1974 election even though it was just a few months after the previous election, because the incumbent minority government was hamstrung.

Imagine that the 2010 election, rather than producing the Coalition Government that it did, had produced a minority Conservative government and that this government took office only to have its legislative proposals constantly voted down. Unable to govern effectively, Prime Minister Cameron might have asked the Queen to dissolve Parliament in the hope that another general election would resolve the problem. Would the Queen automatically have agreed to the Prime Minister's request in these circumstances? Although this was a rather murky constitutional area, most constitutional experts seemed to agree that the Queen did have the right to refuse a Prime Minister's request to dissolve Parliament, if only because of a letter written to The Times in May 1950. The letter was written by George VI's private secretary Sir Alan Lascelles, under the pseudonym 'Senex'. In it he wrote that: *It is surely indisputable that a Prime Minister may ask - not demand - that his sovereign will grant him a dissolution of Parliament; and that the sovereign, if he so chooses, may refuse to grant this request.* He went on to say that the Monarch would not *deny a dissolution to his Prime Minister unless he were satisfied that:*

> *(1) the existing Parliament was still vital, viable, and capable of doing its job;*
> *(2) a general election would be detrimental to the national economy;*
> *(3) another Prime Minister could be found who could carry on the government, for a reasonable period, with a working majority in the House of Commons.*[30]

These 'Lascelles Principles', as they became known, were generally accepted after 1950 as a description of the Monarch's discretion to turn down a Prime Minister's request to dissolve Parliament. But some might find it disturbing that a key constitutional convention such as this simply derives from a letter, written under pseudonym, to a newspaper.

With the passing of the Fixed-term Parliaments Act (FTPA) in 2011 the feeling was that there would now be much more clarity about the dissolution of Parliament. However it didn't quite turn out like that. The genesis of the FTPA lay in the coalition agreement between the Conservative and Liberal Democrat parties. The junior partner in the Coalition Government, the Liberal Democrats, had long campaigned for fixed-term parliaments such as exist in many democracies.[31] In these countries the date of the next election is most often four years after the previous one. A commitment to fixed-term parliaments became part of the Programme for Government that was thrashed out between the Conservative and Liberal Democrat parties in the days after the election, with the FTPA being passed by Parliament

---

[30] Letter to the Editor of The Times. Published 2 May 1950

[31] David Cameron had also given some support to the idea of fixed-term parliaments. In a speech to the Open University in May 2009 he said that a Conservative Government would *seriously consider the option of fixed-term Parliaments when there is a majority government.*

in September 2011.[32] Although the Liberal Democrats could, and did, make sound constitutional points as to why the right to choose the date of an election should be taken away from the Prime Minister (why should one participant in a race get to fire the starting gun?) their main motivation was probably more political. Their concern would have been that if the Coalition Government was seen to be working well in the eyes of the British public, David Cameron might have been tempted to call an early general election at which the bigger of the two parties in the coalition (i.e. his!) would almost certainly be the one to benefit most. The passing of the FTPA would stop Cameron being able to do that.

The act provided for fixed five year parliaments (not four years which, as mentioned, is common in many other countries). This had the effect of removing the Prime Minister's power to bring about an early election simply by asking the Monarch to dissolve Parliament. The act did however allow for a general election to take place before the five years were up. The FTPA said that the trigger for an early election was either where a vote of no confidence in the government by the House of Commons does not lead to a new government being formed within fourteen days, or where the House voted for an early election with at least two-thirds of all MPs voting in favour. (The original Coalition Agreement had mentioned a 55% vote but this had been changed to two-thirds when the bill was published.) This made it rather more difficult to remove a government than was previously the case when a 50% plus 1 vote in the Commons could in effect force a government into an early general election – as happened in 1979 (see below). Although these changes more significantly affected the power of the Prime Minister – an issue that we will return to – they also of course had an effect on the remaining powers on the Monarch. She still formally had to dissolve Parliament but this was now a formality. She would now dissolve Parliament either because the five years were up or because

---

[32] The Coalition: Our Programme for Government
www.gov.uk/government/uploads/system/uploads/attachment_data/file/78977/coalition_programme_for_government.pdf

Parliament itself had voted for an earlier election.

Following the passing of the FTPA in 2011, the subsequent election did indeed take place in May 2015, five years after the previous one. And at the time, one might have been forgiven for thinking that this would be the future pattern of elections for years to come. But, as is well known, the lengths of the next two Parliaments were only two years and two and a half years respectively. It's worth considering how these two early elections came about – and in both cases it was all to do with the British people, in the referendum of 23 June 2016, voting to leave the European Union ('Brexit'). Let's look at each election in turn.

David Cameron resigned as Prime Minister following the British people's rejection of his advice to vote 'Remain' in the EU referendum. The Conservative Party voted to replace him as party leader with Theresa May who was then appointed Prime Minister by the Queen. From the outset, May's administration was dogged by the issue of Brexit. It divided the country and, perhaps even more importantly for her, it divided her party. Theresa May had inherited a majority in the Commons from her predecessor that was never going to be large enough to protect her from rebellions from both the 'hard Brexit' and Remain wings of her party. She therefore took the gamble to hold an early general election. One of the ways in which this could happen under the FTPA, as we have seen, was for the Commons, by a two-thirds majority of those eligible to vote, to vote in favour of an early election. This may seem a rather high hurdle to clear but, put yourself in the position of the Leader of the Opposition – then Jeremy Corbyn – when the Prime Minister puts down a motion in the Commons for an early election. It's actually rather difficult to vote against an election without appearing rather weak. Many in the Labour Party would have been rather cautious about wanting an election in the late spring of 2017 but Corbyn himself seemed quite gung-ho about his party's prospects. Labour therefore supported May's motion, which comfortably passed the two-thirds threshold, leading to the dissolution of Parliament and the general election of June 2017.

The result of that election showed that May's gamble hadn't in any way paid off and that, to some extent at least, Corbyn's optimism had been justified as the Conservative Party lost the small majority it had had in the Commons. May now had to cobble together a deal with MPs from Northern Ireland's Democratic Unionist Party (DUP) to enable her to stay in power. The deal that was done was a long way short of the coalition that her predecessor had agreed with the Liberal Democrats – there were no DUP ministers in the government and its MPs continued to sit on the opposition benches in the Commons. The deal was what is known as a 'Supply and Confidence' agreement which essentially meant that the DUP would support May's government in any 'no confidence' vote and would also support its budget. But no other guarantees were given, in particular regarding the Brexit negotiations.

The disaster for Theresa May of the 2017 general election was instrumental in her eventual resignation as Prime Minister. Without a majority in the Commons and with the support of the DUP tenuous at best, her government was defeated time after time in the Commons, sometimes quite spectacularly.[33] By the summer of 2019 she realised that she couldn't go on and her resignation paved the way for Boris Johnson to become the new Conservative Party leader and Prime Minister.

It was clear that Johnson wanted to hold an early general election. He knew that like his predecessor he was hamstrung without a majority in the Commons and was clearly confident – rightly as it turned out – that he could win a general election largely on the promise to 'get Brexit done'. However, he of course faced the same problem as his predecessor – the Fixed-term Parliaments Act. And this time, the opposition would not be nearly so compliant. More than once Johnson put a motion down in the Commons to prompt an early election and each time he was defeated. The opposition parties were certainly concerned about the idea of a Johnson majority government taking the UK out of

---

[33] For more on this period, see Chapter 7 on the 2017-19 Parliament.

the EU without a deal but they were also no doubt worried about their own prospects in an election when they would be up against the populist 'Boris' promising to get Brexit done.

An early general election therefore seemed impossible under the terms of the FTPA. So the only option for Johnson's government was to introduce legislation to suspend the operation of the FTPA. The 'Early Parliamentary General Election Bill' didn't repeal or even amend the FTPA; it simply stated that 'an early parliamentary general election is to take place on 12 December 2019 in consequence of the passing of this act'.[34] Crucially it would only take a majority of one to pass the House of Commons although, being a bill, it would also have to pass the Lords. Johnson, of course, didn't have a majority in the Commons but once the Liberal Democrats and the Scottish National Party indicated that they would support the bill, Labour fell into line behind them so that when the bill faced its final vote in the Commons, only 20 MPs voted against it. The bill then sailed through the House of Lords (the unelected chamber having little option but to allow such a bill to pass) allowing the election to take place which the Conservative Party won comfortably.

Under the terms of the FTPA, the general election following that of 2019 would take place in May 2024. However, Johnson's government was committed to the repeal of the FTPA and in December 2020 it published a 'Draft Fixed-term Parliaments (Repeal) Bill' to that effect.[35] At the Queen's Speech in May 2021 it was announced that an actual bill would be introduced in the forthcoming session. In fact it was introduced to Parliament and published just a day later. In name this bill was different to the draft bill: 'Dissolution and Calling of Parliament Bill'[36] but it was little different in content. An

---

[34] https://www.legislation.gov.uk/ukpga/2019/29/enacted/data.htm

[35] https://assets.publishing.service.gov.uk/government/uploads/system/uploads/attachment_data/file/940027/Draft-Fixed-term-Parliaments-Act-Repeal-Bill.pdf

[36] https://bills.parliament.uk/bills/2859

important constitutional issue that is unclear in the bill concerns the extent of discretion that the Monarch will in future have to refuse a request from the Prime Minister to dissolve Parliament. As we have seen, prior to the passing of the FTPA, the discretion that the Monarch could exercise in this area was generally accepted as that described by Sir Alan Lascelles in 1950. But the Dissolution and Calling of Parliament Bill isn't clear as to whether the Monarch's discretion will simply revert to the pre-FTPA position. This is an issue into which parliamentarians and constitutional experts will no doubt sink their teeth as the bill progresses through Parliament.

Prorogation of Parliament

Until recently the prorogation of Parliament had rarely been an issue. It is another of these powers that are in theory exercised by the Monarch but in practice by the Prime Minister. Although being able to determine the length of a session, and thereby how long a government has to get its legislation through Parliament, may seem like a potentially controversial power for a Prime Minister to exercise, even where a government has decided to have a two year session (as in 2010-2012) it has caused little controversy. Against that backdrop, the decision by Boris Johnson to seek to prorogue Parliament in September 2019 and cause a constitutional kerfuffle the like of which hadn't been seen in the UK for many years, seems quite extraordinary.

In Boris Johnson's defence, by the late summer of 2019, the session that had started after the general election of 2017 had already been a very long one. Theresa May's government had made it clear at the start that the session was likely to last two years, given the complexity of the Brexit legislation that had to be passed, but by September 2019 the session had run well beyond two years. So why was Johnson's government decision to prorogue Parliament in that month so controversial? Simply put it was because many felt that he wished to prorogue (in effect, suspend) Parliament in order to stop MPs opposed to his Brexit policies passing legislation to delay the UK's departure from the EU. Parliament ever passing legislation against the wishes of the government is a pretty rare event but the issue being Brexit and a minority government being in power was a volatile mix. Earlier in the year MPs had already 'seized the Order Paper' to push through legislation to delay the UK's departure from the end of March to the end of October 2019, against the wishes of Theresa May's government.[37] The Commons was now threatening to do something similar following the introduction of a bill that could further delay Brexit to the end of January 2020.[38] Speculation began to mount as to whether Boris Johnson would seek to prorogue Parliament in order to stop it passing the bill.

At the end of August 2019 the government announced that it was going to do just that (although it claimed rather implausibly that the decision to prorogue Parliament was unrelated to Brexit). Parliament was to be prorogued on 9 September and not return for the new session until 14 October, much too late for it to stop the UK potentially leaving the EU on 31 October without a deal. Given that the gap between Prorogation and a State Opening of Parliament is usually no more than a few days, this caused outrage. The Speaker of the House of Commons, John Bercow, who for a number of months had been facilitating the regular takeover of the Commons' timetable by backbenchers, commented as follows:

> *I have had no contact from the Government, but if the reports that it is seeking to prorogue Parliament are confirmed, this move represents a constitutional outrage. However it is dressed up, it is blindingly obvious that the purpose of Prorogation now would be to stop Parliament debating Brexit and performing its duty in shaping a course for the country.... Shutting down Parliament would be an offence*

---

[37] This was the European Union (Withdrawal) Bill 2019 whose main sponsor was the Labour MP Yvette Cooper.
https://www.legislation.gov.uk/ukpga/2019/16/contents/enActed/data.htm

[38] This was the European Union (Withdrawal) No2 Bill 2019 whose main sponsor was the Labour MP Hilary Benn.
https://www.legislation.gov.uk/ukpga/2019/26/enActed/data.htm

> *against the democratic process and the rights of parliamentarians as the people's elected representatives. Surely at this early stage in his premiership, the Prime Minister should be seeking to establish rather than undermine his democratic credentials and indeed his commitment to parliamentary democracy.*[39]

The Leader of the Opposition Jeremy Corbyn also weighed in by saying that the move was:

> *a threat to our democracy....I am appalled at the recklessness of Johnson's government, which talks about sovereignty and yet is seeking to suspend Parliament to avoid scrutiny of its plans for a reckless no-deal Brexit. This is an outrage and a threat to our democracy.*[40]

His criticisms were echoed by many MPs, including several from the government-side of the Commons but despite this opposition, Johnson decided to push ahead with the Prorogation, despatching the Lord President of the Council, Jacob Rees-Mogg, to Balmoral to seek the Queen's approval of the Prorogation. Whilst there was speculation that the Queen might refuse to give her approval given the circumstances, in reality there was no possibility that she would go against the wishes of her Prime Minister. On the day that Parliament was prorogued there were extraordinary scenes in the House of Commons with chanting, singing and shouts of 'shame on you' aimed at the government frontbench. Speaker Bercow's comments when Black Rod arrived in the Commons to call MPs to attend the House of Lords for the Prorogation ceremony were quite extraordinary:

> *Black Rod, I treat you and what you have to say with respect, and I recognise that our presence is desired by Her Majesty the Queen's Commissioners. They are doing*

---

[39] Quoted in the Independent newspaper 28 August 2019
https://www.independent.co.uk/news/uk/politics/parliament-suspension-john-bercow-boris-johnson-brexit-no-deal-queen-a9081756.html

[40] Ibid.

> *what they believe to be right, and I recognise my role in this matter.... No, I am more than happy if people have the basics of tolerance and manners to listen, they would hear that I am perfectly happy, as I have advised others, to play my part, but I want to make the point that this is not a standard or normal Prorogation....I have already made the point that if people have the manners to listen, which they have not, that I will play my part. This is not, however, a normal Prorogation. It is not typical. It is not standard. It is one of the longest for decades, and it represents, not just in the minds of many colleagues but for huge numbers of people outside an act of executive fiat.* [41]

Meanwhile cases were brought to the English and Scottish courts to challenge the lawfulness of the Prorogation with both eventually being considered by the Supreme Court. On 24 September the President of the Supreme Court, Lady Hale, announced that the Court had judged unanimously that the government had acted unlawfully in proroguing Parliament in the way that it did. In its summary the Court stated that it had been *bound to conclude* that:

> *the decision to advise Her Majesty to prorogue Parliament was unlawful because it had the effect of frustrating or preventing the ability of Parliament to carry out its constitutional functions without reasonable justification.... The prorogation was ... void and of no effect. Parliament has not been prorogued.*[42]

It was a damning indictment of the government's action. Professor Thomas Poole of the London School of Economics, a leading expert on the exercise of such powers by government,

---

[41] https://hansard.parliament.uk/Commons/2019-09-09/debates/F22B450C-0F24-4C12-9A99-DA6634DA779D/MessageToAttendTheLordsCommissioners

[42] https://www.supremecourt.uk/cases/docs/uksc-2019-0192-summary.pdf

described the Supreme Court decision as *quite possibly the most significant judicial statement on the constitution in over 200 years*.[43] Some people, well represented in government, felt that the Supreme Court had overstepped the mark by intervening in this way and had made a political judgement of the like its namesake in Washington DC (a rather different type of judicial beast) might have taken. And quite apart from whether the Supreme Court had reached the right verdict, some even questioned whether issues such as the prorogation of Parliament were a matter for the courts at all. [In its 2019 election manifesto, the Conservative Party said that, if returned to office, it would look at the whole issue of how decisions by government can be challenged in the courts, through the process known as 'judicial review'. In July 2021, Boris Johnson's government published its 'Judicial Review and Courts Bill'.[44] The provisions of the bill, which began its passage through Parliament in the autumn of 2021, perhaps don't fully justify the government's earlier rhetoric about steering the judiciary away from political controversy.]

Once the Supreme Court had judged the Prorogation to be unlawful then, as the Court said in its summary, it hadn't happened. Both Houses simply returned the next day and continued where they'd left off earlier that month. The Prime Minister was forced to return early from a visit to New York to make a statement to the Commons in which he used language that greatly upset many MPs in the House, in particular his description of concerns expressed by a female MP about threats that had been made against her as 'humbug' and his repeated references to the 'Benn Act', which allowed the UK's departure from the EU to be delayed to the end of January 2020, as the 'Surrender Act'.[45] Ironically though, the Benn Act had

---

[43] Thomas Poole, "Understanding what makes 'Miller & Cherry' the Most Significant Judicial Statement on the Constitution in over 200 years" (September 25, 2019)
www.prospectmagazine.co.uk/politics/understanding-what-makes-miller-2-the-most-significant-judicialstatement-on-the-constitution-in-over-200-years

[44] https://bills.parliament.uk/bills/3035

[45] https://hansard.parliament.uk/Commons/2019-09-25/debates/AD2A07E5-

in any case been passed before the unlawful prorogation took place!

For a while then, this relatively obscure and hitherto uncontroversial part of the parliamentary process known as Prorogation had become headline news. For most people, as an issue, it was forgotten following the dissolution of Parliament in November and the triumphant victory of Boris Johnson at the December election. But the incident had left a deep scar on Britain's uncodified constitution. It showed how when the rules weren't properly written down they could be used and abused to suit the ends of those in power. However, more positively, the incident also showed that there are nevertheless limits on how far executive power can be stretched with, in this case, the courts stepping in to place some limits on those powers. That is unless, of course, Parliament in future legislates to limit the courts' ability to do that.[46]

Although the Supreme Court intervened in this case, it wasn't interpreting the rules of Prorogation in the way that the Supreme Court in the USA might interpret what's written in the US Constitution. The British Supreme Court wasn't doing that because there were no rules written down to interpret. What it was rather doing was making a judgement as to whether the Prime Minister had acted reasonably in asking the Queen to prorogue Parliament in these circumstances. The Court's agreement to hear this case was not without controversy as it might have decided not to step into the murky waters of the unwritten constitution at all. If the courts do decide not to intervene (and as previous paragraphs suggest, their power to do this might yet be taken away) then we end up having to rely even more on those in positions of power to act properly. As William Gladstone put it: *the British Constitution presumes more boldly than any other the*

9741-4EBA-997A-97776F80AA38/PrimeMinisterSUpdate

[46] To round off this extraordinary story, it should be added that the government did eventually lawfully prorogue Parliament in early October thereby bringing to an end the 2017-19 parliamentary session. A very short session followed which was itself prorogued as Parliament was dissolved in advance of the general election of December 2019.

good sense and the good faith of those who work it. [47] In other words, they should behave as 'good chaps'. One wonders whether Boris Johnson was behaving as a 'good chap' when he attempted to prorogue Parliament in September 2019. One wonders also what damage might have been done by this event to the relationship between the Queen and her first minister. Of course we'll never hear from the Queen directly; however the Sunday Times Magazine did run an interesting feature on Prince William in March 2021, which suggested that

> *he was not happy about the unenviable position the government put the Queen in with the 2019 proroguing of Parliament...which forced an apology from Boris Johnson to the Monarch. Constitutionally the Queen had no alternative other than to act on the advice of her government, but in William's reign there will be "more private, robust challenging of advice".*[48]

Granting Royal Assent to Bills

The granting of 'Royal Assent' to bills is another constitutional function of the Monarch's. A bill is a piece of primary legislation which, when it has completed its passage through Parliament, becomes an Act of Parliament. For a bill to become an act it has to be passed by both the House of Commons and the House of Lords, unless the Parliament Acts are used. (For more on this see chapter six.) But there is also a third stage: Royal Assent. No bill can become an act until the Queen has assented to it. So is this purely a formality – a traditional, ceremonial, rubber-stamping process – or are there circumstances in which the Queen might withhold her assent? The answer in the early 21st century seemed to be clear: the Monarch would always give Royal Assent to bills. It is what is known as a 'constitutional convention' - a feature of the system of government that is so widely accepted that it almost has the force of law. What would the Queen do if

---

[47] William Gladstone, Gleanings of Past Years, volume 1, p.243. London 1879

[48] Sunday Times Magazine 21 March 2021

Parliament passed a bill to abolish the Monarchy? The only acceptable answer in a parliamentary democracy is that she would assent to it. Can we prove it? No. But every bill presented to the Monarch has been given Royal Assent since Queen Anne refused to agree to the Scottish Militia Bill in 1708 for fear that the proposed militia would not be loyal to the Crown.[49] Even Queen Victoria, who took a very keen and sometimes partisan interest in what her governments were up to, even going as far as sometimes refusing to appoint ministers that the Prime Minister wished to have in his government, gave her assent to every bill that was presented to her.

Because every bill for the last three centuries has received assent, it is now accepted that the granting of Royal Assent – which can only be given while Parliament is sitting - is no longer a 'power' of the Monarch's but merely a 'function'. However, there is still an intriguing question as to what a Monarch might do if she was advised by the Prime Minister to refuse a bill Royal Assent. This was a question that was quite widely discussed when Parliament passed the 'Benn Bill' mentioned above. Was one way for the government to block it simply to advise the Queen to refuse to give it Royal Assent? Constitutional and legal experts were divided and by the time Boris Johnson decided not to go down that highly contentious road no firm agreement had been reached as to its lawfulness. But the important question remains: what *would* happen if a Monarch refused to grant Royal Assent to a bill passed by Parliament? If this were not being done on the advice of ministers, it would certainly create a constitutional crisis of a scale not seen since the 1640s when the King lost his head. Today the Monarch would be unlikely to share that fate, but one cannot see how he or she could survive as a constitutional Monarch. A still more interesting question is whether the Monarch would be *right* to give Royal Assent to a bill that abolished democracy. Is the Monarch there to obey those who are democratically elected or to protect democracy?

---

[49] In 1914, George V was close to withholding his assent to the Irish Home Rule Bill but, on ministerial advice, was persuaded not to.

Queen's Consent

Royal Assent should not be confused with 'Queen's Consent'. This is a stage in the process of a bill going through Parliament where the Queen's agreement is sought to proceed with a bill that affects the constitutional duties, or the personal revenues, property or interests of the Crown. Where legislation affects the Duchy of Cornwall, the Prince of Wales's consent is sought. This is known as 'Prince's Consent'. Queen's Consent and Prince's Consent are usually signified at the third reading of the bill in the House of Commons or at second reading if the extent to which the bill affects the Monarch is particularly significant. Further consent may be required if the bill is subsequently amended before it receives Royal Assent.

Queen's Consent and Prince's Consent have traditionally been considered a largely symbolic part of the legislative process in which the Monarchy exercises no more power than it does than when giving Royal Assent. However, the range of bills in recent years where consent has been required is perhaps surprisingly wide. Those where Queen's Consent was sought during 2020 for example included the Fire Safety Bill, the Agriculture Bill, the Fisheries Bill, the Pensions Schemes Bill and the Coronavirus Bill.[50] The reason why these and many other bills have required Queen's Consent is opaque to say the least. There are however a few examples where legislation has more obviously affected the Queen's personal interests; for example the 'Duchy of Lancaster Act 1988' which had a direct impact on the Queen's personal estate.[51]

In recent times there has been some discussion as to whether the

---

[50] In February 2020 The Guardian published the entire list of 'more than a thousand' bills to which Queen's Consent had been sought during the reign of the current Monarch: https://www.theguardian.com/uk-news/2021/feb/08/royals-vetted-more-than-1000-laws-via-queens-consent. Later, in July 2021, The Guardian published a similar article about 'Crown Consent' which is the equivalent of Queen's Consent for legislation in the Scottish Parliament: https://www.theguardian.com/uk-news/2021/jul/28/revealed-queen-vetted-67-laws-before-scottish-parliament-pass-them.

[51] https://www.legislation.gov.uk/ukpga/1988/10/contents

Monarch and her eldest son are exercising genuine influence over the content of those bills where their consent is required. Although comments about this issue may perhaps have been exaggerated, it is the case that the Military Actions against Iraq (Parliamentary Approval) Bill was denied Queen's Consent in 1999. This was a Private Members' Bill sponsored by the then Labour MP Tam Dalyell that would have required a vote in Parliament before troops were committed to any invasion of Iraq. It is clear, however, that the Queen was acting on the advice of her ministers when she refused to give the bill her consent. Her failure to consent to the bill was, nevertheless, sufficient to halt its progress through Parliament.[52]

The Right to be Consulted

The fact that in most circumstances the Monarch has few, if any, real powers does not mean that the Monarch has no influence at all over what the Government is doing in her name. In *The English Constitution*, published in 1867, Walter Bagehot described three rights enjoyed by the Monarch: *the right to be consulted, the right to encourage, the right to warn*. Most people would accept that these rights persist today. The Prime Minister has frequent (usually weekly) audiences with the Queen. Because this is the one meeting in government that is unminuted and never leaks, we can only really speculate about what is discussed, although some interesting information about the Queen's weekly audiences with Margaret Thatcher was revealed in 2013 following a Freedom of Information request by the Mail on Sunday.[53] What we can pick up though from the memoirs of former Prime Ministers and other briefings, unofficial or otherwise, suggests that the Queen takes a close and informed interest in what her governments are doing. When former Prime Minister Sir John Major was asked by the journalist Andrew Marr

---

[52] As is discussed below, Parliament was nevertheless given a vote on going to war in Iraq just before the hostilities commenced in March 2003.

[53] 'Secret letters reveal what Maggie REALLY thought of audiences with the Queen.' www.dailymail.co.uk/news/article-2523917/Secret-letters-reveal-Maggie-REALLY-thought-audiences-Queen-late-PM-pushed-luck-repeatedly-cancelling-weekly-audiences-Her-Majesty.html#ixzz2set13psu

whether he found these meetings useful, Sir John replied:

> They're very useful. I mean where else can you talk to one person in total certainty ... that is entirely secret; that nobody is going to talk to anybody else about what is said? So they're very free, they're very frank, they're very useful. And of course the Queen has been there for sixty years. Her first Prime Minister was Winston Churchill. Most of the present Cabinet weren't born when the Queen became Monarch. So there's very little she hasn't seen and very little she doesn't understand, and anyone who doesn't listen to her view and consult her where necessary is missing a huge opportunity.[54]

In March 2013, in an ITV documentary, David Cameron spoke about his weekly audience with the Queen as follows:

> I think Tony Blair said it's the only private meeting you ever have because it's just you and the Queen in the room. There are no note-takers, no secretaries, nothing. It's just the two of you. So it's a very frank conversation about anything that's going on in the world that week....There's a very therapeutic side to it because as you explain the particular problem that the government has or a particular problem that the country is facing, sometimes you find it's all becoming clearer as you explain it to this one incredibly experienced person because you're always very conscious that I'm her 12th Prime Minister. She's been listening to this stuff for 60 years. And you get some pretty good questions which you've got to think of some pretty good answers to.

In this very rare public glimpse of the weekly audience, the Queen tells David Cameron how she'd received a phone call from the 'King of Greece' about the financial crisis. *He's very worried about*

---

[54] Interview on the Andrew Marr Show, 5 February 2012

it says the Queen, to which the Prime Minister replies: *oh really?* [55] This brief 'fly-on-the-wall' glimpse of the weekly audience had obviously been authorised by the Queen. What she clearly hadn't authorised for public release were David Cameron's comments a year or so later in a conversation with ex-New York Mayor Michael Bloomberg during which he claimed that the Queen had *purred down the phone* when he spoke to her about the result of the Scottish Independence referendum. Buckingham Palace *declined to comment* on the Prime Minister's remarks.[56]

During the Covid pandemic, Prime Minister Boris Johnson couldn't of course have face-to-face meetings with the Queen. When, in June 2021, the first audience since March of the previous year took place in person, the TV cameras were again briefly allowed in. There was some interest in and amusement at this exchange, which was captured on camera:

> The Queen: *I've just been talking to your Secretary of State for Health, poor man. He came for Privy Council. He's full of...*
>
> Boris Johnson: *Full of beans?*

The Queen went on to tell Boris Johnson that the Health Secretary (Matt Hancock) *thinks things are getting better.*[57] Nothing of great importance was of course heard in this exchange but it was nevertheless interesting to have an opportunity to see the Heads of State and Government together for the weekly audience.

The relationship between the Queen and Boris Johnson had come under more serious scrutiny during the 'unlawful Prorogation' of September 2019 discussed above. Many headlines accused Boris Johnson of 'misleading' or even 'lying to' the Queen over why he wished her to prorogue Parliament. Senior officials in government confirmed that Johnson did speak to the Queen after the Supreme Court

---

[55] 'Our Queen'. ITV documentary shown on 17 March 2013

[56] https://www.bbc.co.uk/news/uk-politics-29335028

[57] https://www.bbc.co.uk/news/uk-politics-57584417

judgment with some sources, as we have seen, going as far as claiming that he 'apologised to the Queen'[58].

As Sir John Major observed, Winston Churchill was the Prime Minister when the present Monarch came to the throne. Boris Johnson is now her fourteenth British Prime Minister. (One should not forget all the Prime Ministers in those Commonwealth nations where she is also Head of State.) She is therefore extremely experienced and it seems likely that any Prime Minister will at least consider very carefully what she has to say on any issue even if they eventually don't take her advice. In the final analysis however, we can really only speculate about the relationship that the Queen has had with any of her Prime Ministers. It is thought she got on well with Sir Winston Churchill, perhaps seeing him as a father figure, and also, perhaps surprisingly, with Sir Harold Wilson, who many claim was her favourite Prime Minister.

An amusing anecdote about the Monarch and Prime Minister concerns the Queen's father, George VI and Clement Attlee's visit to Buckingham Palace to be appointed Prime Minister by him after the 1945 general election. It is said that the King was considerably shocked at the way the British people had turfed out of office the great war hero Winston Churchill in favour of the socialist Attlee. What made the meeting difficult however was less the King's personal views about the election result and more the fact that both he and Attlee were painfully shy men. It is widely reported that the two stood there in a rather awkward silence for a while before Attlee blurted out 'I've won the election' to which the George VI replied: 'I know, I heard it on the six o'clock news'.

Any attempt to analyse in detail the relationship between Monarch and Prime Minister will however always only end up with us wishing we could have been a fly on the wall at some of the meetings between them.

---

[59] https://www.bbc.co.uk/news/uk-politics-49810261, https://www.politicshome.com/news/article/boris-johnson-apologised-to-queen-following-supreme-court-prorogation-ruling and the Sunday Times Magazine article referenced above.

All this points to a fundamental feature of Britain's constitutional arrangements – that Britain is a *constitutional monarchy* where the Monarch is a Head of State with very limited powers.

What are the other key features of the British Constitution?

Other Features of the British Constitution

Cabinet Government

The Cabinet is officially defined as the *ultimate decision-making body of government*.[59] The British system of government is said to be one of Cabinet government, rather than 'prime ministerial' government, because Acts of Parliament generally give powers to ministers (usually Secretaries of State) rather than to the Prime Minister. The Prime Minister has very little formal power in law; it is the ministers who sit around the Cabinet table who exercise these powers, in theory at least. This is explored in more detail in the next chapter.

Parliamentary Democracy

The United Kingdom is a parliamentary democracy. There are two principal features to this: government's accountability to Parliament and ministers' membership of Parliament.

Government's Accountability to Parliament

Government is accountable to Parliament on a day-to-day basis through the system of parliamentary questions, select committees and debates on government policy. But its ultimate accountability to Parliament (or to the House of Commons to be more precise) derives from the fact that it owes its very existence to the Commons. The governing party or parties are in power only because they command a majority on the floor of the House of Commons and at any time the House of Commons has always

---

[59] Ibid. Cabinet Manual paragraph 4.1.

been able to dismiss the Government through a 'vote of no confidence'. Whilst, as we have seen, the Fixed-term Parliaments Act made this a little less straightforward than it once was, it remained the case that if a government lost a vote of no confidence on the floor of the House of Commons it is forced to resign and a general election would follow unless a new administration could be formed within 14 days.

Losing a vote of no confidence in the Commons is a very rare occurrence, it last happening to the Labour Government in 1979. By the spring of 1979 James Callaghan's Government had been operating for some time with no majority in the Commons. The wafer-thin majority that Labour had won in October 1974 had been lost through by-election defeats and defections. For a while the Government had survived by reaching an agreement with the Liberal Party (the so-called 'Lib-Lab Pact') over key areas of policy. This wasn't a formal coalition – there were no Liberal ministers in the government – but it gave the Liberal Party some say over important areas of government policy. Callaghan's Government also received a degree of support from the nationalist parties in Scotland and Wales on the promise that the government would legislate for devolved government in those parts of the UK. When the government failed to deliver on devolution, the nationalist parties withdrew their support and the Leader of the Opposition, Margaret Thatcher, seizing her opportunity, tabled a motion of no confidence in the government.

It was clear in the run-up to the vote that the result would be very close. The votes of MPs from the smaller parties would clearly be crucial and there was some doubt about how they would vote, especially some Northern Irish MPs. All sorts of wheeler-dealering went on prior to the vote, most notably over whether the government would agree to build an oil pipeline between Great Britain and Northern Ireland. The Prime Minister said that he wouldn't allow the government to 'be bought' but, had he agreed to the pipeline, it is highly likely that the unionist MPs from Northern Ireland would have abstained, ensuring the Government's survival. The behaviour of every non-aligned MP became of huge interest to the party whips. For example, one nationalist MP from Northern Ireland, Frank Maguire, rarely attended the House as he spent much of his time at home in Fermanagh running his pub. Would he turn up and, if so, how would he vote? (In the event, Frank Maguire did fly over to Westminster for the debate but mysteriously failed to vote. The then Education Secretary, Shirley Williams, referring to Mr Maguire as *the lost leprechaun*, reputably believed that he got locked in the lavatory! But in retrospect it would appear that it was the views expressed by the nationalist MP from Northern Ireland, Gerry Fitt, during the no confidence debate that proved crucial in persuading Maguire not to support the government.)

Whether sick MPs would be able to vote was of equal interest. The absence from the vote through illness of the Labour MP for Batley, Sir Alfred 'Doc' Broughton, finally proved decisive. James Callaghan initially decided that Broughton should not be brought in and, by the time he changed his mind, it was too late for Sir Alfred to reach the House in time for the vote. The Cabinet minister at the time, Roy (now Lord) Hattersley, speaking on the BBC programme 'A Parliamentary Coup' in 2009, said that the whips had even considered what they would do if Sir Alfred died in Parliament before he could vote. Since no commoner is officially 'allowed to die' in the Palace of Westminster (because the Palace is still classified as a Royal Palace, having once been the residence of the Monarch) one view was that his vote could still be counted!

The then Conservative deputy Chief Whip, Bernard Weatherill, described how his opposite number in the Government's whips' office, Walter Harrison, asked him to honour the 'gentleman's agreement' that sick MPs are 'paired' with an MP from the opposition party, thus reducing the vote on both sides by one. Although Weatherill told Harrison that he had no sick Conservative MP to pair with Sir Alfred, he did agree not to vote himself. If that isn't surprising enough, given what was at stake, astonishingly Harrison replied that this was actually too much to ask of Weatherill and didn't hold him to the agreement. So Bernard Weatherill voted and the government lost by one vote. This forced the government to resign, prompting the 1979 election, which Mrs Thatcher won, heralding eighteen years of Conservative government. (Sadly, Sir Alfred Broughton died a few days after the vote.)

Ministers in Parliament

Members of the government ('ministers') are also members of one or other of the two Houses of Parliament. Most belong to the House of Commons, where each represents a particular constituency in the UK. It is easy – and risky – for those working in government to forget that, because ministers have this wholly separate additional job of being a constituency MP. In practice they are 'part-time' ministers.

But where does it say that ministers have to have seats in Parliament? Nowhere. Is it a constitutional convention, like the requirement of the Monarch to give her assent to all bills that come before her? Probably not, because, while ministers *usually* have seats in Parliament, we don't have to delve too far back into the past to find one who didn't. As recently as 1999 there was a minister who wasn't in the Lords or the Commons. Solicitor-General for Scotland wasn't the most visible of posts but it was nevertheless a ministerial position whose holder wasn't a member of either House.[60]

Perhaps the main reason why all ministers are usually in Parliament is because it is so easy to put them there. If the Prime Minister wants someone as a minister who hasn't been elected to the House of Commons, it's a simple matter to put them in the House of Lords. All Prime Ministers do this.[61] (I look in more detail in chapter five at how members of the House of Lords are appointed but it probably suffices to say at this point that the Prime Minister can

---

[60] When in 1999 devolved government was set up in Scotland, the post of Solicitor-General for Scotland was transferred from the UK Government to the Scottish Administration. The holder of the post at the time, Colin Boyd, did not sit in either House of Parliament. He relinquished the post of Solicitor-General for Scotland in 2000 and now sits as Baron Boyd of Duncansby in the House of Lords.

[61] Examples of this would be: Lord Young, who was appointed to the Lords by Margaret Thatcher to 'allow' him to enter her government; Tony Blair putting his old flat-mate Charlie Falconer into the Lords because he wished him to be a minister; Gordon Brown making some novel and interesting ministerial appointments of people hitherto outside politics such former CBI director Digby Jones and Admiral Sir Alan West, and David Cameron bringing the former banker Sir James Sassoon into his government.

pretty much appoint to the Lords whomever she wants.) Two recent examples of this exercise of Prime Ministerial power were not without controversy. The first concerns Zac Goldsmith who was a minister in Boris Johnson's government at the time of the December 2019 general election. He was also the MP for Richmond Park in south-west London. Bucking the national trend, Goldsmith lost his seat in the election to the Liberal Democrat Sarah Olney. One might have thought that this would mark, temporarily at least, the end of Goldsmith's time as a minister and a parliamentarian. However it marked the end of neither. Boris Johnson simply gave him a seat in the House of Lords and Goldsmith continued in the same ministerial post. The second example concerns Nicky Morgan who was the Secretary of State for Digital, Culture, Media and Sport at the time of the 2019 election. Although Morgan had announced that she wished to step down as an MP at the election, Boris Johnson didn't want to lose her as a Cabinet minister at that point, so he simply gave her a seat in the Lords from where she carried on as Secretary of State. Although Johnson then shuffled her out of his Cabinet just a few weeks later, she remains a member of the Lords for life, if she so chooses.

Although it is not strictly necessary for a minister to be in Parliament, a Prime Minister would probably judge it in the government's interests for a minister to be in the House of Lords rather than outside of Parliament altogether as, in the Lords, the minister will be able to speak on behalf of the government. It would also mean that the minister is accountable to Parliament (albeit to a chamber of Parliament that is wholly unelected). The whole issue of how peers (i.e. members of the House of Lords) are appointed has for very many years, as we shall see, been rather controversial. But the present reality is that the Prime Minister has considerable freedom to make appointments to the House of Lords. Some may find this surprising given that the role of Parliament is to hold the government (of which the Prime Minister is head) to account.

Must the Prime Minister have a Seat in the Commons?

Is it a constitutional convention that the Prime Minister must have a seat in the House of Commons? Although it's certainly not required by any Act of Parliament, the answer to this question must be yes. Any student of British history will know that many of the great Prime Ministers of the past have had seats in the Lords rather than the Commons. During the 19th century Prime Ministers had been drawn interchangeably from the Lords and the Commons. Even in the 20th century Britain had a Prime Minister in the Lords – Lord Salisbury, who left office in 1902. Nowadays though it would be unthinkable for the Prime Minister to have a seat in the unelected House. But in 1902 it was acceptable. So what has changed in the meantime? The constitution has evolved over the last hundred years to a position where it has become a *convention* that the Prime Minister must have a seat in the House of Commons. When did this convention emerge? Most people would say it was in the early 1960s, but perhaps it was earlier – in May 1940.

Britain was at war and the Prime Minister Neville Chamberlain was about to resign. He had lost some support within his own party and Attlee's Labour Party refused to serve in a coalition under his leadership. There were two possible candidates to lead the new government: Winston Churchill, First Lord of the Admiralty, and Lord Halifax, the Foreign Secretary. What seems to have swung things decisively in Churchill's favour was Halifax's concession that it would be *difficult* for him to lead the country from the (unelected) House of Lords. We can only speculate what might have become of Britain had Halifax felt able at that cataclysmic moment to become Prime Minister.

23 years later, in 1963, the question arose again in the peculiar circumstances that led to Alec Douglas-Home's accession to the premiership. In 1963 the Prime Minister Harold Macmillan announced he was stepping down on the grounds of ill health. Until 1965 the Conservative Party didn't elect its leader. Instead, 'soundings' would be taken about who his replacement should be, after which advice would be given to the Monarch about who should be invited to form a government. Consideration began as to who should be recommended to the Monarch as Macmillan's replacement and Lord Home began to emerge as a favoured compromise candidate between two candidates

who represented particular wings of the party. As with Lord Halifax in 1940, his membership of the House of Lords was seen as an obstacle. By 1963 however, an act had been passed allowing hereditary members of the House of Lords to renounce their peerages. This had been done to allow Anthony Wedgwood Benn – Tony Benn as he became known – to renounce the peerage he had inherited on the death of his father, Viscount Stansgate. The law as it had stood before 1963 made it impossible for a peer, which Benn became on the death of his father, to be a member of the House of Commons.[62] However, the Peerage Act allowed Benn to keep his seat in the Commons. Lord Home now used this legislation to renounce his own peerage. The safe Conservative seat of Kinross & West Perthshire was vacant and Home (now Sir Alec) was able to fight and win the by-election, securing a place in the House of Commons.

Curiously then, although Lord Salisbury is usually regarded as the last Prime Minister to sit in the House of Lords, technically it was actually Lord Home, albeit for a very short period between being invited to form a government by the Queen and renouncing his peerage. He was then for a short while a Prime Minister with no seat in either House of Parliament, while he was fighting the by-election. Home's premiership proved very short lived as he lost the 1964 general election but, after the Conservatives were re-elected at the 1970 election, he returned to government as Foreign Secretary, thereby becoming the most recent former Prime Minister to be a minister in someone else's Cabinet.[63] And to complete a highly unusual parliamentary career, which had started in the House of Commons prior to Home inheriting his earldom in 1951, after the Conservative defeat in February 1974 he was re-appointed to the House of Lords, this time as a Life Peer.

So while in 1902 it had been entirely possible for a Prime

---

[62] This law was changed in 1999, after the majority of Hereditary Peers were removed from the House of Lords, so that Hereditary Peers without seats in the Lords could now sit in the Commons.

[63] An earlier high profile example of the same was Neville Chamberlain serving in Churchill's government when the latter replaced him as Prime Minister in May 1940.

Minister to sit in the House of Lords, by 1940 it was seen as 'difficult' and by 1963 it was regarded as impossible. It is therefore now held to be a constitutional convention that the Prime Minister must be a member of the House of Commons.

Must other Senior Ministers have Seats in the Commons?

But what about other senior ministers? In recent times many people have considered it unacceptable for a senior minister such as the Home Secretary, Foreign Secretary or Chancellor[64] to be a member of the House of Lords. Yet in 1982 it seemed acceptable for Lord Carrington to be Margaret Thatcher's Foreign Secretary. And Lord Young was the Secretary of State for Trade and Industry until 1989. In 2003, following the resignation of Clare Short, when Tony Blair made Baroness Amos his new Secretary of State for International Development, concerns were expressed about having even a relatively junior Secretary of State in the unelected House of Lords.[65]

But much more controversy surrounded Peter Mandelson's return to government in October 2008. Having twice had to resign from the Cabinet, the EU Trade Commissioner was brought back into government by Gordon Brown as Secretary of State for Business with a seat in the House of Lords. This was particularly controversial because of the seniority of Mandelson's new post. Since Lord Young had served in Cabinet nearly 20 years earlier, no Cabinet Minister of this seniority had sat in the Lords – an unelected senior Minister accountable to an unelected chamber. And, for most of the time Lord Young had been in Cabinet, there had been another Cabinet minister in the same department with a seat in the Commons. This

---

[64] No Chancellor since the 1830s has sat in the House of Lords. Once the 1911 Parliament Act, which stripped the Lords of their powers over money, was passed, it became unthinkable for a Chancellor to sit in the Lords.

[65] See for example the then Shadow Secretary of State Caroline Spelman's comment in the House of Commons on 11 June 2003. https://hansard.parliament.uk/Commons/2003-06-11/debates/606c33ba-ba69-4505-8b11-a4d7b1102cfc/OccupiedTerritories

arrangement was not repeated when Lord Mandelson became Secretary of State for Business.

Mandelson's subsequent elevation in the reshuffle of June 2009 to the role of 'First Secretary of State' – effectively Deputy Prime Minister[66] – coupled with the simultaneous promotion to the Cabinet of Lord Adonis as Secretary of State for Transport suggested that, in this area at least, rather than being modernised, the British Constitution had actually regressed. The then Shadow Foreign Secretary, William Hague, claimed Gordon Brown had *put so many Lords ...in his Cabinet he's drifting back into Victorian times in terms of less... accountable and less democratic government.*[67] While this may have been an exaggeration, one had to look back to July 1989 to find a British Cabinet with three peers in it and, even then, one of these was the Lord Chancellor who, unlike now, was required to be a member of the Lords.

From the coming to power of the Coalition Government in 2010 until recently, the only full Cabinet Minister to have a seat in the Lords was the Leader of the House of Lords – a ministerial job that requires its holder to be a member of that House.[68] In March 2021 however Boris Johnson appointed Lord (David) Frost as his lead Brexit minister. Although Frost wasn't the most senior minister in his department (that was Michael Gove) he was nevertheless a full Cabinet Minister. Thus there were now two full Cabinet Ministers with seats in the House of Lords.

---

[66] Peter Mandelson has himself confirmed that he was the de facto Deputy Prime Minister: "Some weeks before, the Cabinet Secretary, Gus O'Donnell, had remarked to me that Gordon needed a Deputy Prime Minister to strengthen the centre of government, and that in his view I should do the job. In the event, I became deputy Prime Minister in all but name, partly because of the sensitivity of doing this from the Lords...." Peter Mandelson 'The Third Man: Life at the Heart of New Labour' Harper Press July 2010

[67] Speaking on 'The Andrew Marr Show' 7 June 2009

[68] For some of the time during Cameron's premiership, the Leader of the House of Lords wasn't actually a full Cabinet Minister, much to the irritation of many members of the Lords. The holder did nevertheless attend Cabinet.

So the actions taken by both Gordon Brown and Boris Johnson in this area suggest that modernisation (if that's the right word) is perhaps not irreversible. What might be seen as a huge modernising step would of course be a move to an elected or partly elected House of Lords. This is something we look at in chapter five. Such a change could have a considerable impact on the number of senior ministers in the Lords.

The Separation of Powers

Many democratic constitutions are founded on the principle of the 'separation of powers'. The institutions separated in this principle are the executive (government), the legislature (Parliament) and the judiciary (the judges). The principle of the separation of powers was first identified by the French political philosopher Montesquieu in the 18th century. Montesquieu argued that such separation was essential if citizens were to enjoy the greatest possible liberty.

The American Constitution is a classic example of one based on this principle. In the USA the constitution forbids any overlap in membership of the executive (the President and those who work for him), the legislature (the two Houses of Congress) and the judiciary (although one exception to this rule is that the Vice-President acts as the Presiding Officer of the Senate). Thus, for example, when President Obama brought Senator Hillary Clinton into his administration as Secretary of State, she was obliged to give up her seat in the Senate. Other countries have similar rules. In France, elected members of the National Assembly invited by the President to be ministers must relinquish their seats in the French Parliament. This is why, at elections for the National Assembly, French people elect not only someone to represent their constituency but also a 'suppléant' (what Americans might call a 'running mate') to represent the constituency in the National Assembly should the elected member be invited to join the government.

Unsurprisingly, in the UK things are a little more complicated – although this is an area that has seen some simplification in the last few years. Until recent times in the UK, the executive, legislature and judiciary have been unseparated. As we have already seen, members of the British Government (ministers) almost always have seats in Parliament. This coincidence of the executive and legislature is not unusual; it is found in many other western democracies. More unusual has been the overlap of the legislature and the judiciary. The historic position in terms of the separation of powers in the UK can be shown diagrammatically.

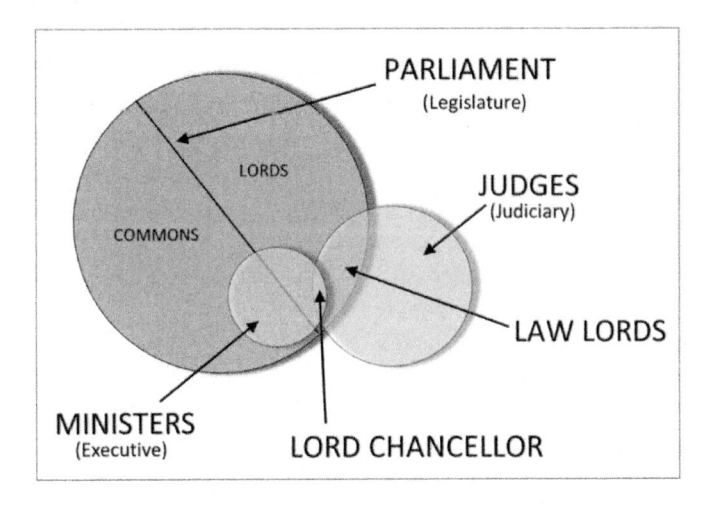

Figure 1

Figure 1 shows the position until April 2006. Ministers sat, as now, wholly within Parliament (although, as we have seen, this is not absolutely always the case). The majority of ministers have seats in the House of Commons rather than the House of Lords. (About 80% of ministers are usually drawn from the Commons and 20% from the Lords.) There was also an overlap between Parliament and the judiciary, and a tiny overlap of all three. The overlap of Parliament and the judiciary reflected the dual role of the House of Lords which was not only one of the two Houses of Parliament (the 'Upper House') but also the highest Court of Appeal in the UK on all matters except those of EU law and Human Rights. In these, respectively, the European Court of Justice (based in

Luxembourg) and the European Court of Human Rights (based in Strasbourg) were the highest Courts of Appeal.[69]

It wasn't the whole House of Lords that acted as the highest Court of Appeal but rather its 'Appellate Committee', although as its name suggested it was technically no more than a committee of the House. The judges in this court were commonly known as the 'Law Lords'.[70] At any one time there were twelve serving Law Lords, with five usually hearing a particular case.[71] These judges were full members of the House of Lords like any of its other members although, in an attempt to uphold the principle that those who *make* the law (Parliament) shouldn't be the same people as those who *interpret* the law (the judges), the Law Lords tended to take a self-denying ordinance when it came to the Lords' legislative role. But the overriding principle, which in a country like the USA would be regarded as sacrosanct, was inherently compromised by the existence of the Law Lords.

This dual role of the House of Lords could cause considerable confusion. A newspaper headline along the lines of *Home Secretary blocked by House of Lords* was not uncommon. But seldom would the story explain which of its two roles the House of Lords was playing in the case in question. For example, if a key government bill ran into difficulty when it is was being considered by the House of Lords, this could prompt such a headline. Equally though, if an individual challenged the Home Secretary on a particular issue in court, and the case was eventually appealed to the Lords in its judicial capacity, with the Lords finding against the government, then once again the headline might have been

---

[69] The House of Lords only acted as the highest Court of Appeal on matters of Scottish law in civil cases. In Scottish criminal cases the highest Court of Appeal is High Court of Justiciary.

[70] They were known formally as the 'Lords of Appeal in Ordinary'.

[71] Nine judges heard the case challenging the validity of the 2004 Hunting Act.

Home Secretary blocked by House of Lords. Consider this extract from an article in the *Guardian* of 27 June 2008:

> Parliament has been forced to legislate because of a House of Lords ruling last week that a double murderer ...was denied a fair trial when key witnesses who identified him as the gunman testified anonymously.... The bill will also have to go through the House of Lords quickly if it is to become law before the summer recess.

This made two references to the House of Lords: one concerning its judicial role, the other its legislative role. But no reference was made in the article to this important distinction. In other countries this confusion would not have arisen. In a similar situation in the USA, this distinction would be between the roles of the Senate and the Supreme Court, two completely separate institutions.

The banning of fox hunting in England and Wales in 2004 illustrated this point well. When the bill to ban fox hunting was in the Lords it was fought tooth and nail by a majority of Lords who wanted fox hunting to continue. Eventually, as we have seen, the bill was passed with the use of the Parliament Acts; fox hunting was duly banned. When, however, supporters of fox hunting then challenged in the courts the validity of this use of the Parliament Acts, the case went to the House of Lords where the Law Lords upheld the act. So here we had a situation where the Lords, acting as part of the legislature, strongly opposed the principle of the legislation, but when that legislation had been passed and was challenged in the courts, the Lords, acting as part of the judiciary, upheld the legislation. So the headline *Legislation to ban fox hunting defeated by Lords* could have been followed some months later by the headline *Lords uphold legislation banning fox hunting* without contradiction.

It was in the office of Lord Chancellor where, until 2006, the executive, legislature and judiciary uniquely came together.

The Lord Chancellor, as a Cabinet minister, was (and still is) a member of the executive. (In June 2003 this became clearer after the Lord Chancellor was also given the title of Secretary of State for Constitutional Affairs and, from May 2007, Secretary of State for Justice.) The Lord Chancellor, as a member of the House of Lords (where he chaired proceedings) was also a member of the legislature. Finally, he was also formal head of the judiciary, which gave him a major role in the appointment of judges. He could, if he wished, also sit as a Law Lord.

This changed, however, with the Constitutional Reform Act 2005. Another important new part of Britain's written constitution, this act was central to the Labour Government's plans for constitutional reform. Its purpose was to make the principle of the separation of powers more of a reality in the UK and to that end it made two important changes.

First, the role of the Lord Chancellor was radically changed. The Government had originally wanted to abolish the post completely. This was controversial, given the post had existed for a thousand years or more, and the legislation predictably ran into opposition in the House of Lords. Meanwhile the Government itself began to have second thoughts when the complications of abolishing the post became apparent (in terms of how much existing legislation would need to be amended). The title of Lord Chancellor was therefore retained, although its holder would no longer chair, nor even have to be a member of, the House of Lords. Instead the Lords would elect its own 'Lord Speaker' and, in July 2006, Baroness Hayman became the first elected Speaker of the House of Lords. (Note that it is the Lord Speaker, not Lords Speaker.) The Lord Speaker serves a five year term before needing to seek re-election and is limited to serving two terms.

More importantly, the Lord Chancellor's role as head of

the judiciary was abolished. The formal titular role of head of the judiciary was passed to the Lord Chief Justice[72] while the power to appoint judges was given to a statutory commission.

While there was some uncertainty about whether the Lord Chancellor at the time, Lord Falconer, was technically able to sit as a judge, the law was clear that his successors never would be. When, in July 2007, Jack Straw became the first Lord Chancellor in history to sit in the House of Commons, one might have enquired why the office was retained, given how many of its powers had been removed. But one important historic role of the Lord Chancellor remained: to represent the views in Cabinet of the judiciary.

After April 2006 the separation of powers looked like this:

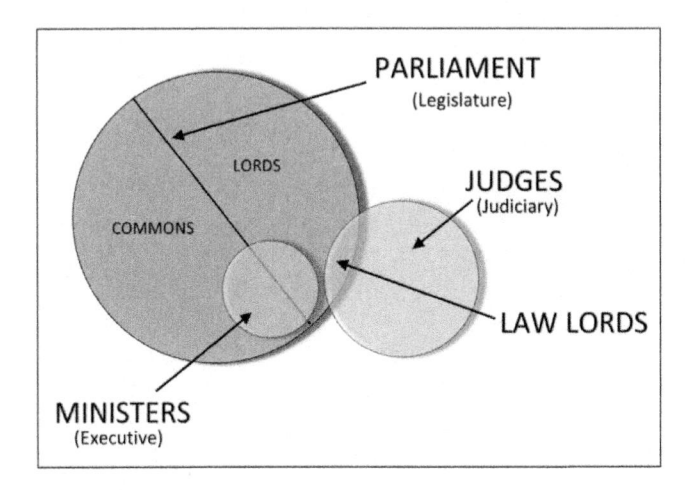

Figure 2

The second and more important reform contained in the

---

[72] The Lord Chief Justice is the Head of the Judiciary in England & Wales. The Head of the Judiciary in Scotland is the Lord President of the Court of Session and in Northern Ireland the Lord Chief Justice of Northern Ireland.

Constitutional Reform Act 2005 concerned the role of the Law Lords. The act provided for a new Supreme Court to be set up to replace the judicial role of the House of Lords. The implementation of this reform was delayed by the difficulty of finding suitable premises for the new court, but once the Middlesex Guildhall – across Parliament Square from the Houses of Parliament – was chosen, the new Supreme Court finally came into being in October 2009. As this new highest Court of Appeal is wholly separate from the legislature (see Figure 3 below) the principle of the separation of powers now has more meaning in the British Constitution.[73]

PARLIAMENT (Legislature)

LORDS

COMMONS

JUDGES (Judiciary – including the Supreme Court)

MINISTERS (Executive)

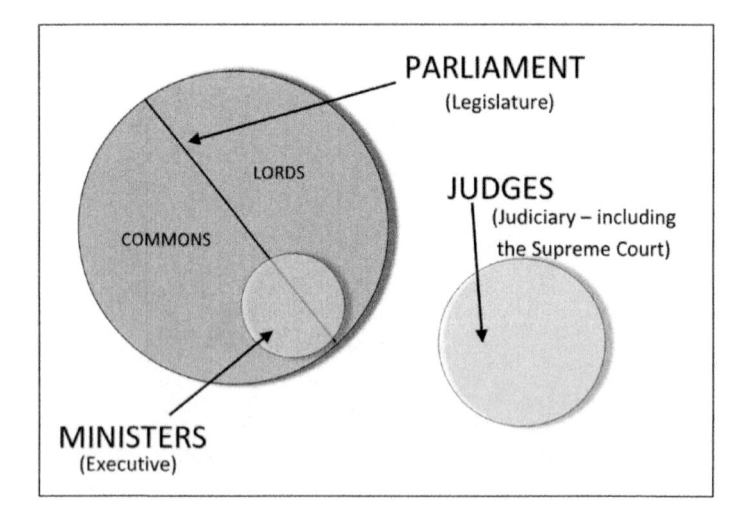

Figure 3

There remains, however, at almost all times, a complete overlap of ministers and Parliament. We have discussed this above, but perhaps before leaving the topic it's worth highlighting

---

[73] The existing Law Lords became the first justices of the new Supreme Court. Although they were disqualified from sitting or voting in the House of Lords, when they retired from the Supreme Court they were allowed to return to the House of Lords as full members. Supreme Court Justices appointed in the future were not, however, given seats in the House of Lords.

the confusion that this can cause. To many people there is no obvious distinction between government and Parliament and it's understandable why. Ask people to think about the Prime Minister at her workplace and they're probably more likely to think of her speaking in the House of Commons – part of Parliament – than they are to think of her working in her office in No 10 or at the Cabinet Table. Many people also assume that all MPs sitting on the 'governing' side of the House of Commons are members of the government. But of course that's not true: only the 80 or so who are ministers are in the government.[74] For those who work as civil servants this is crucially important to understand. Civil Servants work for, and only for, the politicians in the 'executive' circle in Figure 3. Their relationship with any other MP or Peer from the governing party is no different to their relationship with, say, the Leader of the Opposition.

Parliamentary Sovereignty and the Rule of Law

Unlike the legislatures of most other democratic countries, the Westminster Parliament is often described as a 'sovereign' Parliament. In his seminal text of 1902 on the constitution, A. V. Dicey described the principle of parliamentary sovereignty as follows:

> *That Parliament ...has, under the English constitution, the right to make or unmake any law whatever; and, further, that no person or body is recognised by the law of England as having a right to override or set aside the legislation of Parliament.*[75]

The principle of parliamentary sovereignty is not set down in law, but it is a very well established feature of Britain's constitutional arrangements: so well established, in fact, that it is

---

[74] Of these, around 22 ministers are usually full members of the Cabinet. For more information of the various ranks of government minister, see chapter 3.

[75] Introduction to the Study of the Law of the Constitution pp37-38 . A. V. Dicey 1902. Macmillan and Co. London.

sometimes referred to as a 'doctrine' rather than just a principle or convention. So it is Parliament, rather than any other institution of the state, that has the final say. Why are national legislatures rarely sovereign bodies? The answer stems from the fact that most countries, as we have seen, have a formal written constitution that defines people's basic rights and responsibilities and how the system of government operates. Where there is a formal constitution, there needs to be an institution that interprets and upholds the principles enshrined in that constitution. In most countries this is done by the judiciary. In the USA for example, it is the Supreme Court that has the final say on interpreting and upholding the American Constitution.

In the USA, if the legislature (Congress) passes a law that infringes any of the basic rights that people enjoy under the constitution or in any other way is thought to violate the constitution, it is possible for that law to be challenged in the courts, where it can be overturned. Two particular issues illustrate this point well in the USA – abortion and the right to carry weapons. Because the American Constitution upholds the right to life, anti-abortionists in America have in the past challenged legislation liberalising the laws on abortion. If it agrees with the challenge, the Supreme Court can strike down such legislation. Whether the Court agrees or not depends crucially, of course, on its interpretation of 'life' and whether it starts at conception, birth or any other time in between. Similarly, whether Americans should be allowed to carry weapons depends on the interpretation of the 'right to bear arms' included in their constitution. This was a provision written into the American Constitution in a very different era, but the judges alone can interpret its applicability to today's USA. Any legislation passed by Congress to restrict the carrying of weapons by American citizens will always be open to a challenge in the courts on the grounds that it is 'unconstitutional'. Judges, rather than Congress, therefore have the final say in matters concerning the American Constitution. As a result, judges in the USA are often more political than they are in the UK and they have a much more obvious role in *making* law, rather than just interpreting it, than do their British counterparts.

The American President's role in choosing a new Supreme Court judge on the death or resignation of one of the incumbents can therefore be crucial to the overall 'political' position of the Court. And judges at lower levels in the USA are actually elected.

In the UK, parliamentary sovereignty means that the legislature has the final say. Acts passed by Parliament cannot be overturned in the courts. This contrasts with the power of judges to overturn government decisions. A judge may strike down such a decision if a challenge to its lawfulness is successful. What the courts cannot do though is stop government then introducing a new bill in Parliament to allow it to do legally now what it wasn't legally able to do before.

The Human Rights Act

In theory, Westminster can legislate in any way it wishes to without challenge. But the reality is not quite like this, partly because of the passing of the Human Rights Act in 1998. The Human Rights Act (HRA) incorporated into British law the principles set out in the European Convention on Human Rights (ECHR) which was drafted in the years after the Second World War and to which the UK Government was a signatory. Following the implementation of the HRA, people in the UK were able to access through the British courts the basic rights set out in the ECHR. (Before the HRA came into force, the rights of British people were either found in common (i.e. 'judge-made') law or in individual Acts of Parliament that dealt with specific issues.) They no longer had to go through the time consuming and costly process of taking their case to the European Court of Human Rights in Strasbourg. It's perhaps important to stress that the European Court of Human Rights is a quite separate institution to the European Court of Justice in Luxembourg which is the highest court of appeal in the European Union. There has always been confusion, for obvious reasons, caused by short-hand references to the 'European Court'. The European Court of Human Rights is an institution of the Council of Europe, a body which was set up in the 1940s with the UK as a founder member.[76] It may come as some surprise to some people who in 2016 voted for the UK to leave the EU that the UK remains part of the Council of Europe and therefore within the jurisdiction of the ECHR.

Under the HRA, public bodies can be challenged in the British courts for their lack of compliance with the ECHR and the courts are required to interpret legislation as far as possible in a way that is compatible with the Convention.

Why the HRA may be seen to infringe on the principle of parliamentary sovereignty is because it allows challenges to be made in the courts to Acts of Parliament if they are considered to be incompatible with the rights set out in the ECHR. But if the courts uphold such a challenge they can only declare the act as incompatible with the Convention - they can't strike down the legislation. Thus the principle of parliamentary sovereignty is upheld. But in practice such a declaration puts great pressure on government to amend the legislation to remove this incompatibility. As an example, when in 2017 the Civil Partnership Act 2004 was challenged on the basis that it only provided for civil partnerships to take place between same-sex couples, the Supreme Court declared the act incompatible with the ECHR.[77] The 2004 Act was then amended by the Civil Partnerships, Marriages and Deaths (Registration etc) Act 2019 to allow heterosexual couples to enter into a civil partnership.

So how does the challenge to the validity of the Hunting Act 2004 we mentioned above square with the principle of parliamentary sovereignty? That act was in fact subjected to two separate legal challenges. One challenge was on human rights grounds i.e. that banning fox hunting was to deny some people their livelihoods. All the judges had the power to do here was to make a declaration of incompatibility which, as it turned out, they

---

[76] And what causes yet more confusion is that the Council of Europe is something quite different to the European Council and the Council of the European Union, both of which are institutions of the EU.

[77] https://www.supremecourt.uk/cases/docs/uksc-2017-0060-judgment.pdf

didn't do.[78] The second challenge concerned the way that the Parliament Acts were used to override the opposition of the House of Lords (acting as the Upper House of Parliament) to banning fox hunting. The challenge was based on an argument concerning the validity of the Parliament Act 1949 under the terms of which the Hunting Act had been passed. The challenge centred on the fact that the 1949 Act, which itself had been passed under the provisions of the Parliament Act 1911, had unlawfully amended the 1911 Act by reducing from two years to one year the period for which the House of Lords could delay the passage of a Bill. This was a very technical legal argument, which was ultimately not upheld in the House of Lords.[79]

Had the supporters of fox hunting won this case, it would presumably have led to the striking down not only of the Hunting Act but every other act passed under the terms of the 1949 Parliament Act. This would have driven a coach and horses through the principle of the sovereignty of Parliament. Although they did not uphold the challenge, the judges in both the Court of Appeal and the House of Lords did make some interesting observations about the extent to which Parliament (and in particular the House of Commons) can use its sovereignty.

Under the terms of the Parliament Act 1949, for example, the Commons (which in practice usually means the government) would need only to wait one year to amend the Parliament Act 1949 itself and remove the delaying power of the Lords completely. As we have seen, the 1911 Parliament Act left the Lords' veto intact in one particular area, which was the power to extend the life of a Parliament or, to put it another way, the power to delay the date of the next general election beyond the statutory five years. But, under the terms of the Parliament Act 1949, a government would have to wait only one year in order to remove this Lords veto, after which it would be able to delay the date of the next general election indefinitely. A future government could

---

[78] House of Lords judgment 26 November 2007

[79] House of Lords judgment 13 July 2005

in the same way abolish the House of Lords altogether. Should a future government try to use the Parliament Acts to delay a general election or abolish the House of Lords, a major, public, constitutional struggle between the judiciary and the executive would inevitably ensue.

What this illustrates is that, in practice, it is not just what is contained in Acts of Parliament that influences judges in their views. The constitutional principle known as the 'rule of law' is from time to time invoked by judges to justify a particular stance they have taken, usually vis-à-vis the executive. In 1994 the former Lord Chief Justice Lord Woolf stated that if, for example, Parliament *did the unthinkable* and removed the courts' power of judicial review, he would consider it necessary to make clear that *ultimately there are even limits on the supremacy of Parliament which it is the courts' inalienable responsibility to identify and uphold.*[80]

Over recent years the courts have asserted themselves more and more when they think the rule of law is not being upheld. But, as with other areas of the British Constitution, the difficulty is that there is no simple and straightforward description of what the principle of the rule of law actually entails. The Constitutional Reform Act 2005 says in section 1 that the act does not adversely affect *the existing constitutional principle of the rule of law*. It also requires that future Lord Chancellors respect the rule of law. But the act doesn't describe what the rule of law actually is. Perhaps the principle of the rule of law is thought to be so widely understood that it requires no formal definition.

The rule of law is usually taken to require that the rights of individuals are determined by legal rules and not the arbitrary behaviour of authorities; that there can be no punishment unless a court decides there has been a breach of law; and that the courts enforce and define the rights of individuals. Some have argued that the principle of the rule of law also requires governments to

---

[80] 1994 F.A. Mann lecture (published in [1995] PL 57, pp 68-69)

comply with their obligations in international law. But perhaps the most widely understood principles of the rule of law are that everyone, regardless of their position in society, is subject to the law and that the laws of the land should apply equally to all citizens. As former Master of the Rolls, Lord Denning, liked to remind those in authority: *'Be ye never so high, the law is above you'*. Whatever the formal definition of the rule of law, it is certainly a doctrine widely accepted as being central to the British Constitution - perhaps providing a restraint on government that in another country might be included in its codified constitution.

So perhaps there are some limits upon the sovereignty of Parliament. The word 'sovereignty' was much used during the EU referendum campaign, with claims by 'leave' supporters that British sovereignty had been eroded by the UK's membership of the European Union. By 2016 a significant proportion of the legislation that governed the lives of British people (and all other citizens of the EU) was now made in Brussels, Strasbourg and Luxembourg rather than in Whitehall and Westminster. Sometimes EU legislation is directly applicable to member states and at other times it has to be implemented via national legislatures but either way it must be applied. Where there is an incompatibility between EU legislation and domestic legislation, national courts have the power to 'disapply' acts of Parliament that conflict with EU law.[81] Thus, so long as the UK was a member of the EU, in all areas where the EU had competence to make law, there had been a transfer of sovereignty from the UK Parliament to the EU. The sovereignty of the UK Parliament had therefore been compromised by Britain's membership of the EU – although, of course, when the UK Parliament, following the referendum, legislated to take Britain out of the EU, all of the sovereignty that had been surrendered returned.

The setting up of devolved governments in the non-English parts of the UK is a topic that we will discuss in some detail in chapter eight of this book. However it's an issue worth briefly raising here

---

[81] This position was established by the second *Factortame* case in 1991

because of its apparent effect on the sovereignty of the UK Parliament. The devolved legislatures that were created in Belfast, Edinburgh and Cardiff in 1999 all have substantial powers to legislate within their own jurisdictions over major areas of domestic policy such as education and, as we particularly saw during the Covid pandemic, health. So in a practical sense, the sovereignty of Westminster has been reduced in these and other policy areas, with the UK Parliament in these areas really only acting as a legislature for England.

There is nothing, however, in the legislation that established devolved government in Scotland, Wales and Northern Ireland to prohibit Westminster from legislating in *any* area, whether devolved or not, across the whole of the UK. That Westminster doesn't generally legislate in devolved areas is because successive UK Governments have usually chosen not to introduce such legislation since it would make a mockery of the whole principle of devolution if it did. But there is nothing legally stopping the UK Parliament legislating across the UK, against the wishes of the devolved administrations, on devolved matters, and, as we shall see, in recent years it has done so more often than before. Furthermore, because the legislation that set up devolved government in Scotland, Wales and Northern Ireland is *Westminster's* legislation, Westminster could at any time amend or even repeal it. In theory, a one-vote majority in the Commons could abolish devolved government in Scotland, Wales and Northern Ireland. So theoretically at least, the creation of devolved government across the UK hasn't impinged on the sovereignty of Westminster.

The Royal Prerogative

Much of what the Prime Minister can do, she does not as a consequence of legislation but of what are known as 'prerogative powers'. These are powers, once exercised by the Monarch, that have since been transferred to ministers (and to the Prime Minister in particular) but have never been put under the control of Parliament. (We have already looked at some of these prerogative powers in the form of Royal Assent and the prorogation and dissolution of Parliament.) Ministers' powers to take executive action are usually found in Acts of Parliament but, in areas that come under the Royal Prerogative, Parliament has never passed any legislation and so ministers are free to act without the consent of Parliament. Is this therefore another restriction on the principle of parliamentary sovereignty? Not really, since at any time Parliament could legislate to bring any part of the Royal Prerogative within its control.

The areas of government in which the Royal Prerogative has most often operated surround what might be described as 'the ancient powers of the state'. Historically they have included a number of aspects of foreign and defence policy, managing the Civil Service and the granting of appointments and honours.[82] A key feature of Gordon Brown's proposals for constitutional change, first set out in a consultation document published in 2007,[83] was to bring a number of existing areas of the Royal Prerogative under the control of Parliament. And whilst not all of these proposals became law, when the Constitutional Reform and Governance Act was passed shortly before the 2010 general election it did for the first time put the Civil Service and its core values on a statutory footing and give Parliament the right to vote against the ratification of treaties.[84]

War Powers

Perhaps the most controversial area of the Royal Prerogative concerns a government's power to make war. A formal

---

[82] Whilst it's difficult to produce a definitive list of prerogative powers, they include those in paragraphs 2.7 – 2.9 of this government document: https://assets.publishing.service.gov.uk/government/uploads/system/uploads/attachment_data/file/742221/Queen_s_and_prince_s_consent_pamphlet__September_2018___accessible_.pdf

[83] The Governance of Britain CM7170 The Stationery Office https://assets.publishing.service.gov.uk/government/uploads/system/uploads/attachment_data/file/228834/7170.pdf

[84] www.legislation.gov.uk/ukpga/2010/25/contents

'declaration of war' is a technical issue under international law. Although Britain hasn't actually declared war on any country since January 1942, when it reciprocated Siam's declaration of war, according to Peter Hennessy, Margaret Thatcher's Government did consider such a declaration when the Falkland Islands were invaded in 1982:

> *A declaration of war against Argentina was considered over what one might call the "Falklands weekend" in the first days of April 1982 and the 1939 file on how to do it was sent for. It could not be found. A search was mounted in what was then a called the Public Record Office. Still no file was found. It turned up 12 years later in 1994. It was just two sides of paper, drawn up for the Foreign Secretary, Lord Halifax, by the Foreign Office's legal adviser, Sir Gerald Fitzmaurice, on the day of the Molotov-Ribbentrop Pact, 23 August 1939. On 12 September 1939, it had been consigned to the FO's registry in a collection known as "General and Miscellaneous" and therefore lost for 55 years.* [85]

Under the Royal Prerogative, the government has the power to put British troops into action, whether or not following a formal declaration of war, without the consent of Parliament. This doesn't mean that Parliament will not debate the issue. But it had meant, until quite recently, that Parliament never debated a formal motion to authorise military action. An adjournment debate is a technical device used in Parliament (though less so now) to allow a debate on a particular issue without a formal motion being voted on. Until March 2003 this had been used by governments to hold a debate without expressing a formal view on the issue of putting British troops into action.

In 2003 this changed when Britain went to war in Iraq. The Government decided to put a formal motion before the House of

---

[85] https://publications.parliament.uk/pa/ld201314/ldhansrd/text/131128-0003.htm

Commons that *support[ed] the decision of Her Majesty's Government that the United Kingdom should use all means necessary to ensure the disarmament of Iraq's weapons of mass destruction.*[86] For the first time the Commons was allowed formally to debate and authorise the use of military force even though its authorisation wasn't constitutionally required. Whether this helped Tony Blair's government is a matter of debate. Certainly it allowed ministers subsequently to say that 'Parliament' had authorised the war in Iraq, but the motion was carried only when a large majority of Conservative MPs voted in its favour. 139 Labour MPs rebelled by supporting an amendment that rejected the immediate use of force. A few Conservative MPs, every Liberal Democrat MP and some MPs from the minor parties also voted against the Government. This Labour rebellion continues to represent the largest ever in the House of Commons by MPs from a governing party.

In May 2007 the House of Commons passed a resolution stating that *this House welcomes the precedents set by the Government... in seeking and obtaining the approval of the House for its decisions in respect of military action against Iraq; is of the view that it is inconceivable that any Government would in practice depart from this precedent...*[87]

Later, in March 2011, the then Cabinet Secretary, Sir Gus O'Donnell, wrote to the Political and Constitutional Reform Committee of the House of Commons in the following terms:

> *The Government believes that it is apparent that since the events leading up to the deployment of troops in Iraq, a convention exists that Parliament will be given the opportunity to debate the decision to commit troops to armed conflict and, except in emergency situations, that*

---

[86] https://publications.parliament.uk/pa/cm200203/cmhansrd/vo030318/debtext/30318-06.htm#30318-06_head1

[87] https://hansard.parliament.uk/Commons/2007-05-15/debates/07051555000001/ArmedConflict(ParliamentaryApproval)

debate would take place before they are committed. [88]

And when in that same month the Coalition Government decided to take part in military action against Libya there seemed to be no question as to whether there should be a vote in the House of Commons. Such discussion as there was about Parliament voting on this military action concerned the fact that the vote was taken after the action had begun rather than just before, as in the case of Iraq.[89] So it therefore seems now to have been established as a pretty firm convention that the consent of the Commons is required for military action to take place. During the debate on this military action, the Foreign Secretary, William Hague, actually pledged that the government would *enshrine in law for the future the necessity of consulting Parliament on military action.*[90]

Soon after this pledge was made, in response to a recommendation made by the House of Commons Political and Constitutional Reform Committee in its report *Parliament's Role in Conflict Decisions*[91], the Coalition Government made the following addition to the Cabinet Manual:

> In 2011, the Government acknowledged that a convention had developed in Parliament that before troops were committed the House of Commons should have an opportunity to debate the matter and said that it

---

[88] Written evidence to the Political and Constitutional Reform Committee's inquiry into the role and powers of the Prime Minister, Session 2010-12:
www.publications.parliament.uk/pa/cm201011/cmselect/cmpolcon/write v/842/m11.htm

[89] On this occasion the government had a rather more comfortable victory in the House of Commons with only 13 MPs voting against military action, one of whom was an MP from the governing party – the Conservative MP John Baron.

[90] https://hansard.parliament.uk/commons/2011-03-21/debates/1103219 000001/UnitedNationsSecurityCouncilResolution1973

[91] www.publications.parliament.uk/pa/cm201012/cmselect/cmpolcon/ 923/92302.htm

proposed to observe that convention except when there was an emergency and such action would not be appropriate.

It was however just a convention. No legislation has since followed. The Coalition Government did however confirm its adherence to the convention set out in the Cabinet Manual when, in August 2013, it was surprisingly defeated on a motion that would pave the way for the UK's militarily intervention into the crisis in Syria. Following the vote, the Prime Minister David Cameron was challenged by the Leader of the Opposition, Ed Miliband, to *confirm to the House that, given the will of the House that has been expressed tonight, he will not use the royal prerogative to order the UK to be part of military action before there has been another vote in the House of Commons.* David Cameron's response was clear:

> *I can give that assurance....I strongly believe in the need for a tough response to the use of chemical weapons, but I also believe in respecting the will of this House of Commons. It is very clear tonight that... the British Parliament, reflecting the views of the British people, does not want to see British military action. I get that, and the Government will act accordingly.*[92]

This vote in the Commons, compared to those on Iraq and Libya, rather more significantly confirms the existence of a constitutional convention in this area given that the government was defeated. That ministers felt bound by the vote clearly established the principle that the Commons now exercises a real veto over a government's power to engage in military action. Indeed the Syria vote may have wider ramifications, since a crucial difference between this vote and those on Iraq and Libya was that it was only a preliminary vote on principle: there was a clear promise of a further vote before any military action was undertaken. And unlike the vote on Iraq, there was no suggestion

---

[92] https://hansard.parliament.uk/commons/2013-08-29/debates/1308298 000001/SyriaAndTheUseOfChemicalWeapons

that any ground troops would be deployed.

The Syria vote raised some wider issues about the freedom of governments to act in foreign and defence matters. Did, for example, the vote prevent the British Government giving logistical or intelligence support to the Americans had they decided to take military action against Syria alone? The answer to this isn't clear. If it *is* the case that Parliament can now stop a hitherto executive action such as this, it suggests that the convention that has evolved since 2003 in the area of war powers may have developed more widely than many had thought. This is an issue of concern for some. As Alistair Burt, a Foreign Office minister at the time of the Syria vote argued:

> *If we are now in the position of having to convince half of Parliament plus one before difficult foreign policy executive action can be taken, not through a taking of voices by the whips, or being merely reliant on the arithmetic of Commons composition, but by vote, then what can Government commit itself to in discussions with allies, or preparation in advance for regional strategic defence? If Iran threatens not shipping lanes and British interests directly, but a smaller Gulf state friendly to the UK which asks for our assistance, do the Prime Minister and Foreign Secretary decide, and expect support, or do backbenchers?* [93]

It's an interesting question, the answer to which is still unclear.

A Permanent and Impartial Civil Service

Another feature of the British Constitution that sets the United Kingdom apart from most other countries is that it has a politically impartial Civil Service that does not change

---

[93] Patrick Wintour & Nicholas Watt, 'Alistair Burt Reveals Anger over Syria Vote at Westminster' The Guardian (London, 30 December 2013). https://www.theguardian.com/politics/2013/dec/30/alistair-burt-anger-syria-westminster

when a new government takes power. In other countries around the world, civil services tend to be politically appointed, at least at the most senior levels. For example, when a new American President is elected, even when he or she is replacing a President from the same party, there follows a wholesale removal of senior civil servants from the federal government in Washington, to be replaced by officials loyal to the new President. By contrast, in the UK, when a new Conservative-Liberal Democrat Government came to power in 2010 after thirteen years of Labour rule, no civil servants were removed – not even at the very top, where the Cabinet Secretary and Head of the Home Civil Service, Sir Gus O'Donnell, stayed in post. Nor were there any changes when Labour replaced eighteen years of Conservative rule in 1997. This feature of the UK system of government makes the relationship between ministers and civil servants rather different from that in other countries.

In chapter three we will explore the principles on which the British Civil Service is based – principles that go back to the reforms of the 19th century. One of those principles, impartiality, enables the British Civil Service to serve governments of any political hue. Before the Constitutional Reform and Governance Act was passed in 2010, no act of Parliament had ever enshrined the principles on which the Civil Service was based. All that had existed to protect those principles were the Civil Service Code – no more than a code of practice that ministers could ignore without any legal consequences, and the Civil Service 'Order-in-Council' – a law made not by Parliament but by ministers using their prerogative powers.[94] (Such 'executive legislation' can be created and amended very easily by ministers, without reference to Parliament.)

---

[94] Technically such law is made by what is known as 'The Queen in Council' – the Council being the Privy Council. To make an Order-in-Council under the Royal Prerogative, all it requires is for a group of Privy Counsellors to be in the presence of the Monarch and the law can be made.

So, while the principles on which the Civil Service is based may have remained largely unchanged for around 160 years, the political reality is that, until recently, any government since the mid-19th century could have changed them at any time almost on a whim.

Constitutional Reform

It is impossible to calculate precisely the proportion of the British Constitution that is written down because there will always be some debate about what is and what isn't a constitutional document. We have mentioned above a number of acts, ancient and modern, that certainly belong to the written part of the British Constitution. But this written part does not consist solely of acts. What about Erskine May – the 'bible' of parliamentary procedure?[95] This book, originally written in 1844 by a Commons clerk of that name, is really an interpretation of the standing orders of Parliament, describing its function and processes. As a manual that is regularly consulted by the Speakers of both Houses, other members of the two Houses and parliamentary staff, it is widely regarded as forming part of the constitution of the UK. Similarly the Cabinet Manual, as a document in which many previously unwritten conventions have been written down, is regarded by many as part of the British Constitution. The Cabinet Manual itself says that the *constitutional order...consists of various institutions, statutes, judicial decisions, principles and practices that are commonly understood as 'constitutional'*.[96] And the Brown Government's 'Governance of Britain' Green Paper described the British Constitution as having four principal sources: *statute law, common law, conventions and works of authority, such as those of Walter*

---

[95] The full name of Erskine May is "Erskine May's Treatise on the Law, Privileges, Proceedings and Usage of Parliament". A digital version can be found here: https://erskinemay.parliament.uk/

[96] Ibid. Cabinet Manual Paragraph 4

Bagehot and A.V. Dicey.[97]

But whatever our 'definition' of the constitution, what we can be clear about is that much more of Britain's constitutional arrangements are written down now than was the case before 1997. The Labour Governments of 1997-2010 stood out from their 20th century predecessors for their willingness to make reforms to Britain's constitution as did the Coalition Government, within which its Liberal Democrat element pushed hard for extensive constitutional reform.

The years since 1997 have seen major changes to the separation of powers and in particular to the House of Lords. Legislatures with substantial powers have been set up in Scotland, Wales and Northern Ireland with smaller amounts of power devolved to regional authorities in England. A Human Rights Act has been introduced, giving British people for the first time access to fundamental human rights enshrined in British law: the rights that are set out in the European Convention on Human Rights. All of this – and other changes – has been brought about through Acts of Parliament. Legislation was passed, as we have seen, to bring in fixed-term parliaments and a referendum was held in May 2011 on changing the electoral system to the Alternative Vote (a referendum in which the British people voted 'No'). Further legislation on reforming the Upper House was introduced in 2012 but later withdrawn (see chapter five).

Since 2015, constitutional change has arguably moved at a slower pace; but let us not overlook the one huge change to the UK's constitutional arrangements that has taken place since the time of the Coalition Government: Brexit. Devolution represented a major change to the way in which the UK is governed, but will the impact of Brexit be any less? That may still remain to be seen, but the Johnson administration has made clear that it too is interested in further constitutional reform. The 2019 Conservative

---

[97] Ibid. Governance of Britain Paragraph 211

manifesto committed to considerable constitutional reform proposals including, as we have seen, the repeal of the Fixed-term Parliaments Act (FTPA) as well as an 'update' of the Human Rights Act. It also said that a 'Constitution Democracy and Rights Commission' would be created to consider wider constitutional matters.

As the amount of constitutional law increases, so debate continues to grow about whether Britain should, like most other countries, have a formal single written document as its constitution. An important feature of this debate concerns the fact that 'constitutional' Acts of Parliament are legally no different to any other act passed by Parliament. The American Constitution requires the assent of the President, two-thirds of both Houses of Congress and three-quarters of the 50 states before it can be amended. But in the UK, unusually in the modern world, there is no concept of 'entrenched constitutional law' as a form of law higher – and harder to change – than other laws. There are many laws that are regarded as being part of the constitution, and we have mentioned a number of them here but, in their making and amending, such laws are no different from any other. Acts that reform the House of Lords or enshrine human rights into law are made – and therefore potentially amended and repealed - in exactly the same way as the Dangerous Dogs Act. [98]

---

[98] There is, however, a view, held by some lawyers, that there are some constitutional Acts that are so important that they are 'protected' from what is known as 'implied repeal'. In other words, they can only be repealed explicitly by another Act. Their repeal cannot be simply 'implied' by a future, contrary Act. The Human Rights Act and, until its repeal, the European Communities Act might be considered to fall into this category of primary legislation. The Civil Contingencies Act 2004 (www.legislation.gov.uk/ukpga/2004/36/section/23), under which ministers can use emergency powers to amend primary legislation by regulation, specifically mentions that the act cannot be used to amend the Human Rights Act (HRA). This suggests that the HRA, and perhaps other constitutional acts, have a status which is higher than other Acts. Indeed the explanatory notes to the Civil Contingencies Act (www.legislation.gov.uk/ukpga/2004/36/notes/division/5/22) state that 'Parliamentary Counsel have advised that the effect of the normal principles of the construction of delegated powers is that substantive amendments could not be made by emergency regulations to provisions

Some key parts of the British Constitution remain unwritten. Those dealing with the functions of the Monarch were almost entirely in this category until recently and even now, they have only been written about in a 'manual for the executive' (the Cabinet Manual) which is a far cry from legislation, let alone a formal written constitution. And few of the Prime Minister's powers are enshrined in acts. But much of the constitution is now written down. The debate about constitutional reform may traditionally have been seen as an issue only for the 'chattering classes', but it was given a much more public profile by the furore that followed the breaking of the MPs' expenses scandal in 2009. MPs' expenses may have been a rather prosaic issue to provoke a debate about constitutional reform amongst the British public but it did prompt discussion about the merits of Britain having a formal written constitution. Speaking in the House of Commons in June 2009, the then Prime Minister Gordon Brown stated that *it is for many people extraordinary that Britain still has a largely unwritten constitution. I personally favour a written constitution.*[99] And a decade later we saw the unlawful proroguing of Parliament, as described above. That further increased interest in the idea of having a formal written constitution for the UK.

But the debate around whether or not Britain should have a formal written constitution can sometimes be too simplistic. Britain's current constitutional arrangements can be justifiably criticised, but simply to argue for 'a written constitution' as an alternative raises more questions than it answers. At the most basic level, a written constitution could be a bad written constitution. (The constitution of Weimar Germany didn't, after all, stop Adolph Hitler coming to power.) And if the UK were to have a formal written constitution, what sort of constitution should it be? Some constitutions around the world have proved to be relatively simple to change. The current

---

of an enactment which are of constitutional significance'. This would suggest that any act of 'constitutional significance' was protected from amendment by the Civil Contingencies Act.

[99] https://hansard.parliament.uk/commons/2009-06-10/debates/090610620 00005/ConstitutionalRenewal

constitution of France (the Constitution of the Fifth Republic) might be seen as an example of that, with Charles de Gaulle being able to amend it without even going through the proper procedures laid down in the constitution itself. Is that a good thing? Or is the American model, where the constitution is very difficult to change, preferable? Instinctively one might feel it is good if the rulebook can't be easily messed around with, but look at the problems that the USA often faces on knotty policy issues that have to be considered within a set of rules drawn up in the late 18th century. The 'right to bear arms' is an obvious example of this.[100] One of the downsides of a constitution that is difficult to change is that the interpretation of it by the judiciary becomes crucially important. This in turn can lead to the politicisation of the judiciary. Many people will be familiar with the current politicisation of the Supreme Court in the USA, whose members can usually be readily identified as 'liberals' or 'conservatives'. But there has also long been a strong division of opinion on the US Supreme Court between those who might be described as supporters of 'originalism' and those who support the concept of a 'living constitution'. Whereas the former argue that the constitution should be interpreted in its original context, the latter argue that it should be interpreted within the context of the present day. It's not difficult then to see how different judges can come to very different conclusions as to what the 'right to bear arms', given to Americans in the late 18th century, might mean in current times. So yes, it may be a good thing that there is some consideration these days as to the merits of the UK having a formal written constitution, but how the country might move towards adopting one would need to be thought through very carefully.

Peter Hennessy has caricatured Britain as having *a 17th century system… with general elections occasionally bolted onto it.* [101] Gordon Brown's statement in the Commons in 2009 might

---

[100] This right wasn't in the original US Constitution but was added to it in 1791 as the second amendment.

[101] Giving evidence to the House of Commons Select Committee on Public Administration on 11 March 2004.
www.publications.parliament.uk/pa/cm200304/cmselect/cmpubadm/212/4031106.htm

have heralded a shift away from this model. But whatever the desire of the Labour Government and its Coalition successor to bring about constitutional reform, change has been piecemeal. That doesn't mean that it hasn't been or won't continue to be substantial, but it remains unlikely in the extreme that the United Kingdom will have a formal written codified constitution any time in the near future. Apart from any other considerations, drawing up such a document would be a mammoth task, taking up a huge amount of time in government and Parliament. It's hard to imagine any future government, even one that strongly believed in constitutional reform, finding the time to go down that road.

2

The Prime Minister and Cabinet

I'll start this chapter with three observations about British Prime Ministers that may be of interest. First: when one considers a new Prime Minister taking office, one tends to think of him or her winning a general election and being invited by the Queen to form a new government following the resignation of the losing Prime Minister. After all, that is what happened to Clement Attlee (in 1945), Winston Churchill (1951), Harold Wilson (1964 and February 1974), Edward Heath (1970), Margaret Thatcher (1979), Tony Blair (1997) and David Cameron (2010). But what of our other post-war Prime Ministers: Anthony Eden, Harold Macmillan, Alec Douglas-Home, Jim Callaghan, John Major, Gordon Brown, Theresa May and Boris Johnson? None of them, more than half the total, came to power for the first time as the result of a general election. All of them, rather, entered Downing Street following the resignation of their predecessor. They were therefore not elected on a mandate from the British people. Was that to their disadvantage? When you look at that list, particularly those who didn't later win an election in their own right, you might think so.

Second: these days Prime Ministers tend to be given one go at winning a general election and if they don't, they're out, often in a rather ruthless way. Edward Heath was forced out soon after losing in October 1974 (though, to be fair, he had been given another chance by his party after the 'hung' result of February

1974.) John Major resigned as party leader within hours of losing the 1997 general election and left the Commons after the following election. Gordon Brown did the same. And if Theresa May managed to stick around for a couple of years after the 2017 election that is only because she didn't quite lose it. This is rather different to how things were in earlier times. Churchill was surprisingly defeated in 1945 but returned to power six years later, as did Harold Wilson four years after his defeat in 1970. But such 'returns' seem to be a thing of the past. Some former Prime Ministers do remain in Parliament after their resignation for at least until the following general election (as Margaret Thatcher and Gordon Brown did and Theresa May continues to do) but others, like Tony Blair and David Cameron, weren't seen for dust in Parliament once they'd stepped down as Prime Minister. When you combine this phenomenon with the fact that Prime Ministers tend to come to power at a rather younger age than they used to, it arguably means there is a lot of talent and experience in the form of ex-Prime Ministers who fill their time writing books, running think tanks or making a lot of money on the lecture circuit. One wonders whether that talent isn't sometimes rather wasted.

Third: new Prime Ministers in recent decades, on arrival in the job, have been much less experienced in government than their predecessors. Consider the last five Prime Ministers from Blair to Johnson. Between them they had served in just three 'offices of state' prior to becoming Prime Minister. These were Chancellor (Gordon Brown), Home Secretary (Theresa May) and Foreign Secretary (Boris Johnson). The former two did at least spend a long time in those single offices but they hadn't enjoyed the breadth of some of their predecessors' experience. Then compare these five Prime Ministers with the five that immediately preceded them: John Major, Margaret Thatcher, James Callaghan, Harold Wilson and Edward Heath. Those five between them had worked in 23 offices of state prior to becoming Prime Minister.[102] One wonders how helpful this experience was for these five when

---

[102] According to the prime ministerial biographer, Sir Anthony Seldon, speaking on an Institute for Government podcast in June 2021

they entered the office of Prime Minister and how the lack of such experience affected the premierships of their successors.

The experience that some new Prime Ministers had of being Leader of the Opposition might have been useful too. Having the 'most difficult job in British politics', as some have described the role of Leader of the Opposition, may not provide experience of government, but it does offer the incumbent the opportunity to hone the political leadership skills which are so important to any Prime Minister. Is there something to be learned from the fact that David Cameron, Tony Blair and Margaret Thatcher spent substantial periods of time as Leader of the Opposition before becoming Prime Minister, whereas Boris Johnson, Theresa May, Gordon Brown and John Major did not?

Prime Ministerial Power

The British Prime Minister is arguably one of the most powerful heads of government in the democratic world (not in global terms but within the context of the domestic system of government). But if we hunt for documentary evidence of the extent of her powers, they would be hard to find because few are formally defined or written down.

We know that the Prime Minister has powers to appoint a vast array of people and to chair the Cabinet but these and her other powers do not come from Acts of Parliament. Only a handful of acts actually mention the words 'Prime Minister' and, with the exception of those concerning her oversight of the security agencies (for example the Security Service Act 1989 and the Intelligence Services Act 1994), they are of little constitutional importance. (For example, the right of the Prime Minister to use the country seat of Chequers and her right to be paid a salary are established, respectively, in the Chequers Estate Act 1917 and the Ministerial and Other Salaries Act 1975.)[103]

---

[103] The Fixed-term Parliaments Act was another of the few Acts of Parliament to mention the Prime Minister.

Generally speaking, acts give powers to Cabinet ministers rather than to the Prime Minister. Most prime ministerial powers are not 'statutory' in nature but are powers that successive Prime Ministers have inherited and developed from their predecessors. Over the last half century, those powers have developed markedly.

Although the British Prime Minister is not as powerful as the American President as a world leader, the extent of her control of the domestic levers of power can only be marvelled at by the leaders of other democracies. Bill Clinton is reported to have acknowledged this when he addressed Tony Blair's Cabinet as American President in May 1997. Like all American presidents he was limited by the checks and balances that exist in the American Constitution and also, in his case, by the fact that both Houses of Congress were under the control of the Republican Party. Contrast this with the position of his host, the newly elected British Prime Minister, with his majority in the House of Commons of 177, a House of Lords in which he could place his close confidants without any need of an election, free rein to appoint whomever he wished to key positions in the state without any need to consult Parliament, and a constitution where a lot of the rules were unwritten (particularly those concerning his own position) and where there was no Supreme Court to guard them.

The first time that the words 'Prime Minister' were used officially seems to be when Benjamin Disraeli used the title when signing the Treaty of Berlin in 1878.[104] Before then, the term 'Prime Minister' might have been considered an insult. The Head of Government more often would have been referred to as the 'King's Minister' and might also have used the title 'First Lord of the Treasury'.

The traditional description of the British Prime Minister is that she is *primus inter pares* or 'first among equals'. No one would describe the American President as 'first among equals' –

---

[104] https://history.blog.gov.uk/2012/01/01/the-institution-of-prime-minister/

'first' certainly, but constitutionally no one is his equal. So why, despite her considerable power within the system, is the Prime Minister only 'first among equals'? The answer lies in the British system of *Cabinet* government, rather than the chief executive-style or presidential government of the USA. The Cabinet system has a collective body of ministers at its head, not an individual, and these ministers, who form the Cabinet, hold power in their own right. Acts of Parliament generally give powers to 'the Secretary of State' whilst very few give powers to the Prime Minister. British Cabinet ministers are not, therefore, the 'Prime Minister's men and women' in the way that those who work in the American administration may be described as 'the President's men and women'. The American Constitution gives powers to the President who in turn may delegate those powers to those who work for him or her, whereas British Acts of Parliament give senior ministers powers in their own right.

If this is the case, why is the British Prime Minister such a dominant figure? The office has not always been as powerful as the institution became in the 20th century. Many of the powers widely accepted today as being for the Prime Minister's exclusive use have not always been the Prime Minister's alone. For example, although today the Prime Minister chooses and appoints ministers, at one time the Monarch would have had a considerable say in these appointments. It wasn't until the late 19th or early 20th century that the power to call a Cabinet or to decide the date of the general election became the Prime Minister's. This transfer of power has happened not, as we have seen, because any legislation has been passed to grant the Prime Minister these powers, but simply because Prime Ministers have been allowed by their Cabinet colleagues to assume these powers.

Whilst determining the power of any particular Prime Minister cannot be an exact science, it is undoubtedly true that the power of the office of Prime Minister has increased, particularly since 1979. But the general trend disguises shorter-term fluctuations of power, not just from one Prime Minister to another but within the period of office of some individual Prime

Ministers. Let's look briefly at the fluctuations in prime ministerial power that have occurred over the last 40 or so years.

Margaret Thatcher

Margaret Thatcher will forever be regarded as a very powerful Prime Minister, but it is easy to forget the difficulties she had in the first few years of her premiership – as papers released from the Thatcher Archive Trust in March 2012 show[105] - when the more liberal wing of the Conservative Party (the 'wets' as they were then known) still formed a majority in her Cabinet. It's widely thought that the person who came to her rescue was the Argentinean leader, General Galtieri, whose invasion of the Falkland Islands in 1982 and Britain's subsequent recapture of them were decisive in Margaret Thatcher's landslide victory in the 1983 election. Victory in the Falklands certainly helped, but so did the British electoral system and an anti-Conservative vote that was split almost equally between the Labour Party and the newly formed Liberal-Social Democratic Party Alliance.[106]

Margaret Thatcher's power probably peaked soon after the 1987 election and no one would have believed, even in the summer of 1990, that she would be gone by Christmas. But on 22 November of that year she resigned, to be replaced, after two rounds of balloting amongst Conservative MPs, by her Chancellor John Major. The rise and fall of Margaret Thatcher provides a telling case-study of prime ministerial power. She was a powerful, resolute Prime Minister, whose sometimes rather sexist caricature of her 'hand bagging' her ministers into submission on every issue was widely believed.

(When in April 2013 tributes were being paid in the House of Commons following Margaret Thatcher's death, the late Michael Meacher MP told the following amusing anecdote:

---

[105] www.bbc.co.uk/news/uk-17397224

[106] The vote won by the Conservative Party in 1983 was 46.0% of the total whereas in 1979 it had been 43.9%

The Prime Minister and Cabinet

> *I recall a story I recently heard while sharing a platform with my very good friend John Gummer.... When he was Secretary of State for the Environment in the 1980s, he complained that he could not get his Department to take climate change seriously. He rang Mrs Thatcher to ensure that he had the necessary support. When he explained the situation, she said to him, "John, you really shouldn't worry. There are two persons in the Cabinet who are committed over climate change—you and me, so we are in a majority".[107])*

But what finally forced Margaret Thatcher to resign? Electoral failure? Policy failure? Unpopularity in the country? In the main, it was her own Cabinet. When the result of the first round of the ballot for the Conservative leadership was announced, she had actually won enough votes to continue into the second round.[108] At an impromptu press conference she announced that she would be 'fighting on' but, very soon after, she was gone – because she had lost the support of her Cabinet. When her senior ministers filed in one by one to see her (one of them was reported to be in tears) they told her that, while they would support her in the second ballot, they believed that she would lose it. In other words, it was time for her to go. Of any event in the post-war period this is the one that most clearly 'proved' that Cabinet government was still a reality.

John Major

John Major's power as Prime Minister is often regarded as somewhat less than that of his immediate predecessor and

---

[107] https://hansard.parliament.uk/Commons/2013-04-10/debates/130410 4000001/TributesToBaronessThatcher

[108] In the first ballot for the Conservative leadership, Margaret Thatcher defeated the only other candidate, Michael Heseltine, by 204 votes to 152, but under the rules this left her four votes short of outright victory. When she resigned on 22 November, Heseltine was joined in the second round of balloting by John Major and Douglas Hurd.

successor. But it wasn't until after the 1992 election or, more specifically, September 1992 and 'Black Wednesday' when sterling crashed out of the European Exchange Rate Mechanism, leaving the Government's economic policy in tatters, that John Major was particularly weakened. For the first year or so of John Major's premiership he certainly benefited from a honeymoon period, rather as Gordon Brown did (for a short period at least) after he became Prime Minister in June 2007. (For a while almost all new Prime Ministers are popular simply because they are not their predecessors!) It's all too easy to explain John Major's difficulties as Prime Minister in terms of his personality. Clearly he wasn't a Margaret Thatcher. He was less inclined to lead from the front in the way that both his predecessor and successor did. But did that necessarily make him a 'weak' Prime Minister? Britain's first post-war Prime Minister, Clement Attlee – 'a sheep in sheep's clothing' as Churchill once described him – was said to run a model of collective government, where everyone was allowed to have their say before a decision was reached. No one, however, would have described him as a weak Prime Minister. He conducted Cabinet business with decisive efficiency, sacking ministers with clinical ruthlessness.[109]

In politics it is easy to allow the characters to blind us to the plot. Consider the circumstances surrounding John Major in 1992. Two specific issues made life very difficult. One was Britain's relationship with the EU, which, not for the last time, was tearing the Conservative Party apart. The Cabinet was itself divided on the issue, with the Prime Minister famously referring (when he didn't realise he was on air) to the eurosceptic 'bastards' in his Cabinet.[110] Perhaps more important was the size of the

---

[109] It may be of passing interest that Clement Attlee's grandson, the 3rd Earl Attlee, became a Conservative minister in the Coalition Government formed after the 2010 general election.

[110] Following an interview with ITN's Political Editor Michael Brunson in July 1993. The 'bastards' weren't named by Major but were widely thought to be Michael Howard, Peter Lilley and Michael Portillo.

Conservative majority in the House of Commons following the 1992 election. Many pundits had predicted a very close result at the election. In fact, in terms of votes, it wasn't particularly close, but widespread tactical voting meant that the votes won by the Conservative Party didn't translate into the number of seats that would usually follow.[111] With a majority of 21 seats, Major's party confronted problems similar to those James Callaghan had faced in the late 1970s. A series of by-election defeats and a few defections meant that for quite some time before the 1997 election Major's government was operating without a majority.

Governing with a small majority is difficult; governing with no majority – as Theresa May was later to discover - is almost impossible. Because in the British system ministers remain MPs, in circumstances where every vote counts they must drop whatever they are doing and attend the Commons, where their individual vote may make the difference between a major government bill being won or lost – or even the government winning or losing a confidence motion. How can the Foreign Secretary attend a crucial summit in Tokyo if at the same time she needs to be in the House of Commons to vote? Major's government suffered because of its small majority, although it did at least avoid the ignominy of being thrown out by the Commons in the way that Jim Callaghan's was.

Tony Blair

Tony Blair, of course, had no such problems. Prime ministerial power soared during the night of 1 May 1997, not just because of the government's massive majority in the House of Commons but also because Blair was so obviously in complete control of his party, and therefore of the government, in a way that Major never could be. Blair's style was more like Margaret Thatcher's than that of Attlee or Major. He didn't welcome debate

---

[111] At the 1992 election the Conservatives won 41.9% of the vote and 336 seats. In 1987 they had won 376 seats with only a slightly larger proportion of the vote (42.3%).

around the Cabinet table. Like Mrs Thatcher, he preferred his colleagues to know up front exactly where he stood on any particular issue.

At the height of Blair's power, Cabinet meetings became very short, occasionally as short as half an hour. There were complaints that sometimes Cabinet was by-passed altogether, with Blair preferring a 'sofa style' government of informal meetings with close confidants to formal, minuted meetings of Cabinet or Cabinet Committees. Some ministers who resigned or were sacked from the Cabinet were subsequently very critical of his approach to Cabinet. In her resignation speech of May 2003, Clare Short expressed her view:

> *The problem is the centralisation of power into the hands of the Prime Minister and an increasingly small number of advisers who make decisions in private without proper discussion.... There is no real collective responsibility because there is no collective; just diktats in favour of increasingly badly thought through policy initiatives that come from on high.* [112]

It is important, however, to remember that ex-ministers' views are often coloured by the circumstances of their departure. But Clare Short was not alone in making these kinds of criticisms; Mo Mowlam expressed similar concerns.[113]

Tony Blair's power began to wane some time before his eventual departure for perhaps two principal reasons. One was the decision he took (and it was very much a prime ministerial decision) to support the Americans in their invasion of Iraq in March 2003. Rather like the issue of Europe for many

---

[112] https://hansard.parliament.uk/commons/2003-05-12/debates/96356b80-3893-41e6-8324-7e5faf33f095/PersonalStatement

[113] For example, on the BBC television programme 'Cabinet Confidential' screened in November 2001, Mo Mowlam said of Tony Blair: 'He is not inclusive. He thinks of Cabinet government as irrelevant'.

Conservative Prime Ministers, this decision divided the governing party, although crucially for Blair it didn't have too divisive an effect on the government itself. One Cabinet Minister, Robin Cook, resigned before British troops were sent in and another, Clare Short, resigned later. A handful of junior ministers also resigned. But the government still held together in a way that Major's was unable to do. (In June 1995, one of Major's Cabinet ministers, John Redwood, had actually resigned from the Cabinet to stand against Major for the party leadership.)

The other reason for the decline in Blair's power was his unusual, perhaps unique, announcement of his departure some months in advance of it actually happening. This might seem a sensible approach – better perhaps than surprising everyone (including his own Cabinet) as Harold Wilson did in 1976 or being ejected like Margaret Thatcher in 1990 – but it undermined the Prime Minister's power as people turned their attention away from him and towards his successor.

Tony Blair's premiership will rightly be remembered as one where power in government became increasingly centralised. It was, in the words of Peter Hennessy, *the most commanding of command-premiership models*. But, as Hennessy also points out, it was *operated by a Prime Minister who presided over the most comprehensive dispersal of central power ever in his Government's devolution programme*.[114] At the same time as power was being transferred from the UK Government to other institutions (in particular the devolved administrations), within central government power was steadily accruing to the centre.

While there were similarities between the way Margaret Thatcher and Tony Blair ran their governments, there was at least one important difference. This concerns the machinery surrounding the Prime Minister in Number 10 Downing Street. When Mrs Thatcher replaced Jim Callaghan as Prime Minister,

---

[114] Whitehall. Part Six: Epilogue. Peter Hennessy Pimlico; 2nd revised edition (Sep 2001)

the machinery in Number 10 barely changed. But when Blair became Prime Minister the size of the Number 10 machine increased substantially. The number of political special advisers (as opposed to permanent civil servants) in Number 10 trebled, and a handful of individuals became very powerful indeed: particularly the Chief of Staff Jonathan Powell and Director of Communications Alastair Campbell. (I explain how special advisers fit into a government department's hierarchy in chapter three.)

Gordon Brown

Gordon Brown's style of leadership provided an interesting contrast to his predecessor's. Brown was more inclined to use the formal processes of collective government, with longer Cabinet meetings and more use of Cabinet Committees. He seemed less inclined to adopt the 'sofa-style' government for which Tony Blair was much criticised. Whether that made Gordon Brown's style of government any less 'prime ministerial' than Tony Blair's is, though, open to question. He was much more prone to involve himself in the detail of policy. Those who worked closely with him describe how Gordon Brown liked to work incredibly long hours, how he could be heard hammering away at his computer keyboard in the small hours of the morning, and that he was inclined to send emails to startled civil servants at all times of the day and night. One can only speculate how prime ministerial government might have been had Gordon Brown become Prime Minister in 1997 rather than Tony Blair.

Perhaps the most fundamental difference between the Brown and Blair regimes was that Gordon Brown 'didn't have a Gordon Brown'. Because he had no major political rival in the Labour Party, even when from the autumn of 2007 problems began to mount, there was no obvious challenge to him. This was particularly apparent in the 'failed coup' of June 2009 that followed the resignation of a number of Cabinet ministers. And, structurally, the Treasury under Brown's premiership did not operate as the semi-independent powerhouse that it was during

Blair's premiership.

David Cameron

The huge difference between Cameron's first government and those of all other Prime Ministers since 1945 was that he was leading a coalition government. This limited his power in a number of ways, but most obviously in his ability to appoint whomever he wished to the Cabinet and to other ministerial positions. All Prime Ministers to some extent have to take political considerations into account when making ministerial appointments which may require them to appoint ministers who they wouldn't otherwise necessarily choose. But the reality of coalition government is that the Prime Minister is forced to accept ministers in his government from another party. This was made clear by the 'Coalition Agreement for Stability and Reform' that was agreed by the two coalition parties after the 2010 election:

> *The Prime Minister, following consultation with the Deputy Prime Minister, will make nominations for the appointment of Ministers. The Prime Minister will nominate Conservative Party Ministers and the Deputy Prime Minister will nominate Liberal Democrat Ministers.... Any changes to the allocation of portfolios between the parliamentary parties during the lifetime of the Coalition will be agreed between the Prime Minister and the Deputy Prime Minister.*[115]

During the period of the Coalition Government there were five Liberal Democrat ministers in the Cabinet. When the Liberal Democrat Chief Secretary to the Treasury David Laws was forced to resign just a few days after taking office after the 2010 election, the decision to replace him with Danny Alexander was made by the Liberal Democrat leader and Deputy Prime Minister Nick Clegg, not by the Prime Minister. And Danny Alexander's

---

[115] Coalition Agreement for Stability and Reform paras 1.3-1.4. www.gov.uk/government/uploads/system/uploads/attachment_data/file/78978/coalition-agreement-may-2010_0.pdf

replacement as Scottish Secretary had to be a Liberal Democrat, again selected by Nick Clegg. Interestingly, the new Scottish Secretary, Michael Moore, was not even a junior minister at the time he was appointed to the Cabinet. (The requirement for the job holder to be both a Liberal Democrat and have a Scottish seat rather limited the pool from which he was selected.) Subsequent changes to the ranks of Liberal Democrat ministers – both in and outside of Cabinet – were again the decision of the Deputy Prime Minister.

Formal processes become more important in coalition government which was bound to strengthen the role of Cabinet and Cabinet Committees. (For more about these, see below.) Parliament becomes more important as well. The Coalition Government may have had a nominal majority in the House of Commons in the mid-70s but how dependable was that majority, particularly when the House was considering legislation that was fully supported by only one of the two coalition parties?[116] That majority was most put to the test when, in August 2013, the House of Commons voted on the motion, mentioned above, that would have paved the way for military action against the Syrian Government. The government's defeat on that vote, albeit more at the hands of Conservative backbenchers than Liberal Democrats, was a serious blow to David Cameron's standing in government, in his party and in Parliament.

A further important difference between the Coalition Government and its predecessors concerned the role of the Deputy Prime Minister. Some, but not all Prime Ministers in the past have had a deputy. Some of these have been very important figures in the government (Michael Heseltine and John Prescott being good examples); others less so. But in coalition government the role of the Deputy Prime Minister becomes much more important. The relationship between the Prime Minister and his deputy has to be seen as a genuine partnership – one in which the Deputy Prime

---

[116] In the first major test of the Coalition's majority in the Commons – the vote on university tuition fees in December 2010 – the Coalition's majority was cut by almost three-quarters to 21.

Minister, whilst clearly the junior partner, carries considerable clout. It was clear for all to see that the personal relationship between David Cameron and Nick Clegg was absolutely crucial to the success of the Coalition Government.

Also crucial to the success of the coalition was the operation of the 'Quad' – a committee consisting of David Cameron, George Osborne, Nick Clegg and Danny Alexander – where a lot of issues were initially brokered. This committee was described by the Liberal Democrat minister David Laws as operating *in some ways...almost as an inner cabinet.*[117] But important though this committee was, all the business that it discussed would still subsequently be considered by a cabinet committee for formal discussion and agreement.

In some respects then the personal power of the Prime Minister in a coalition government is inevitably weakened, but does that mean that during the Coalition Government the power of "the Centre" - i.e. the machinery that operates around and supports the Prime Minister - was weakened? Like Tony Blair, David Cameron made some very influential political appointments in the form of Chief of Staff Ed Llewellyn (who went to school with him), Director of Communications Andy Coulson and Head of Strategy Steve Hilton. And the Deputy Prime Minister Nick Clegg had his own team of political advisers who worked very closely with those of the Prime Minister. He also had his own special advisers in key positions in No 10 such as the Deputy Heads of the No 10 Press Office and of the No10 Policy Unit. His team was further strengthened by the appointment in late 2011 of six additional advisers covering policy areas in particular where the Liberal Democrats had little ministerial representation.

---

[117] In evidence to the House of Lords Constitution Committee's Inquiry into 'The Constitutional Implications of Coalition Government'. www.parliament.uk/documents/lords-committees/constitution/coalitiongovernment/Final-evidence-volume-coalition-gov-070214.pdf

It's fair to say that David Cameron had a rather more 'hands off' approach than some of his predecessors and successors. This probably was a personal choice rather than one forced on him by the realities of coalition government. But the political realities that Cameron faced in the year or so after the 2015 general election, at which he won a slender majority, were really quite different to those he faced when leading a coalition government. Looking back at the period either side of the 2015 election it's reasonable to conclude that Cameron probably found life as the head of a coalition government rather more easy than as head of a single-party government with a small majority when his party continued to be so divided on the question of 'Europe'. Had he not won that slender majority in 2015 he would almost certainly have once again formed a coalition with the Liberal Democrats. If that had come about, it's questionable as to whether the EU referendum would ever have been held: his eurosceptic backbenchers would not have been able to exercise the same degree of power that they actually did after the election and it's hard to imagine Cameron's Liberal Democrat partners allowing the referendum, which brought about his downfall, to take place.

Theresa May

Theresa May's government was of course dogged by one huge issue: Brexit. It's what brought her to power and it's what removed her from power. Brexit was an issue that divided the country and, possibly even more importantly from her personal perspective, it divided her party. With the small majority she inherited from David Cameron, her divided party was perhaps just about manageable but once she lost that majority, following her personally disastrous decision to call a general election in 2017, there was probably only one direction that she could now head and that was out.

May's government for the year or so between her becoming Prime Minister in July 2016 and the election of 2017 in some ways looked like Tony Blair's, with strong control from the centre. When she became Prime Minister she brought with her two key special advisers from her time as Home Secretary: Fiona Hill and Nick Timothy. They exercised the same sort of clout around Whitehall that Alastair Campbell and Jonathan Powell had when Blair was Prime Minister though anecdotal evidence suggests that they used to frustrate those working in the wider government machine (even) more than did Campbell and Powell. Timothy and Hill were instrumental in May's decision to call the 2017 election and when that turned out to be disastrous, they had to go. It's clear that Theresa May rather struggled without these two key advisers. As a sort-of replacement she gave the job of Chief of Staff to Gavin Barwell who had just lost his seat at the general election, but he was no Hill or Timothy.

Running a government without a majority is always extremely difficult. Running one against the background of Brexit was next to impossible. Theresa May's government suffered defeat after defeat in the House of Commons – 33 in total, compared to Tony Blair's four in 10 years – and some of these were of huge importance to the process of the UK leaving the European Union. After the 2017 election the opposition parties alone had enough votes to defeat her in Parliament (if joined, as they sometimes were, by the government's 'allies' in the Democratic Unionist Party) but when significant numbers in her own party – on both sides of the Brexit divide – were prepared to rebel, governing became very difficult. Events in Parliament between the two elections of 2017 and 2019 were probably unique in parliamentary history. (They were so extraordinary that we have devoted a specific chapter of this book to that period.)

Theresa May, like Margaret Thatcher, was finally removed from office by losing the support of her party. In Thatcher's case, as we have seen, she lost the support of her Cabinet. In May's case it was more a case of her losing the support of her parliamentary party. She survived some of her MPs bringing a motion of no-confidence in her as party leader in December 2018[118] but when in June 2019 she tried to bring to Parliament

---

[118] This shouldn't be confused with a no confidence motion that might be moved in the House of Commons against a government and its Prime

her European Union Withdrawal Agreement Bill, she realised that the votes in the Commons simply weren't there to support it. Lacking support on such a crucially important issue meant she then really had no option but to announce her resignation. Looking back, in many ways it's surprising that Theresa May lasted as long as she did following the disaster of the 2017 general election. The setback she suffered in the House of Commons on her Brexit deal in January 2018, when her government incurred the biggest ever defeat for a governing party in the history of the House of Commons would be sufficient for many other Prime Ministers to have resigned.[119] One could praise her doggedness but it could equally be argued that following a defeat of such magnitude on an issue of such importance, she really *should* have resigned.

Boris Johnson

If in July 2019, when Boris Johnson became Prime Minister, we had asked ourselves what would be the major issue to dominate the early part his premiership we would almost certainly have said 'Brexit'. If someone had told us that it would actually be 'Covid' our response would without doubt have been 'what's Covid?' But, even if Johnson remains Prime Minister for a very long time, it seems that his time in office will inevitably forever be associated, for good or for bad, with the pandemic. Just as Blair's premiership is so often looked back on through the lens of Iraq (which some argue unfairly disguises so much else that happened during that period), so people are likely to forever judge Johnson on how he handled the pandemic.

When Boris Johnson became Prime Minister in July 2019 he of course inherited Theresa May's minority position in the House

---

Minister, as happened to James Callaghan in 1979. This was a motion of no confidence moved by some Conservative MPs in Theresa May as party leader. It was wholly a party matter and nothing formally to do with Parliament.

[119] This was the first so-called 'meaningful vote on May's Brexit deal. It is discussed further in the chapter 7.

of Commons and so faced many of the same problems she had. (Actually, whereas May, as we have seen, was defeated in the Commons 33 times in three years, Boris Johnson lost the first seven votes that took place in the Commons after his coming to power including three in the space of 24 hours!)

When Boris Johnson formed his first government he gave barely a nod to the fact that he had to work with a divided party and a Parliament of which he wasn't in control, forming a Cabinet consisting largely of 'Brexiteers', Nicky Morgan and Amber Rudd being perhaps the two highest profile 'remainers' to whom he did give Cabinet posts. Nicky Morgan had been sacked as Education Secretary by Theresa May when she became Prime Minister in July 2016 and returned to government under Boris Johnson as Secretary of State for Digital, Culture, Media and Sport; and Amber Rudd stayed in the post of Work and Pensions Secretary given to her by Theresa May, resigning less than two months later in protest against Johnson's policies on Brexit and his decision to withdraw the whip from 20 Conservative MPs. But the vast majority of his appointments were committed Brexiteers.[120] Of perhaps greater interest than the membership of his Cabinet was who he brought in to Downing Street to work directly to him. Of particular note were his Senior Adviser Sir Eddie Lister, his EU negotiator David Frost, his Communications Director Lee Cain and, of course, Dominic Cummings. Having previously been a special adviser to Michael Gove at the Department for Education (a job from which David Cameron claims he sacked him[121]) Cummings had led the Vote Leave campaign in the EU referendum before being given the job as 'Chief Aid' and de facto Chief of Staff to Boris Johnson. These men, and in particular Cummings, carried huge authority around Whitehall.

---

[120] For a full list of Johnson's first government, see here:
https://www.gov.uk/government/news/full-list-of-new-ministerial-and-government-appointments-july-2019

[121] David Cameron says he sacked Dominic Cummings twice "but he kept coming back". Times Radio 17.9.20
https://www.youtube.com/watch?v=FlHd-k2EQDM

Whilst it might be a something of an exaggeration to say that Alastair Campbell became a household name during Tony Blair's time in government, that description certainly would be accurate in respect of Dominic Cummings and largely for all the wrong reasons. His role as head of the leave campaign had already made him quite a recognisable figure (all the more so after his portrayal by Benedict Cumberbatch in the Channel 4 drama of January 2019 'Brexit: The Uncivil War') by the time he was given his position in Downing Street by Boris Johnson. In March 2019 Cummings had been held in contempt of Parliament for refusing to give evidence to a select committee of the House of Commons.[122] This didn't however stop Boris Johnson giving him his very senior post in government just a few months later.

However that issue was as nothing compared to the notoriety Cummings would gain for his apparent breaking of lockdown rules in April 2020 during the early stages of the Covid pandemic and his explanation of why he decided to drive his wife and child to Barnard Castle in County Durham during the lockdown as 'to test his eyesight'.[123] The fact that he stayed in his post despite the outcry that this caused across the country said something about his importance to the Prime Minister. But when he did eventually leave his job in Downing Street in November 2020, the fallout from his departure was quite spectacular. The evidence Cummings gave in May 2021 to the joint Health & Social Care and Science & Technology Select Committees' inquiry into the lessons learned from the management of the Covid pandemic provided quite a lurid insight into the rather chaotic workings of the Johnson Government. People might be wise not to take at face-value everything Dominic Cummings says, but nor should

---

[122] The House of Commons' Privileges Committee's explanation of why Cummings had been held in contempt can be found here: https://publications.parliament.uk/pa/cm201719/cmselect/cmprivi/1490/149003.htm. For more on this episode, see the section on select committees in chapter 6.

[123] You can see Cummings' extraordinary explanation of his actions, given during a press conference in the garden of No 10 Downing Street, here: https://www.youtube.com/watch?v=IGLRBwYZEHs

they perhaps dismiss out of hand his comments about Boris Johnson and the way he runs his government. So despite Cummings' self-aggrandisement and use of hyperbole, it's still worth hearing what he has to say about his time in government. His description of the events of 12 April 2020 to the select committee inquiry is particularly revealing:

> *That is how the day started off, with us thinking, "Okay, today is going to be all about Covid and whether or not we are going to announce the household quarantine. We then got completely derailed because, in the morning of the 12th, suddenly the national security people came in and said, "Trump wants us to join a bombing campaign in the Middle East tonight and we need to start having meetings about that through the day with Cobra as well." So everything to do with Cobra on Covid that day was completely disrupted because you have these two parallel sets of meetings. You had the national security people running in and out talking about, "Are we going to bomb the middle east?" and we had the Cobra meeting being delayed and whatnot as we were trying to figure out what we were going to do with household quarantine.*
>
> *Then, to add to that day - it sounds so surreal it couldn't possibly be true - The Times had run a huge story about the Prime Minister and his girlfriend and their dog, and the Prime Minister's girlfriend was going completely crackers about this story and demanding that the press office dealt with that.*
>
> *So we had this completely insane situation in which part of the building was saying, "Are we going to bomb Iraq?"; part of the building was arguing about whether we are going to do quarantine or not do quarantine; the Prime Minister has his girlfriend going crackers about*

something completely trivial.[124]

At the same hearing, when Cummings was asked whether he thought Johnson was *a fit and proper person to get us through the pandemic,* his answer was a simple *no.*[125] People can question whether, after the 'Barnard Castle incident', the words of Dominic Cummings can be fully trusted. They can also speculate as to what extent his words were motivated by a desire for revenge. But it might be wrong to dismiss out of hand an opinion of the Prime Minister such as this, expressed by the person who had been his right-hand man in No 10.

So the Covid pandemic will have a huge impact on how people view Johnson's premiership. At the time of writing, Johnson may still be in the relatively early stages of his time in No 10, and there must be every probability that he will lead his party into the next general election. As a Prime Minister he has been quite different to any of his post-war predecessors – a populist and brilliant communicator who retained his popularity despite the UK having one of the worst death tolls in the world during the Covid pandemic. And although to most people this will be of far less importance, he was also found to have unlawfully prorogued Parliament.

The Functions of the Prime Minister

While a Prime Minister's formal functions and powers are difficult to define, with no proper written constitution and few Acts of Parliament that mention any, we can identify ten principal functions in which she wields considerable power.

First, as Head of Government she is a national leader. Constitutionally, the Monarch is Head of State but at important international gatherings and 'summits' the nation is represented by the Prime Minister alongside the American President or French President (who are Heads of State), or the German Chancellor or

---

[124] https://committees.parliament.uk/oralevidence/2249/html/ Question 1003

[125] Ibid. Question 1228

Italian Prime Minister (who are Heads of Government). For many years the Prime Minister has been seen as 'in charge' of British foreign policy. Who remembers who the Foreign Secretary was at the time of the Suez crisis in 1956? For how long will we remember who was Foreign Secretary when the UK invaded Iraq in March 2003? And who was the Foreign Secretary when the UK departed the EU? All of these events will forever be associated with the Prime Ministers of the day – Anthony Eden, Tony Blair and Boris Johnson. This is because British foreign policy has for a long while been seen as 'prime ministerial'. The growth of prime ministerial power over the years has seen the Prime Minister's influence over other areas of policy widen considerably too.

Government policy is often portrayed in the media as the Prime Minister's policy, whether it's 'Margaret Thatcher taking on the coal miners', 'Tony Blair's schools policy', 'Gordon Brown's plans for dealing with the financial crisis' and 'Boris Johnson's handling of the coronavirus pandemic'. At one time policy wouldn't have been identified with the Prime Minister in this way. Health policy was for the Health Secretary – the creation of the National Health Service in 1948 was strongly associated with Aneurin Bevan – and education policy was for the Education Secretary – the Education Act of 1944 was often described as Rab Butler's Act – and so on. This personal focus on the Prime Minister is not always an advantage. While Prime Ministers are unlikely to object to being associated with successful policies, they may feel less enthusiastic about their names being linked with unsuccessful policies or disasters. Boris Johnson will be delighted to take credit for the success of the Covid vaccine roll out; he might be less happy about having to take responsibility for the Test and Trace failure or the number of deaths in Britain due to Covid.

Government policy across the board is increasingly identified with the Prime Minister because the Prime Minister has become increasingly influential in every area of government. But it is also because the media likes to focus on one individual. With today's 24/7 media the Prime Minister is almost never out of the spotlight. She needs an effective response to any question thrown at her on any issue. This in turn has led to Number 10 becoming more involved in the details of what is going on in government departments to ensure that the Prime Minister is fully briefed to appear in the media. The growing importance over the years of Prime Minister's Questions in the House of Commons has had the same effect. Before Mrs Thatcher's time, questions about subjects which were the responsibility of particular departments were directed to the appropriate minister. Since then, at her weekly appearance in Parliament the Prime Minister can be asked about absolutely anything and therefore needs to be briefed accordingly.

Second, the Prime Minister appoints and dismisses all ministers from the most senior to the most junior. (We noted above how this was different during the period of the Coalition Government.) The Prime Minister doesn't simply appoint the Cabinet who in turn appoint their own departmental ministers. This is clear when a minister resigns. Whoever they are, it is to the Prime Minister that they address their resignation letter, not their immediate superior in the department. The Prime Minister can, however, consult Cabinet ministers before appointing junior ministers in their departments.

Third, the Prime Minister chairs the Cabinet. As well as choosing its members, she sets the Cabinet's agenda, decides who speaks and when and, crucially, sums up at the end of each agenda item. The Prime Minister also dictates the remit and membership of Cabinet Committees. (I discuss Cabinet and Cabinet Committees in some detail below.)

Fourth, the Prime Minister, at least until 2011, could request a dissolution of Parliament. At one time the decision to ask the Monarch for a dissolution of Parliament was taken by the whole Cabinet, but in 1918 Lloyd-George took the decision himself and it has remained a prime ministerial decision since. As was explained above, this power was limited by the passing of the Fixed-term Parliaments Act, but one only has to look at both 2017 and 2019 to see that it was still very much the Prime Minister's decision to hold an early election, even if the final decision over whether to do so rested with Parliament.

Fifth, the Prime Minister can commit Britain's armed forces to action. This was discussed earlier, but one further aspect of interest is that only the Prime Minister can activate the codes to launch a nuclear strike. Every new Prime Minister is taken through the procedure on appointment and is required to leave instructions in a sealed envelope to advise the military what to do (that is, whether to retaliate or not) in the event of the government being wiped out. This is perhaps the ultimate in prime ministerial decision-taking.

Sixth, the Prime Minister recommends the award of honours and peerages. The honours system is an area of government that, despite some recent reforms, is still shrouded in mystery. It is, of course, the Monarch who actually bestows honours but it is the Prime Minister who submits the honours list to her. (Exceptions to this are the handful of honours, like the Order of Merit and appointments to the Royal Victorian Order, which remain in the personal gift of the Monarch.) Of particular importance is the Prime Minister's power to create peerages. Although there are conventions governing the appointment of peers and a commission to nominate the 'non-political' peers and to oversee the appointment of political peers, it remains the case that the Prime Minister has the sole right of nomination to the Monarch. (This is developed further in the chapter seven.)

Seventh, the Prime Minister has considerable powers of patronage under the Royal Prerogative to make important appointments, including to the House of Lords and Regius Professorships at Oxford and Cambridge.[126] She also makes appointments to the senior ranks of, amongst other organisations: the Civil Service, the armed forces and the intelligence services. Although civil servants are generally

---

[126] The Brown Government's proposals for constitutional reform included ideas to limit the Prime Minister's powers in this area. See *The Governance of Britain – Constitutional Renewal* paragraphs 254-256. www.official-documents.gov.uk/document/cm73/7342/7342_i.pdf

recruited, promoted and dismissed independently of ministers, at the most senior levels ministers, and the Prime Minister in particular, are involved. When it comes to appointing the most senior civil servant, the Cabinet Secretary, there is no standard process. Some in the past have been direct prime ministerial appointments but, in more recent years, Cabinet Secretaries have been appointed through a more formal process with the Prime Minister interviewing a number of candidates. This process is supervised by the Civil Service Commission which oversees civil service recruitment. And under the terms of 2010 Constitutional Reform and Governance Act the Cabinet Secretary's appointment, as with all other civil service posts, has to be on merit and on the basis of fair and open competition. It should not be a political appointment.

The Prime Minister also has the final say over who should be recommended for appointment as a Church of England bishop. The words that the Church itself uses to describe this is that *following the approval of Her Majesty the Queen on the advice of the Prime Minister, the announcement of the new bishop is made by No 10 Downing St.*[127] Until the mid-1970s the Prime Minister had, in theory at least, an unfettered power to recommend to the Monarch whomsoever he wished to be appointed as a bishop. This changed in 1976 when a 'Crown Appointments Commission' was created which would henceforth suggest two candidates to the Prime Minister, one of whose names he or she would put forward to the Monarch.

In practice, some Prime Ministers have taken a rather more active role in this area than others. The constitutional expert Professor Vernon Bogdanor cites three examples of where the advice given to the Monarch by Margaret Thatcher was based more on political than ecclesiastical grounds – over the choices of the new Bishop of London in 1981 and Bishop of Birmingham in 1987, and in 1990 when she recommended George Carey rather

---

[127] https://www.churchofengland.org/about/leadership-and-governance/crown-nominations-commission#na

than John Habgood as Archbishop of Canterbury.[128]

And in 1997 it was reported that Tony Blair rejected both of the candidates put to him to succeed David Shephard as Bishop of Liverpool. According to The Sunday Times, while the *workings of the [Crown Appointments Commission] are shrouded in secrecy, it is thought to be the first time in its 20-year history that a prime minister has rejected its recommendations.*[129]

Gordon Brown, who had been brought up as a member of the Church of Scotland, decided to take a rather more hands-off approach. His 'Governance of Britain' Green Paper published in 2007 said that in choosing how *best to advise* the Queen on church appointments, the government believed *that, where possible, the Prime Minister should not have an active role in the selection of individual candidates.*[130]

As the case of Gordon Brown demonstrates, it's entirely possible that a Prime Minister who is exercising this power to nominate bishops is not him- or herself a member of the Church of England, but this isn't seen as a problem - unless, perhaps surprisingly, he or she is a Roman Catholic. It is a misconception that the Prime Minister cannot be a Roman Catholic. The bar to this was removed with the passing of the Roman Catholic Relief Act of 1829 which lifted the ban on Catholics sitting in Parliament. However, the act didn't remove all discrimination against Catholics. It remained the case that Catholic priests could not become MPs until that section of the 1829 Act was repealed in 2001. And it continues to be the case that no 'person professing the Roman Catholic religion' is allowed to advise the Monarch on the appointment of Church of England bishops. The punishment

---

[128] Vernon Bogdanor, Monarchy and the Constitution, Oxford: Oxford University Press, 1995, p226.

[129] "Blair blocks church choice for bishop", The Sunday Times, 14 September 1997. Quoted in House of Commons Library Paper. Ibid.

[130] Ibid. 'Governance of Britain' Green Paper. Paragraphs 62-63

for doing so would be for them to be 'disabled for ever from holding any office, civil or military, under the Crown'.[131] Whether this influenced Tony Blair to wait until after he ceased being Prime Minister before converting to Roman Catholicism is unknown.

This is also relevant to Boris Johnson as Prime Minister. When Johnson married his fiancée Carrie Symonds in Westminster Cathedral in May 2021, the cathedral authorities confirmed that 'bride and groom are parishioners and baptised Catholics'.[132] If this is the case, then the 1829 Act would seem to bar him from advising the Monarch on the appointment of Church of England bishops. Media reports at the time of his marriage suggested that Johnson had converted to Roman Catholicism just before his wedding. If so, this would mean that the one appointment he had already made - the new bishop of Chelmsford in December 2020 – was bona fide. Those reports also suggested that Boris Johnson's role in the appointment of bishops would in future be carried out by the Lord Chancellor.[133]

Eighth, the Prime Minister decides the structure of government. Decisions of this kind are taken on advice from the Cabinet Secretary but the decision is the Prime Minister's. On coming to power, many Prime Ministers reorganise 'Whitehall' but such reorganisations also often take place during any Prime Minister's time in office. Some sceptical commentators suggest that Prime Ministers engage in this as a kind of displacement activity when everything else is going wrong! The ease with which Whitehall can be reorganised at the whim of the Prime Minister has been criticised by some, for example by the Public Administration Select Committee of the House of Commons which in 2008

---

[131] https://www.legislation.gov.uk/ukpga/Geo4/10/7/section/18

[132] https://rozenberg.substack.com/p/boris-can-no-longer-pick-bishops

[133] House of Commons Library Paper: https://researchbriefings.files.parliament.uk/documents/CBP-8886/CBP-8886.pdf

reported:

> We are not calling for primary legislation for every government reorganisation, but, for major changes to the machinery of government, new secondary legislation should be subject to a debate and vote in Parliament to ensure proper scrutiny and analysis of the consequences. This would require a fundamental change to the way that Government is structured. It would mean giving statutory functions to Government Departments, rather than just to interchangeable Secretaries of State.[134]

Nothing, however, has changed in this area.

Ninth, the Prime Minister is responsible for ministerial procedures and conduct. This might sound dry and dusty, but her power to write, revise and interpret the Ministerial Code – the rulebook for ministers – is a very important one. In a system of government where there is no formal written constitution, codes and rulebooks can be very important. When a minister breaches the rules set out in the Ministerial Code, the Prime Minister is essentially the judge and jury in deciding whether the minister can stay in post or has to go. The code, for example, says that *Ministers who knowingly mislead Parliament will be expected to offer their resignation to the Prime Minister.*[135] (It doesn't, however, say what should happen if it is the Prime Minister who is misleading Parliament.) It is for the Prime Minister initially to decide whether a minister's behaviour should be referred to the 'Independent Adviser on Ministers' Interests' and ultimately, whether or not that minister should resign. The Prime Minister's powers in this respect were very apparent in

---

[134] Select Committee on Public Administration Eighth Report: Machinery of Government Changes: Further Report May 2008
www.publications.parliament.uk/pa/cm200708/cmselect/cmpubadm/514/51402.htm

[135] www.gov.uk/government/uploads/system/uploads/attachment_data/file/61402/ministerial-code-may-2010.pdf   Paragraph 1.3c Paragraph 1.3c

November 2020 when Boris Johnson decided not to ask for his Home Secretary, Priti Patel's resignation when she was found by the Independent Adviser, Sir Alex Allan, to have breached the Ministerial Code by bullying her staff. In his report, Sir Alex had said:

> *My advice is that the Home Secretary has not consistently met the high standards required by the Ministerial Code of treating her civil servants with consideration and respect. Her approach on occasions has amounted to behaviour that can be described as bullying in terms of the impact felt by individuals. To that extent her behaviour has been in breach of the Ministerial Code, even if unintentionally.*[136]

Patel herself had actually previously resigned as Secretary of State for International Development in 2017 after holding a series of undisclosed meetings with Prime Minister Benjamin Netanyahu and other officials, while on holiday in Israel. By failing to inform both the Foreign Office and the British embassy in Israel in advance of the meetings, she accepted that she had breached the code and therefore resigned, without, in this instance, the case being referred to the Independent Adviser. It may be relevant though that this resignation took place whilst Theresa May was the Prime Minister.

Whilst there had been examples in the past of Prime Ministers not referring issues of alleged ministerial misconduct to the Independent Adviser, the 2020 case was the first time – at least in recent years - that a Minister had not resigned after being found by the Independent Adviser to have breached the Ministerial Code. As a result, Sir Alex resigned from his post, making the following very brief statement:

> *"I recognise that it is for the Prime Minister to make a*

---

[136]https://assets.publishing.service.gov.uk/government/uploads/system/uploads/attachment_data/file/937010/Findings_of_the_Independent_Adviser.pdf

> *judgement on whether actions by a Minister amount to a breach of the Ministerial Code. But I feel that it is right that I should now resign from my position as the Prime Minister's independent adviser on the Code.*"[137]

Sir Alex resigned in November 2020. It took five months for his successor, the Queen's former Private Secretary, Lord Geidt, to be appointed. It's worth emphasising again though: the ultimate choice was the Prime Minister's alone and the new incumbent, like his predecessors, is able to carry out investigations only at the Prime Minister's request.

We saw earlier that Gordon Brown's government accepted the case for putting the Civil Service Code on a statutory footing, but no similar change was made to the Ministerial Code.[138] It has seemed, therefore, that the Ministerial Code is no more than a code of conduct that Prime Ministers can interpret in whichever way they wish. However, following Johnson's decision to disregard the findings of the Independent Adviser, the Civil Service trade union, the First Division Association (FDA), successfully sought the permission of the High Court to have the decision judicially reviewed. The government opposed the application on the grounds that the Ministerial Code was separate from the law but the judge didn't accept that view.

---

[137] https://www.gov.uk/government/news/statement-from-sir-alex-allan

[138] When the then Minister for the Cabinet Office, Ed Miliband, was quizzed about this by the Public Administration Committee in April 2008 he said: '[the] implication of [making the Ministerial Code statutory] would be to make justiciable the question of compliance with the Ministerial Code, in other words put into the courts potentially the question of whether ministers were or were not complying with the Code. I think ministers should be held to account by Parliament. Ultimately, as we know, it is for the Prime Minister to choose who is and who is not in government, but ministers are held to account by Parliament and in the court of public opinion. To open up the question of whether a minister complied with the Ministerial Code into judicial review does not seem to me to strike the right balance between the proper functions of the Executive, Parliament and the courts in this country.' Transcript of Oral Evidence to the Public Administration Select Committee 29 April 2008. Published as HC 499-ii.

As the FDA's case is essentially that the Ministerial Code should be subject to the rule of law, the outcome of the case may have implications for the status of codes in a system of government where formal rules are often lacking.

In addition to all of these functions and powers, the Prime Minister, as mentioned earlier, also bears the title 'First Lord of the Treasury'. (It is the words 'First Lord of the Treasury' that appear on the letter box on the front door of No 10 Downing Street.) As such, he is technically the senior Treasury Minister. In practice, Prime Ministers have tended to devolve most of this power to their Chancellors, but if they need any excuse to interfere in matters of economic or monetary policy, this provides it. In his exchange of texts with the industrialist Sir James Dyson during the Covid pandemic, Boris Johnson reminded us that he held this title of First Lord of the Treasury. Sir James had texted the Prime Minister, clearly frustrated that he hadn't received a response from the Chancellor, Rishi Sunak, concerning an issue about the tax treatment of his staff. In his response to Sir James, Boris Johnson said: *James I am first lord of the treasury and you can take it that we are backing you to do what you need.*[139]

Finally, Prime Ministers also carry the title 'Minister for the Civil Service'. This is a function enshrined in legislation that gives the Prime Minister responsibility for the central co-ordination and management of the Civil Service, although, in practice, day-to-day responsibility for Civil Service matters lies with the Minister for the Cabinet Office.

These are the ten principal functions and powers of the Prime Minister as Head of Government. But, as well as being the Head of Government, the Prime Minister is also the leader of her party and a Member of Parliament. Leadership of the party will carry many additional duties, including chairing party committees, meeting with the party's parliamentarians and attending the annual conference. And even the Prime Minister can't ignore the

---

[139] https://www.bbc.co.uk/news/uk-politics-56839459

fact that she is the Prime Minister only because the people of her constituency have elected her to the House of Commons. The Prime Minister may have immense affairs of state to worry about, but she cannot afford to ignore her constituents, whose support she will need at the next general election if she is to continue as Prime Minister.

The Cabinet

The Cabinet Manual describes the Cabinet as the ultimate decision-making body of government.[140] The Ministerial Code tells us that the Cabinet's business *consists in the main of...questions which significantly engage the collective responsibility of the Government because they raise major issues of policy or because they are of critical importance to the public.*[141] In short, the Cabinet is the most senior committee in government. There is a statutory maximum of 22 ministers (to include the Prime Minister) who can be paid as Cabinet ministers, but there are sometimes full Cabinet Ministers in excess of the maximum by dint of them not being paid.[142]

The Privy Council

All members of the Cabinet – as well as a number of other senior ministers - are Privy Counsellors. The Privy Council, of which the Cabinet is technically just a committee, dates from the earliest days of the monarchy when it comprised those appointed by the King or Queen to advise on matters of state. These days, the

---

[140] Ibid. Cabinet Manual Paragraph 4.1

[141] Ibid. Ministerial Code Paragraph 2.2

[142] A full list of all government ministers can be found here: https://www.gov.uk/government/ministers. The Ministerial and Other Salaries Act 1975 sets the maximum number of paid ministerial posts at 109 and The House of Commons Disqualification Act 1975 provides that there may be no more than 95 ministers in the House of Commons. There is no legal restraint on the number of Ministers in the Lords.

business of the Privy Council (for example, the making of Orders-in-Council under Acts of Parliament or the Royal Prerogative) is usually carried out by ministers who are Privy Counsellors. Members of the Privy Council have the title 'The Right Honourable'. Other people will be members of the Privy Council too: senior bishops and judges, for example, and senior figures in opposition parties. Members of the Privy Council swear an oath which dates back to Tudor times. It requires those taking it to *keep secret all matters...treated of in Council*. By swearing the oath, a Privy Counsellor may be given information 'on Privy Council terms' that would not be given to those who are not Privy Counsellors. On this basis, from time to time the Prime Minister will brief senior members of opposition parties on matters to do with national security.

Privy Counsellors are appointed for life. (David Laws entertainingly describes the process of being sworn in as a Privy Counsellor, which *involved kneeling on a stool, but with only the right knee, and in an uncomfortable 'squatting' pose that seemed designed to cause maximum awkwardness.*[143]) Only six Privy Counsellors have resigned from the Council since the start of the 20th century but, coincidentally, three of these resignations all occurred during 2013. Chris Huhne resigned after pleading guilty to perverting the course of justice; John Prescott resigned over how the Council would handle the issue of press regulation; and Denis MacShane resigned before a High Court hearing at which he pleaded guilty of false accounting and for which was subsequently imprisoned.

Secretaries of State

The majority of, but not all, Cabinet ministers are the Secretaries of State who head the main government departments. The Prime Minister himself is not a Secretary of State, nor is the Chancellor of the Exchequer. Other ministers who are not Secretaries of State include the Leaders of the House of Commons

---

[143] Ibid. David Laws p. 226

and House of Lords, the Chief Secretary to the Treasury and the Minister for the Cabinet Office (who often also goes by the title of 'Chancellor of the Duchy of Lancaster').[144] The fact that these ministers are not Secretaries of State is significant because Acts of Parliament generally give powers to 'the Secretary of State',[145] powers which therefore cannot be assumed by ministers who are not Secretaries of State. If powers need to be given to the Chancellor of the Exchequer, the act must state that it is to that office that these powers are being given. It was noted earlier that in more recent times the title of "First Secretary of State" has been given by the Prime Minister to one senior member of the Cabinet. While it's largely used as a courtesy, it does give the holder the right to use powers given to "the Secretary of State" if they don't otherwise have that title, as for example was the case for some of the time when John Prescott was Deputy Prime Minister.

Other Ministers who attend Cabinet

Other ministers also attend Cabinet although they are not full Cabinet members (because they can't legally be paid as such). Following the September 2021 reshuffle there were seven ministers who regularly attended Cabinet without being a full member of it. These were the Minister of State at the Ministry of Justice and Home Office, Kit Malthouse; the Chief Secretary to the Treasury, Simon Clarke; the Minister without Portfolio at the Cabinet Office, Nigel Adams; the Minister of State at the Department for Education, Michelle Donelan; the Leader of the House of Commons, Jacob Rees–Mogg; the Chief Whip, Mark

---

[144] The post of Chief Secretary to the Treasury was created in 1961 with a specific remit over the management of public expenditure. The holder of the office is usually a Cabinet Minister. Thus the Treasury is a department that has two Cabinet ministers (three if you include the Prime Minister as 'First Lord of the Treasury').

[145] In theory there is only one office of Secretary of State, but several ministers may be given the title and powers of the office. The powers and functions given to 'the Secretary of State' can therefore be exercised by any Secretary of State. There are exceptions to this where an act mentions a specific Secretary of State, but this is unusual.

Spencer and the Attorney General, Suella Braverman.

The Operation of Cabinet and the Prime Minister's Control over it

From 1963, Thursday had traditionally been the day when Cabinet would meet but since 2007 the meeting has moved backwards and forwards between Tuesdays and Thursdays. Since 1856 Cabinet meetings have taken place in the Cabinet Room at Number 10 Downing Street, although very occasionally the Cabinet meets elsewhere such as in January 2020 when it convened in Sunderland to mark the UK's departure from the EU.[146] Ministers sit round what has sometimes been described as a 'coffin-shaped' table. Since 1937 Prime Ministers have sat at the middle of one of the long sides of the Cabinet table, in front of the fireplace and in the only chair that has arm-rests. The shape of the table is far from ideal for a meeting of this size and, from where she sits, the Prime Minister doesn't have the best view of all of her ministers. So where a particular Cabinet minister sits at the table is important. The more senior ministers tend to sit close to the Prime Minister. A key determinant of who sits where is the order of precedence that is published after every Cabinet reshuffle.[147] This order is influenced not only by the importance of the post but also by how long the post holder has been in the Cabinet. Ministers in what may seem to be less important Cabinet posts may therefore be high on the precedence list simply because they have been in the Cabinet a long time.[148]

Some ministers take quite seriously their position at the Cabinet table. In his book about life with Tony Blair and Gordon Brown, Peter Mandelson describes the first meeting of the

---

[146] During the pandemic the Cabinet met virtually.

[147] On this list, Cabinet ministers appear in order of precedence: https://members.parliament.uk/Government/Cabinet

[148] So, other than for the most senior of Cabinet posts, there is very little correlation between the order of precedence of Cabinet ministers and the 'pecking order' of government departments.

Cabinet following his return from Brussels in the autumn of 2008:

> *Seating arrangements around the cabinet table are always politically sensitive, and I was curious to see where I would be allocated a place. Those who are regarded as most senior or important are invariably seated opposite the Prime Minister. The further you are from the centre, especially if you are on the same side of the table as the Prime Minister, the more difficult it is to catch his attention when you want to speak. I was relieved, therefore, to find myself placed opposite Gordon, alongside Alistair Darling. I was equally fortunate to have Douglas Alexander on my other side. He was one of the wittiest members of the cabinet, and with Alistair's dry humour on my other flank, I knew that at least I would be kept quietly and occasionally amused.*[149]

And David Laws, who briefly served as Chief Secretary to the Treasury following the formation of the Coalition Government, gives his own interesting insight into the position of ministers around the Cabinet table. In his book on the creation of the Coalition Government, he describes how, at the first Cabinet meeting of the Coalition Government:

> *we were ... ushered into the Cabinet Room, and had to find the places which had been allocated to us. As one of the more junior members of the Cabinet, I was not surprised to find myself close to the end of the great table, second from the end....However, I had the advantage of being on the other side of the table from the Prime Minister, so it was easy to see him, watch his reactions to the points being made, and signal a desire to contribute when necessary.*[150]

---

[149] Ibid. Peter Mandelson

[150] Ibid. David Laws

Who sits where around the Cabinet table was clearly an issue in earlier governments too. In his book 'A History of Modern Britain', Andrew Marr describes how in 1962, the Foreign Secretary, Lord Home

> walked into the cabinet room in Number Ten to find the Prime Minister quietly reshuffling the place-names around the table. He asked the cabinet secretary what was going on. Had someone died? No, came the reply, it was all to do with Enoch Powell: 'The Prime Minister can't have Enoch's accusing eye looking at him straight across the table any more'. And Enoch was put way down on the left where Harold [Macmillan] couldn't see him.[151]

At the Prime Minister's right sits the Cabinet Secretary. Until 1917 the 'Cabinet Letter' written to the Monarch by the Prime Minister in his own hand was the only record of decisions taken in Cabinet. But the complexity of decision taking in war required a more formal process for managing Cabinet and recording its decisions. The Cabinet Secretariat and the position of 'Secretary of the Cabinet' or 'Cabinet Secretary' were born. For most of the time since, the Cabinet Secretary has also held the position of Head of the Home Civil Service. The first Cabinet Secretary, Sir Maurice Hankey, would take the formal minute of what was agreed by the Cabinet, but these days the Cabinet Secretary is helped in this by other senior Cabinet Office officials who sit at a small table at the end of the main Cabinet table. As these officials attend only for that part of the meeting concerning their particular responsibilities, their table is near the Cabinet room door to allow easy entrances and exits.

The past 70 years have seen considerable variation in the length of Cabinet meetings and there is a degree of correlation between this and the importance of Cabinet. Whilst a graph plotting prime ministerial power might show a marked increase

---

[151] Andrew Marr 'A History of Modern Britain' Macmillan May 2007

since the Second World War, a graph plotting the power of Cabinet might show a trend in the opposite direction. But it would be simplistic to suggest that prime ministerial power and Cabinet power is a zero-sum game. Certainly, over the last 40 years the general trend in the number and length of Cabinet meetings has been downward, although the average length of meetings may these days be slightly longer than under Tony Blair when, as we have seen, some Cabinet meetings were as short as half an hour.

Prime Ministers have always enjoyed considerable control over their Cabinets. As well as having the power to appoint, dismiss and reshuffle her ministers at any time, in Cabinet meetings she has three specific powers: setting the agenda, deciding who speaks when, and summing up. Regarding the agenda of Cabinet, the Cabinet Manual says that *there are no set rules about the issues that should be considered by Cabinet itself and it is ultimately for the Prime Minister to decide the agenda, on the advice of the Cabinet Secretary.* [152] The formal agenda of Cabinet rarely changes from meeting to meeting as it consists of a number of 'stock items' when senior ministers report on important legislation that is currently going through Parliament or on the key home and foreign affairs issues. There may sometimes be specific papers for the Cabinet to discuss. But, despite this rather free agenda, the Prime Minister will have decided in advance, in consultation with the Cabinet Secretary, what specific issues she wishes to be raised in Cabinet. Individual Cabinet ministers may ask the Cabinet Secretary for a particular issue to be discussed in Cabinet, but the decision always rests with the Prime Minister.

Although Cabinet discussions are now less formal than they once were – Blair introduced first names rather than formal titles – it is still very much for the Prime Minister to decide who speaks and when. As all discussion goes through the chair, the Prime Minister can to a certain extent steer the discussion. Senior ministers and those with a direct interest in the issue would normally expect to be able to give their views early on in the

---

[152] Ibid. Cabinet Manual Paragraph 4.18.

discussion, but it shouldn't be assumed that all Cabinet ministers express their views on every issue. In shorter Cabinet meetings this is not feasible.

The minutes of Cabinet meetings are by no means a blow-by-blow account of what was said. Rather, for any particular issue, there will be a summary of the main points made in the general discussion, followed by the Prime Minister's summing up. This summing up by the Prime Minister is crucial as, once it is in the minutes, it becomes the official decision of government. Cabinet ministers may from time to time wish to challenge a Prime Minister's summing up but they may not always be successful, as the 1970s Labour Cabinet Minister Shirley Williams suggests: *(Harold) Wilson's summing up of Cabinet discussions was masterly. I once challenged his conclusion, busily counting heads myself. The Prime Minister abruptly reminded me that summing up was his prerogative.*[153] But however the Prime Minister has summed up, once the decision has been reached, the 'doctrine of collective responsibility' applies.

Collective Responsibility

The doctrine of collective responsibility requires all members of the government, whether they were involved in the discussions or not, publicly to support the decision that has been reached. It was a doctrine developed in the 18th Century as a means of ensuring that ministers presented a united front to the Monarch. Where ministers cannot accept the restrictions placed on them by the doctrine, they are usually required to resign from the government as Robin Cook and Clare Short did over the Blair Government's policy on Iraq. Although Clare Short actually resigned in May 2003 after the main hostilities were over, her anti-war views were well known throughout both the build-up to the invasion and the invasion itself. It might therefore be argued that the principle of collective responsibility was rather flexibly interpreted by Tony Blair before Short finally left office. Perhaps an even more

---

[153] Shirley Williams 'Climbing the Bookshelves' p.200. Virago Press 2009.

celebrated case was Michael Heseltine's resignation from Margaret Thatcher's government in 1986 over the issue of the Westland Helicopter Company. An apparently unimportant issue to force the resignation of a senior Cabinet Minister, it was the way in which the decision had been reached that prompted Heseltine's resignation. The Cabinet was split over the question of who would be allowed to buy the British company. The split came to a head at a Cabinet meeting in January 1986 when, complaining at the lack of collective decision-making on the issue, Heseltine is said to have picked up his papers and walked out of the Cabinet room, telling his rather surprised colleagues that he could no longer be a member of Margaret Thatcher's Cabinet. He then walked out of the front door of Number 10 Downing Street and announced his resignation to the journalists waiting outside.

This doctrine of collective responsibility continued formally to exist under the Coalition Government - except in a few policy areas where the Coalition Agreement explicitly set it aside[154] – though it was tested on a number of occasions, most notably in January 2013 when, for the first time, Conservative and Liberal Democrat Ministers entered different voting lobbies in the House of Lords over the question of whether to reduce the number of parliamentary constituencies in the UK.[155]

Cabinet usually meets once a week when Parliament is sitting. This often means it is meeting fewer than 40 times a year. Given this, and the length of the meetings, it is therefore understandable that some have questioned whether the Cabinet truly is *the ultimate decision-making body of government*. The

---

[154] It was set aside by the Coalition Agreement in the policy areas of the electoral reform referendum, tuition fees, nuclear power, the replacement of Britain's nuclear deterrent and transferable tax allowances for married couples.

[155] This was a vote on adding a clause to the Electoral Registration and Administration Bill that would delay the reduction in the number of constituencies, as required by the Parliamentary Voting System and Constituencies Act 2011, until 2018.

https://publications.parliament.uk/pa/ld201213/ldhansrd/text/130114-0002.htm

criticism often levelled at Tony Blair and Margaret Thatcher was that too many decisions were taken by the Prime Minister outside the Cabinet room, perhaps in the company of a small coterie of advisers or individual ministers, and then presented to the Cabinet ministers as *faits accomplis*. Peter Hennessy has been a particular critic of the decline in Cabinet Government, particularly so when the Blair Government was in power. In evidence given to the Public Administration Select Committee in 2008 he described Tony Blair's Cabinets as *the most supine since World War II*. And when a committee member said that Hennessy seemed to be suggesting that the Cabinet was *just a vegetable patch*, Hennessy's reply was: *That gives a false impression of vigour, actually. Vegetables grow!* [156]

Actually, opinion is divided as to how much proper Cabinet discussion there was on key issues during the Blair premiership. Robin Cook resigned from the Cabinet in March 2003 when he could not support the government's position on Iraq. His criticism, however, was more that the wrong decision had been reached, and perhaps based on faulty evidence, rather than that Cabinet had not discussed it sufficiently. But Clare Short's and Mo Mowlam's comments, as we know, were more critical of Blair's conduct of Cabinet.

Gordon Brown and David Cameron, as we have seen, operated a more collective style of government although to some extent that was imposed on Cameron, at least for his first five years as Prime Minister, due to him leading a coalition government. Theresa May perhaps tried to operate a more prime ministerial style of government only for this to be made next to impossible by divisions not only within her party but within the Cabinet itself.

So what of Boris Johnson and his style of Cabinet? At the select committee hearing of May 2021 already referenced,

---

[156] Transcript of oral evidence to the Public Administration Select Committee 24 April 2008. Published as HC 499-i.

Dominic Cummings was asked about the role played by the Cabinet in the big decisions during the Covid pandemic. His responses to Carol Monaghan MP are quite revealing:

> Carol Monaghan: So you were pressing for a circuit breaker lockdown in September?
>
> Dominic Cummings: Yes.
>
> Carol Monaghan: So if the Prime Minister wasn't persuaded, in your words, of the importance of this, whose advice was he taking?
>
> Dominic Cummings: He wasn't taking any advice; he was just making his own decision that he was going to ignore the advice.
>
> Carol Monaghan: Did his Cabinet agree with his decision?
>
> Dominic Cummings: The Cabinet wasn't involved or asked.
>
> Carol Monaghan: Did you hear anything from Cabinet members about these decisions?
>
> Dominic Cummings: There were different views, I think....But there wasn't any formal Cabinet meeting to discuss it, or, if there was, it was a purely Potemkin exercise. It wasn't a real discussion that actually affected anything. [157]

This certainly supports the view, held by many, that Johnson runs a very centralised, 'presidential' style of government with a Cabinet that is arguably the weakest in living memory. Indeed it was reported in June 2021, after a string of damaging revelations from Dominic Cummings and a bad by-election result in Chesham

---

[157] Ibid. Questions 1158-1161

and Amersham, that Cabinet ministers themselves were tiring of Johnson's centralised approach.[158]

This approach can be seen in a number of ways. Special advisers have come more directly under control of No 10 rather than of the Cabinet Ministers they nominally serve. Within one month of Johnson coming to power, Dominic Cummings had sacked the Treasury special adviser Sonia Khan, without even consulting the Chancellor. This ultimately led to the departure of the Chancellor, Sajid Javid, from government. He was replaced by Rishi Sunak but not before Sunak had accepted control by No 10 over his Treasury special advisers. Special advisers in the Johnson government now clearly know that they serve at No 10's pleasure. There has similarly been a takeover by No 10 of the communications operation in government without any obvious consultation with Cabinet ministers. It is therefore reasonable to suggest that Boris Johnson has downgraded the role of Cabinet, with a marked shift away from collective cabinet government to a system that is being run almost entirely from the centre and in the name of the Prime Minister. So if Peter Hennessy described Tony Blair's Cabinets as having less vigour than vegetables, one wonders how he might describe Johnson's.

Tony Blair and Prime Ministers since have tried to make the Cabinet Office and No 10 more of a Prime Minister's department, without an enormous amount of success. Under Johnson this might yet happen, with perhaps those parts of the Cabinet Office which manage the collective aspects of government being moved out of the Cabinet Office into No 10 (see paragraphs on 'The Cabinet Office' below). This sounds like a dry organisational matter but it would indicate a real shift away from Cabinet government to a more prime ministerial, even presidential style of government. Who could stop this move happening? The Cabinet Secretary and other senior officials in the Cabinet Office carry

---

[158] https://www.theguardian.com/politics/2021/jun/20/ministers-urge-boris-johnson-to-consult-cabinet-on-key-decisions

some clout, but in the final analysis it could only really be stopped by members of the Cabinet themselves. Ministers in the current Cabinet however know full well that they are in their senior positions only because of Boris Johnson. It was he, not them, who promised to 'get Brexit done' and it was he, not them, who won the 2019 general election. At the moment there is very little evidence that ministers in the current Cabinet would stand up to the Prime Minister if they felt he was taking the way government operates in a direction that was too prime ministerial.

Cabinet Committees

Below the Cabinet sit a number of Cabinet Committees, some of which have sub-committees. These are groups of ministers that 'can take collective decisions that are binding across government'.[159] They are made up of ministers, some of whom will be Cabinet ministers and some who won't. (It's noticeable how few non-Cabinet ministers sit on the Cabinet Committees of the Johnson Government.) The Committees' powers may wax and wane like those of the Cabinet, but they always have an important role to play in the decision making processes of government. A number of people close to the Blair premiership stressed the importance of Cabinet Committees during that time. In his immensely entertaining diaries, the former Labour MP and junior minister Chris Mullin mentions a discussion he had with the Home Secretary Jack Straw:

> We talked about Cabinet meetings. Jack confirmed what others have said, that little in the way of serious debate takes place [in Cabinet]....The important work, he said, is done in the sub-committees.[160]

And Tony Blair's Chief of Staff, Jonathan Powell, in

---

[159] https://www.gov.uk/government/publications/the-cabinet-committees-system-and-list-of-cabinet-committees

[160] Chris Mullin 'A Walk-On Part: Diaries 1994-1999' p.383. Profile Books 2011

evidence to the House of Lords Constitution Select Committee in 2009 said:

> *Cabinet Committees… are an essential instrument of government decision making: all the relevant people can be there (and not the irrelevant), they are focussed on particular decisions, properly prepared and they have as much time as they need to reach a decision. In my view therefore rather than arguing about the death of Cabinet government, when it in fact died a long time ago, we should spend more effort reinforcing the Cabinet Committees and their supporting infrastructure as a key part of government decision making.*[161]

Most Prime Ministers reorganise the Cabinet Committee structure when they come to power. Under the Coalition Government their structure inevitably had to change. Overnight, Cabinet Committees became rather more important because they provided a vital forum for thrashing out disagreements that existed between the coalition partners. Every committee not only had a chair but also a deputy chair from the other coalition party. Cameron at the same time took the important step of creating a 'National Security Council' which is 'the main forum for collective discussion of the government's objectives for national security'.[162] This committee of senior ministers is also attended, when required, by the Chief of the Defence Staff and the heads of the 'agencies': MI5, MI6 and GCHQ.

As of March 2021 there were 15 Cabinet Committees and sub-committees covering all the main areas of government. Two of these committees were devoted to the Covid pandemic and two to post-Brexit arrangements. The most recent of the 15 to be created was the 'Union Policy Implementation Committee', set up in February 2021 to 'support the delivery of the Government's

---

[161] Written memorandum to the Constitution Committee, appended to the Committee's report on 'The Cabinet Office and the Centre of Government'. www.publications.parliament.uk/pa/ld200910/ldselect/ldconst/30/30.pdf

[162] https://www.gov.uk/government/groups/national-security-council

priorities in relation to the Union of the United Kingdom'.

The number of members that a committee has varies enormously. The current 'Domestic and Economic Strategy' committee has just five members whereas the 'Domestic and Economy Implementation' committee has 22.

Cabinet Committees exist to bring the collective will to bear on decision-making by allowing issues that are not discussed by the Cabinet itself to be considered by ministers from across government. Decisions reached in Cabinet Committees do not have to go to the full Cabinet, even for formal ratification. Cabinet Committee decisions become government policy and are covered by the doctrine of collective responsibility as if they were decisions of the full Cabinet. So, broadly speaking, Cabinet Committees provide for the collective consideration of those major policy issues that do not go to the full Cabinet.

Prime Ministers can also create other types of ministerial committee. For example, David Cameron created implementation taskforces, designed to drive the delivery of the government's most important cross-cutting priorities. Boris Johnson scrapped these when he became Prime Minister but a few months later, in response to the Covid pandemic, created four 'implementation committees' focusing on healthcare, the general public sector, economic and business, and international response. These were in turn scrapped in June 2020 and replaced by two full Cabinet Committees: 'COVID-19 Strategy' and 'COVID-19 Operations'.

The Cabinet Office

While the staff of Number 10 Downing Street directly support the Prime Minister in her role as Head of Government, the traditional role of the Cabinet Office – as well as acting as a kind of 'corporate head office' for government – is to support the collective decision-making process in government. The machinery within the Cabinet Office that supports the Cabinet and Cabinet Committees is known as the 'Cabinet Secretariat'. Until 2016 the major secretariats were the Economic and Domestic Secretariat, the National Security Secretariat, Civil Contingencies Secretariat and European and Global Issues Secretariat. When Theresa May became Prime Minister she disbanded the latter and it became part of the new Department for Exiting the European Union. Boris Johnson's government hasn't officially announced its secretariats but, according to the Institute for Government, it is likely that the National Security and Civil Contingencies secretariats still exist.[163]

With the growth of prime ministerial power, the Cabinet Office's role in directly supporting the Prime Minister has gained in prominence. The Cabinet Office currently describes itself thus:

> *We support the Prime Minister and ensure the effective running of government. We are also the corporate headquarters for government, in partnership with HM Treasury, and we take the lead in certain critical policy areas.*[164]

This explicit reference to supporting the Prime Minister first appeared in the early years of this century and it represented a real change given that supporting the Cabinet had always been the traditional role of the Cabinet Office going back to its foundation in the early 20th century. Because Number 10 is a very small organisation to support the British Head of Government, it is perhaps inevitable that, with increasing power concentrated on the Prime Minister, the Cabinet Office has assumed a greater share of this role. As far back as 2001 the then Deputy Prime Minister, John Prescott, told the House of Commons Select Committee on Public Administration: *The Cabinet Office is the department of the Prime Minister at the end of day.*[165]

---

[163] https://www.instituteforgovernment.org.uk/explainers/cabinet-office

[164] https://www.gov.uk/government/organisations/cabinet-office/about

[165] www.publications.parliament.uk/pa/cm200102/cmselect/cmpubadm/262/1101808.htm

The concern about calling the Cabinet Office 'the Prime Minister's Department' is that it would lend weight to the claim that in practice modern Britain has a system of prime ministerial, rather than Cabinet, government. Perhaps the best way of describing the collective function of the Cabinet Office and Number 10 is as the 'Department of the Prime Minister and Cabinet'. What is undeniable though is that there are now a number of functions, many of which sit in the Cabinet Office, which are prime ministerial in nature.

Cabinet or Prime Ministerial Government?

Britain has a system of Cabinet government where theoretically power lies in the hands of ministers who sit round the Cabinet table. But, as the power of the Prime Minister progressively increased during the second half of the 20th century and into the 21st, so the power of the Cabinet has waned. The extent to which this has happened is open to debate. An extreme view is that Cabinet has become no more than a cipher for the Prime Minister whose diktacts come down from on high to a subservient group of men and women whose sole allegiance is to him. That was a view occasionally heard during the Blair administration and it was perhaps a bit of an exaggeration. It is though a description that perhaps fits the Johnson Cabinet.

A less extreme view might be that, while Cabinet in the late 20th and early 21st centuries was clearly a lesser force than it had been previously, it still had two vital roles to play in government. First to ensure that government as far as possible operated collectively and, second, to provide an essential check on the office of Prime Minister, the rules governing whose powers and functions are almost entirely unwritten. At the current time, both those roles are less evidently being played than they have been in the past.

3

Ministers, Civil Servants and Departments

Ministers

As we saw in the previous chapter, there are some statutory limits placed on the number of ministers that the Prime Minister may appoint. In departments there are three levels of seniority to the ministerial hierarchy: Cabinet ministers, Ministers of State and Parliamentary Under Secretaries of State (PUSSs). The latter are sometimes referred to, more simply, as Parliamentary Secretaries. Collectively, Ministers of State and PUSSs are sometimes described as 'junior ministers'. A fourth categorization of minister are the whips. Although their role is almost entirely political, they are paid by the taxpayer for the work they do in government and are therefore classified as ministers. (For more on the work of the whips, see chapter four.) There is also another group of politicians who work in government but aren't actually ministers: Parliamentary Private Secretaries (PPSs). PPSs are MPs from the governing party whose primary role is to help keep their minister in touch with the party in Parliament. Although they receive no ministerial salary in addition to their salary as an MP, they are regarded as members of the government and are generally expected to abide by the principles of collective ministerial responsibility. (Beware the abbreviation PPS, which can also mean Principal Private Secretary: the senior civil servant running a senior minister's private office.)

The hierarchy within a department will vary substantially from department to department. Whilst most departments would have only one Cabinet minister (the Treasury being the regular exception), the number of Ministers of State and PUSSs will vary considerably, with some departments having more of the former and others more of the latter. One shouldn't therefore think of there being a formal hierarchy of ministers in a department whereby the PUSSs report to a Minister of State and the Ministers of State report to the Secretary of State. Rather, each Minister of State and PUSS will have their own specific portfolio in the department and each will report to the Secretary of State. Because of the discrete nature of the roles of some ministers at Minister of State and PUSS level, they will have a specific title such as 'Minister for Sport' or 'Minister for Public Health'.

As an example, the ministerial structure of the Home Office in July 2021 was as follows:

- Secretary of State (Home Secretary) – Priti Patel
- Minister of State (Security) – James Brokenshire
- Minister of State (Crime and Policing) – Kit Malthouse
- Minister of State – Baroness Williams of Trafford
- Minister of State (Building Safety and Communities) – Lord Greenhaigh
- Parliamentary Under Secretary of State (Safeguarding) – Victoria Atkins
- Parliamentary Under Secretary of State (Future Borders and Immigration) – Kevin Foster
- Parliamentary Under Secretary of State (Immigration Compliance and Justice) – Chris Philp

> Priti Patel's Parliamentary Private Secretary – Mike Wood

In most departments, one or more of the ministers will have a seat in the House of Lords. (In the Home Office example above, there are two: Baroness Williams and Lord Greenhaigh.) In some cases they will have been specifically given a seat in the Lords by the Prime Minister on becoming a minister. (We discuss the Prime Minister's power to make appointments to the Lords in chapter five.) More often though they will have been drawn from the existing membership of the Lords when appointed a minister. Within the department, a Lords minister will have a specific portfolio for which they are responsible. When speaking in the Lords however, if they are the only Lords minister from their department, they will be answerable for everything for which their department is responsible. As an example, whilst the Foreign Office minister Lord Ahmad may have specific responsibilities in the department for South Asia and the Commonwealth, in the Lords he will need to be able to speak about any foreign policy issue. Ministers in the Lords will therefore often need rather more briefing from their officials on certain issues than might their counterparts in the Commons. Where a department doesn't have a Lords minister, someone else who is from the governing party in the Lords, usually a government whip, will speak on behalf of the government.

Civil Servants

There is no single accepted definition of what a civil servant is but, to say that they are the staff of government departments is, for most purposes, sufficiently accurate. There are around 465,000 civil servants in the United Kingdom. The large majority of these – perhaps 80% - are carrying out executive functions such as issuing driving licences and passports and paying benefits. Perhaps around 5% are working closely with ministers, devising, advising on and communicating policy. The remainder will be carrying out human resource, finance, IT and other functions.

Until the middle 1990s there was a uniform pay and grading system operating across the whole of *Whitehall* (the name often used for the Civil Service, based on the street in London where a number of government departments continue to be based). Since then there has been a considerable decentralization in and fragmentation of the Service. However, all ministerial departments are headed by the Permanent Secretary (or Permanent Under-Secretary (PUS) in the case of the Foreign, Commonwealth & Development Office and the Ministry of Defence). The Permanent Secretary is the administrative head of the department whose relationship with the department's political head, the Secretary of State, is extremely important. Below the Permanent Secretary, in most departments, will be found Directors General, Directors and Assistant Directors. Across the Civil Service these grades are classed as the 'Senior Civil Service' - approximately the 3,500 most senior civil servants. Below the Senior Civil Service, there will be different pay and grading systems operating across the various departments,

Private Office

Immediately outside a minister's office in a government department will be the private office. In the private office work a number of civil servants whose job it is to manage the minister's departmental life, making sure he or she is in the right place at the right time with the right papers and ensuring that the minister knows what they should be doing and who they are meeting. Having good private office staff is absolutely vital to ministers and it is crucially important that the minister and private office work well together. The size of the private office will vary with the seniority of the minister. The largest private office in a department will be that of the Secretary of State. This will be headed by the Principal Private Secretary who will also be responsible for the staff of the private offices of the other ministers in the department. The private office acts as a bridge between the department and the minister, in particular managing the flow of written communications between officials and their minister. Crucial to this is the 'red box'. This is a large red attaché case which is usually filled with paperwork for the minister to take home each evening. At the weekend there may well be more than one red box. The private office staff have to consider carefully what should and shouldn't go into the overnight box, bearing in mind that the minister may not start to go through it until late at night.

A crucially important member of the private office staff will be the minister's diary secretary. The diary secretary manages the moving target that is the minister's diary, liaising with officials throughout the department as well as the party, the constituency office, special advisers and the minister's family. Engagements are inserted, re-arranged, postponed and cancelled constantly, and the diary secretary's responsibility is to ensure that no important engagements are missed, that business is conducted efficiently and that no one is offended.

Ministers in the UK government are extremely busy people, not least because most of them have to juggle their ministerial life with their life as a constituency MP – not to mention their private life. The diary secretary will face a constant battle to ensure that as well as being able to attend meetings, spend time in Parliament etc, he or she will also have time to look after their constituents. Permanent civil servants should have nothing to do with the minister's life as a constituency MP but they have to be aware that this other job exists and make sure that there is time in the diary for the minister to pay attention to it. An excellent minister may cease being a Member of Parliament, let alone a minister, if their constituents consider that she or he has failed to look after them!

Civil Service Principles

Civil Servants serve ministers in the government of the day and through them, Parliament and the public. The two key principles that underpin the British Civil Service are those of political impartiality and objectivity, both of which are associated with the further principle that ministers have no (or perhaps little) say over the recruitment, promotion and dismissal of civil servants.[166] The British Civil Service is therefore a permanent organisation: even at its most senior levels its staff do not come and go with ministers. It is there to serve the government of the day, whatever its political complexion.

These principles, which were first established by the Northcote-Trevelyan report of the mid-19th century, are key to the good governance of the United Kingdom. We contrasted above what happens to the Civil Service in the UK when there is a change of government (effectively nothing) to what happens in the USA where the senior levels of the federal Civil Service are made up of political appointments. When Joe Biden replaced Donald Trump as US President in January 2021, something like 4,000 senior posts had to be filled by the new President. Just imagine the hiatus that caused and the corporate memory that was lost. This is a problem that the UK system avoids. And, perhaps even more importantly, permanence allows civil servants in the UK to 'speak truth to power'; in other words, to tell ministers what they need to know rather than what they want to hear. It's human nature to want to bring one's boss good news, so it's important that a British civil servant's boss, in terms of their hiring, firing and promotion, is another civil servant, not the minister.

These key principles were first codified in the mid-1990s when John Major's government published the Civil Service Code[167] and were further entrenched in 2010, as mentioned above, when the principles set out in the Code were enshrined in an Act of Parliament for the first time: the Constitutional Reform and Governance Act. The Code clearly sets out how civil servants must act with political impartiality. This part of it is worth quoting in full:

---

[166] Ministers do have some say over the appointments of the most senior civil servant in the department – the Permanent Secretary – as well as the staff who work in their private offices. Many people would accept such influence as valid, assuming the appointments are not influenced in any way by party political considerations.

[167] https://www.gov.uk/government/publications/civil-service-code/the-civil-service-code

You must:

- *serve the government, whatever its political persuasion, to the best of your ability in a way which maintains political impartiality and is in line with the requirements of this code, no matter what your own political beliefs are*

- *act in a way which deserves and retains the confidence of ministers, while at the same time ensuring that you will be able to establish the same relationship with those whom you may be required to serve in some future government*

- *comply with any restrictions that have been laid down on your political activities*

You must not:

- *act in a way that is determined by party political considerations, or use official resources for party political purposes*

- *allow your personal political views to determine any advice you give or your actions*

A crucial part of that extract is the requirement for civil servants to retain the confidence of those they *may be required to serve in some future government.* It's always important for a civil servant to keep in mind that they could quite soon be working for the politicians who are currently on the other side of the House of Commons and Lords attacking their ministers. Are you sure that what you are doing for this government you'd also do for the other side? And is there anything you're doing for this government that might make it difficult for a new government to have confidence in your advice? This has been particularly important in recent decades when we have tended to have long periods of one party in power: 18 years of Conservative rule after the 1979 election followed by 13 years of Labour in power and now the Conservatives again in power for over 11 years (five of those being in coalition with the Liberal Democrats). In the run up to the 1997 election Labour politicians were heard to question whether civil servants would really be able to work for them after 18 years of Conservative government.[168] Similar comments were made by Conservative politicians in the run up to the 2010 election and we'll no doubt hear more from the opposition if and when this current period of Conservative rule seems to be coming to an end. I think ministers both after the 1997 and 2010 elections did generally accept that the Civil Service had been able to make a fairly seamless transition from one government to the next and did rapidly feel confident in the advice they were being given by civil servants who for many years had worked for the 'other side'.

Also of great importance is the requirement under the Code for civil servants *not (to) deceive or knowingly mislead Ministers, Parliament or others.* Whilst the job of a civil servant is to give objective and impartial advice to ministers, it is also to help ministers present their decisions and policies in the best possible light whilst being factually accurate and not misleading. This can be quite a challenge for a civil servant, particularly if they happen to disagree with the policy or the decision. But this is part of a civil servant's job, particularly those who help ministers communicate publicly through answering parliamentary questions, making speeches, replying to letters etc.

Special Advisers

Close to the private office will be found the advisers who have been appointed to give political advice to ministers that permanent civil servants are not allowed to provide. These are known as 'special advisers' (or 'SpAds'). Special advisers are temporary civil servants who have been appointed directly by ministers (increasingly, these days, by the Prime Minister) but are not allowed to manage or give orders to permanent civil servants.

---

[168] One Labour MP, who became a minister in Tony Blair's government, strongly expressed this view when speaking to the author and other civil servants not long before the 1997 election. He did later admit that he had got this wrong. (Private Information.)

Special advisers have worked in government for some time but it was when Tony Blair became Prime Minister that the numbers increased substantially (although the doubling of the number in May 1997 was almost entirely accounted for by the threefold increase of special advisers in No 10 Downing St.) But even during the Blair/Brown period, the number of special advisers in government was only around 75. The Coalition Agreement of May 2010 promised to put a cap on the number of special advisers, and the formal numbers did decline a little in the months following the election of the Coalition Government. However, as it became increasingly apparent to ministers that special advisers had a vital role to play in oiling the wheels of coalition government, the number of special advisers was allowed to increase significantly above the numbers in post when the Coalition Government had come to power. By October 2013 there were 97 special advisers in government, 23 of whom worked for the Prime Minister and 20 for the Deputy Prime Minister. The rest were spread across the various Whitehall departments. Since then the total number has hovered around the 100 mark, with close to 50% working directly for the Prime Minister.

With the private office, special advisers, who formally work for the Secretary of State, form part of the machinery at the centre of a department that helps ministers carry out their functions efficiently and effectively. Special advisers' advice is, almost by definition, political. The advice of permanent civil servants, as we have seen, should be impartial and objective. Ministers should take advice from both before reaching a decision. Special advisers are not always regarded in a positive light by civil servants and others. Often this is because they are seen to be acting as some kind of filter or gateway between the officials in the department and the minister. Certainly, special advisers who behave in this way are not acting in the best interests of the minister since the minister will not be making a decision based on all the facts if a special adviser has filtered officials' briefing before it reaches the minister. On the other hand, special advisers can be very useful for permanent civil servants to have around. Without special advisers, permanent civil servants would come under more pressure from ministers to do things that they should not be doing.

Ministers, Civil Servants and Special Advisers Working Together

The successful interaction of these three sets of players is crucial to the smooth running of a department and of the government as a whole. It is extremely important that all who work in the department are aware of the rules that govern their work and behaviour, most of which are written down in the Ministerial Code, the Civil Service Code and the Special Advisers' Code.

The Ministerial Code is clear that ministers must not ask civil servants to engage in any activity that might be seen as party political and it also requires ministers to treat their civil servants with respect. Furthermore it tells ministers that they must take very seriously their appearances in Parliament and in particular not to knowingly mislead Parliament in any way. The extent to which these requirements have been adhered to in recent times has become questionable. We saw above how the Home Secretary Priti Patel was found to have breached the Ministerial Code in 2020 for bullying her staff and yet didn't resign.

The behaviour of some civil servants has also been questioned in more recent times, in particular concerning their role in helping ministers present their policies and decisions in the best possible light *while not being misleading.* In October 2020 the Institute for Government (IfG) gave three examples of civil servants being involved in public comments that should not have been made. First was the tweet by the Department for International Trade that month which claimed that soy sauce *will be made cheaper thanks to our trade deal with Japan.* This was presumably written by a civil servants and it wasn't accurate. When this was pointed out to the department, rather than accept what it had said was wrong, it issued an elaborate clarification that soy sauce *will be cheaper than it otherwise would be under WTO terms, on which we would be trading with Japan from 1 Jan if we had not secured the UK-Japan trade deal.* This might seem rather trivial but it wasn't the only time that departmental twitter accounts had put out misleading information. Second was the Northern

Ireland Office's continual assertion that in the post-Brexit era *there will be no border in the Irish Sea between GB & NI,* despite all the evidence to the contrary. And third, an example highlighted by the IfG of civil servants engaging in public comment that was neither objective nor impartial when the Home Office made a video for its twitter account that talked about *activist lawyers* trying to *delay and disrupt returns* of migrants. The Permanent Secretary of the Home Office publicly admitted that this was wrong.[169]

The role of special advisers was brought into sharp relief in particular by the behaviour of Boris Johnson's senior special adviser Dominic Cummings. As we have seen, Cummings was held in contempt of Parliament for refusing to appear before a select committee of the House of Commons, was severely criticised for the way in which he behaved towards the civil servants and other special advisers that he worked with and, most infamously, in the eyes of most people, though not, it seems, in the eyes of ministers, broke the lockdown rules during the Covid pandemic.[170]

All of the above has recently put some strain on working relationships in government. Pressure has been put on civil servants to work in ways that many deem as not impartial. And many very senior civil servants have been forced out of their jobs by ministers who have become frustrated at their officials' insistence on giving their ministers objective advice, rather than telling them what they want to hear. Many would regard the principles on which the British Civil Service is based as one of the great strengths of the British system of government and so any move towards a more politicised Civil Service is to the great detriment of the efficient and effective running of the country.

---

[169] https://www.instituteforgovernment.org.uk/blog/government-communications-fall-flat-over-great-british-bake

[170] There are numerous examples of government ministers claiming that Dominic Cummings didn't break the lockdown rules. Here is one: https://www.bbc.co.uk/news/av/uk-52804626

Departments, Agencies and other Public Bodies

Central government stretches much more widely than the departments in which ministers are based. In government we also find non-ministerial departments, executive agencies and non-departmental public bodies as well as a host of other public bodies that don't readily fit into any particular category.

Departments of State

Those departments with ministers are known as 'Departments of State'. These are the traditional government departments that usually have a minister representing them at the Cabinet table and include not only those that have the word 'department' in their names but the Ministries of Defence and Justice, the Treasury, the Home Office, the Cabinet Office and the Foreign, Commonwealth and Development Office. Departments of State are not statutory bodies – in other words their existence and key functions are not set down in an Act of Parliament.[171] This means that Prime Ministers can set up, abolish, and change the names and functions of such departments largely at will. As an example, Theresa May created two new departments when she became Prime Minister: the Department for International Trade and the Department for Exiting the European Union. The latter was abolished when the UK left the EU at the end of January 2020.

Non-Ministerial Departments

Departments without ministers are known as 'Non-Ministerial Departments'. These are almost always statutory bodies set up by Act of Parliament. Such departments have been consciously set up to put some distance between their day-to-day operation and

---

[171] An exception to this rule is the Ministry of Defence which was created by the Ministry of Defence Act 1946 and the subsequent mergers between 1964 and 1971 of the Admiralty, the War Office, the Air Ministry, the Ministry of Aviation and the Ministry of Defence itself.

ministers. Non-Ministerial Departments are still staffed by civil servants, and ministers account to Parliament for their activities, including answering parliamentary questions on their performance and policies.

An example of a Non-Ministerial Department is the Food Standards Agency (FSA), which was set up in 2000 as a direct result of the BSE crisis of the late 1990s. Until its creation, responsibility for food safety lay with the old Ministry of Agriculture, Fisheries and Food (MAFF). MAFF was, however, also the sponsor department of the agricultural industry and therefore faced a potential conflict of interest. As a consequence, the FSA was established as a statutory body, at 'arm's length' from ministers, to oversee food safety across the UK. Other examples of Non-Ministerial Departments are the Crown Prosecution Service, HM Revenue and Customs and the energy regulator OFGEM, for whom the Attorney General, Treasury ministers and ministers in the Department for Business, Innovation and Skills are respectively answerable.

Executive Agencies

Many Departments of State and Non-Ministerial Departments have their own 'executive agencies'. This innovation dates from 1988 when Robin Ibbs, who in 1983 had been recruited from ICI by Margaret Thatcher to run the government's Efficiency Unit, published a report entitled *Improving Management in Government: The Next Steps*.[172] Ibbs's report concluded that, since around 95% of civil service functions were executive – rather than policy making – in nature, such functions should be hived off into executive agencies, with clear objectives and targets, each headed by a chief executive who would be directly accountable to ministers for the agency's performance. Each chief executive would enjoy substantial freedom to run the organisation, including setting a pay and grading system for the agency, subject to the constraints of the budget allocated by the parent

---

[172] Martin Stanley has placed a copy of the original Ibbs report on his excellent website:
https://www.civilservant.org.uk/library/1988_improving_management_in_government_the%20_next_steps.pdf

department. These organisations would be part of the department and therefore staffed by civil servants, but their day-to-day operations would be at 'arm's length' from ministers...

Executive agencies come in all shapes and sizes, ranging from HM Prisons and Probation Service (an executive agency of the Ministry of Justice), which employs over 50,000 people, to the Wilton Park conference centre (an executive agency of the Foreign, Commonwealth and Development Office), which employs fewer than 100. And, although all executive agencies conform to the same model, the extent to which they have genuine freedom from ministers and senior civil servants in the parent department varies considerably. Two executive agencies of the Department for Health and Social Care (DHSC) had high profiles during the Covid pandemic: Public Health England and the Medicines and Healthcare Products Regulatory Agency (MHRA). Most people wouldn't realise that both of these were part of the DHSC, staffed by civil servants of that department.[173] One could be forgiven for thinking from the way they were discussed in the media – and perhaps this has been in the interests of ministers – that they were bodies wholly independent of ministers when they were not. Whilst not questioning at all the MHRA's views on whether any particular Covid vaccine was safe to use, it is perhaps worth keeping in mind the fact that its staff, including the Chief Executive, are accountable to the Secretary of State for Health. (For the same reason it would be wrong to regard the UK Government's Chief Medical Officer, Chris Whitty, or its Chief Scientist, Sir Patrick Vallance, as people working independently of ministers. In fact they both work for the ministers they often found themselves standing alongside at Covid press conferences. As public servants these appearances, and those of many others like the Chief Executive of the MHRA or the Chief Nursing Officer, constitutionally looked a little odd.)[174]

---

[173] The functions of Public Health England were largely subsumed into the new UK Health Security Agency (UKHSA) in October 2021. The UKHSA is also an executive agency of the DHSC.
[174] In March 2021, the Conservative MP Charles Walker made a reference in the Commons Douglas to the fact that 'we allow unelected officials to have lecterns at No. 10 to lecture us on how to live our lives'.

Non-Departmental Public Bodies

A Non-Departmental Public Body (NDPB) is usually defined as follows:

> NDPBs have a role in the process of national government but are not part of a government department. They operate at arm's length from ministers, though a minister will be responsible to Parliament for the NDPBs.[175]

They are sometimes loosely described as 'QUANGOS', which is usually taken to stand for 'Quasi-Autonomous Non-Governmental Organisations' but this is rather misleading because NDPBs are very much part of government.

Because a key feature of Non-Departmental Public Bodies is that they are not generally staffed by civil servants, the arm in these particular 'arm's length' bodies is rather longer than it is in executive agencies. The larger Non-Departmental Public Bodies are known as 'Executive Non-Departmental Public Bodies' in that they have specific executive functions to carry out. An example of one of these would be the Environment Agency. (Note that the word 'agency' can be used in the title of different types of public body – executive agency, Non-Ministerial Department and Non-Departmental Public Body. No inference should be made as to the status of a particular body based simply on the word 'agency' appearing in its name.)

Given that NDPBs receive their funding through a government department and that their senior staff are appointed

---

https://hansard.parliament.uk/Commons/2021-03-25/debates/9701394F-FF53-4364-85E1-F017B13CE921/Coronavirus

[175] From: 'Classification of Public Bodies: Guidance for Departments' published by the Cabinet Office.
https://assets.publishing.service.gov.uk/government/uploads/system/uploads/attachment_data/file/519571/Classification-of-Public_Bodies-Guidance-for-Departments.pdf

by the Secretary of State, their description as 'independent' seems something of a misnomer. But the fact that their staff are not civil servants is important because it affects their accountability to Parliament. For example the staff of Non-Departmental Public Bodies who appear before select committees of Parliament do not speak on behalf of ministers as civil servants do. (For more on this, see chapter six.)

A few NDPBs, known as 'Crown Non-Departmental Public Bodies', are, however, staffed by civil servants. Examples of these are the Health and Safety Executive, the Advisory, Conciliation & Arbitration Service and the Office for Budget Responsibility. These are the only organisations outside government departments and their executive agencies that employ civil servants.

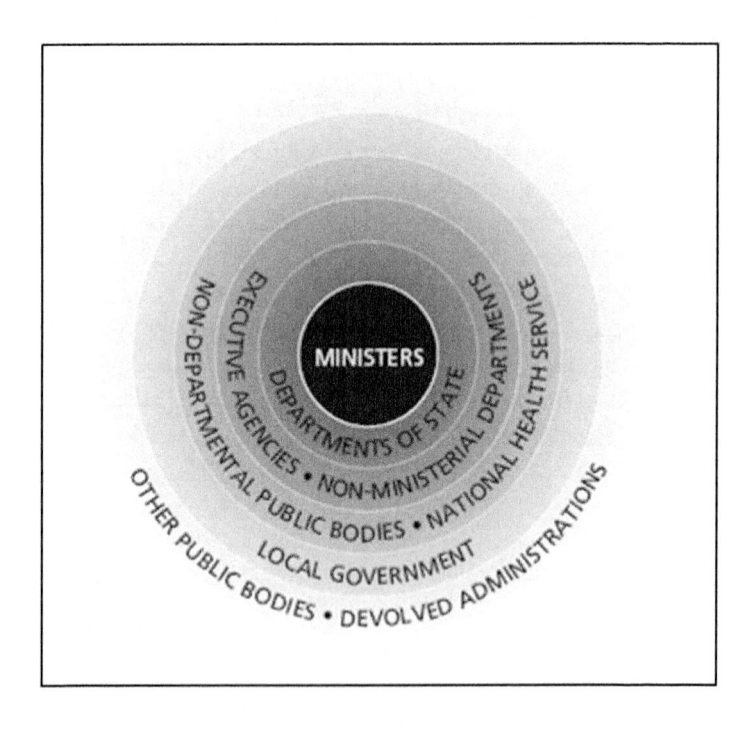

Figure 4

Other Public Sector Organisations

Figure 4 gives a view on the relative distance from ministers of Departments of State, executive agencies, Non-Ministerial Departments and Non-Departmental Public Bodies. It also shows other public sector organisations. The National Health Service is unique and cannot really be categorised under any formal heading. It is not staffed by civil servants and its distance from ministers may be a matter of some debate. Ministers are not usually involved in the day-to-day running of the NHS but it is common for ministers to be challenged in Parliament over the standard of care received by individual members of the public. Local Government, which is not a topic of discussion in this book, is still further from ministers, as are various other public bodies such as the nationalised industries and the BBC. The devolved administrations (which are discussed in chapter eight) are, of course, under the direction of their own ministers.

The reality though is actually rather less clear than the diagram suggests. Executive agencies, Non-Ministerial Departments, Non-Departmental Public Bodies and the NHS may be described as 'arm's length bodies' but how long is the arm? And this isn't a question only when comparing these different categories of public body; the arm will vary in length within each category too. Ministers are always going to be more closely involved in the running of some public organisations because of their political sensitivity. Equally there are other organisations whose independence ministers will be keen to stress. As suggested above, during the Covid pandemic, ministers always stressed the independence of the Medicines and Healthcare Products Regulatory Agency given its importance to the public trust of vaccines.

In reality, the way in which government bodies are classified is a bit of a mess. This was noted by the Public Administration Select Committee of the House of Commons in its 2014 report 'Who's accountable? Relationships between

Government and arm's-length bodies'.[176] In the summary to that report the Committee noted that:

> ...arm's-length Government is confused and opaque. Organisational forms and names are inconsistent. Most public bodies answer to Ministers but some are directly accountable to Parliament. There is no agreement on how many types of body exist. There are overlaps and blurring between categories. Accountability arrangements and reforms so far have been ad hoc.
>
> The Government has reviewed non-departmental public bodies, but it should review all forms of arm's-length Government, including executive agencies and non-ministerial departments. The Government should establish a clear taxonomy of public bodies: constitutional bodies, independent public interest bodies, departmental sponsored bodies, and executive agencies. All public bodies should sit in one of the categories, so that it is clear how each is to be governed and sponsored. This is essential in order to clarify who is accountable for what.

Little however has changed as a result of that report.

---

[176] https://publications.parliament.uk/pa/cm201415/cmselect/cmpubadm/110/11003.htm

4

The House of Commons

Like many other countries, the UK has a 'bicameral' Parliament – a Parliament with two chambers. The House of Commons is the 'Lower House' and the House of Lords the 'Upper House'. The British Parliament has one of the most famous homes in the world, sitting in that mid-19th century neo-gothic building, properly known as the 'the Palace of Westminster', on the north bank of the River Thames beside Westminster Bridge. In the middle of the 16th century, following a fire which had prompted Henry VIII to leave the Palace of Westminster, eventually to reside in the nearby Palace of Whitehall, his son Edward VI gave the Palace of Westminster to Parliament to use as a permanent home. The House of Commons used as its chamber St Stephen's Chapel within Henry's Palace. Because Members of Parliament then sat in the old chapel's choir stalls, they still now sit in rows of benches opposite each other, rather than in the semi-circular layout of most parliaments.

In 1834 the Palace was so badly damaged by fire that only the ancient Westminster Hall, built in Norman times, and the Jewel Tower, which is now across the road from the Palace, survived. In 1941 the Palace was again badly damaged, this time by bombing. With the chamber of the House of Commons almost completely destroyed, the members of the Commons moved into the House of Lords, with the Lords moving into the 'Robing Room' which is used by the Monarch at the State Opening of Parliament. Many of

Winston Churchill's famous wartime speeches were therefore given in the chamber of the Lords, not the Commons, and the dents in the wooden table in the House of Lords are attributed to Churchill thumping his ring finger on the table as he made his speeches.

The post-war rebuilding of the House of Commons offered an opportunity to modernise and enlarge. The chamber of the old House of Commons could seat only about 430 people – far fewer than the 640 MPs of the immediate post-war period or the 650 there are now. But Churchill in particular was very keen that the House should be rebuilt as it had been before the bombing. Thus it is still the case that only two-thirds or so of MPs are able to sit down when the Commons is busy. If there is no room for them to sit down, MPs stand behind the Speaker's chair or below the 'bar of the House' at the opposite end of the chamber to the Speaker's chair. It may seem strange to people that a parliamentary chamber in the 21st century isn't large enough to seat all its members; stranger still though is the fact that MPs who are forced to stand won't be called by the Speaker to speak, either because, if standing below the bar of the House they are not technically in the chamber or, if they are standing behind the Speaker's chair, because quite simply he can't see them.

Most people, on their first visit to Parliament, remark on how small the two chambers are. Between them, the Lords and the Commons probably take up no more than 5% of the ground floor area of the Palace. Their compactness, and the closeness thus created, can spark an electric atmosphere – especially in the Commons when it is full. Much of the time the chamber is emptier but, for set piece occasions such as Prime Minister's Questions, the Chancellor's budget speech and major debates, the House will be packed and buzzing.

Method of Election

MPs have always been elected using the simple and straightforward 'first past the post' system, in which all that is required for victory in any constituency is winning one more vote than any other candidate. Apart from its simplicity, an advantage of this system has traditionally been that it usually produces a clear majority for a particular party, and therefore leads to stable government. But whilst that might be true of the 2019 election, it wasn't true of any of the three general elections that preceded it. The 2010 election produced a hung Parliament and coalition government (arguably more stable than the governments that followed both of the next two elections.) The 2015 election gave a small majority to the Conservatives but the seeds of David Cameron's downfall can be found in that small majority, being forced as he was into holding the EU referendum. And the 2017 election produced another hung Parliament with all the problems that followed for Theresa May and her government (which we explore in more detail in chapter seven).

But even when an election does produce a clear majority for one party and therefore a stable government, the advantages are bought at a cost: the number of seats won is not proportional to the number of votes cast for any particular party. In 2019, for example, the Conservatives won 56.2% of the seats in the House of Commons having only won 43.6% of the vote. So the 'resounding majority' that Boris Johnson won was only a majority in terms of the seats his party won. In terms of votes cast, his party won fewer than half. At the same election the Liberal Democrats won fewer than 1.7% of the seats with 11.5% of the vote. The Liberal Democrats are particularly penalised by the electoral system because their vote is more evenly spread across the country and they therefore come second in many constituencies. This is in marked contrast to the Scottish National Party whose vote, of course, is contained within Scotland. At the 2019 election they succeeded in winning 7.4% of the seats in the Commons with just 3.9% of the votes cast across the UK.

Over the years there have been calls to change the Westminster electoral system to one that is more proportional. The Labour Government after 1997 accepted the case for proportional systems of election to the European Parliament, as well as to the new Parliament in Edinburgh and the new Assemblies in Belfast, Cardiff and London. Tony Blair's Government set up a commission, under the Liberal Democrat peer (and former Labour Home Secretary) Lord Jenkins, to consider options for Westminster. But, while Labour's 2001 manifesto promised to review Jenkins's report, which had recommended a rather complex form of proportional representation, nothing came of it.

Electoral reform disappeared from the political agenda until towards the end of Labour's time in power. As an amendment to the Constitutional Reform and Governance Bill, in March 2010 the Labour Government tabled proposals to require the holding of a referendum soon after the forthcoming general election on the adoption of the Alternative Vote (AV) system but these proposals were lost when Parliament was dissolved in advance of the election. Labour then proposed in its 2010 election manifesto that a referendum should be held on whether to introduce AV. But of course the Labour Party lost that election and so electoral reform became one of the key issues discussed by the Conservative and Liberal Democrat parties when the Coalition Agreement was negotiated after the election. AV doesn't necessarily produce a more proportional result than the current system (which is why the Liberal Democrats have always supported more proportional systems[177]) but it would be likely to be of some benefit to parties like the Liberal Democrats whose votes are more evenly spread across the country than those of Labour and the Conservatives. Under AV, instead of simply marking an X on the ballot paper, voters rank the candidates in order of preference. If no one candidate gains 50% of first preference votes, second preferences of the bottom candidate are redistributed until someone reaches the 50% threshold. Thus every MP could claim to be elected by at least 50% of those who voted in his or her constituency. Although

---

[177] There are many forms of proportional systems such as those used for the European Parliament (Regional Lists), for the Northern Ireland Assembly (the Single Transferable Vote) and for the Scottish Parliament and National Assembly for Wales (the Additional Member System). For more on elections to the devolved legislatures, see chapter 8.

not the preferred choice of the Liberal Democrats (or of the Conservatives who supported the status quo), it was this system that appeared in the Coalition Agreement as the one that would be put to the test, unsuccessfully as it turned out, in the referendum of May 2011.

Composition

The composition of the House of Commons in July 2021 was as follows:

Party	Men	Women	Total
Conservative	276	87	363
Labour	96	103	199
Scottish National Party	29	16	45
Liberal Democrat	4	8	12
Democratic Unionist Party	7	1	8
Sinn Féin	5	2	7
Independent	4	2	6
Plaid Cymru	2	1	3
Alba	2	0	2
Social, Democratic & Labour Party	1	1	2
Alliance	1	0	1
Green	0	1	1
Speaker	1	0	1

Figure 5

A few points are worth noting about the figures above. First: the seven Sinn Féin MPs that were elected in Northern Ireland. Although they were elected to the House of Commons, like all their Sinn Féin predecessors they refused to take their seats because, as an Irish Republican party, they don't recognise the jurisdiction of the Westminster Parliament over what they call 'the north of Ireland'. Interestingly though, Sinn Féin members do take their seats in the Northern Ireland Assembly in Belfast.

Second: there are six 'independents' shown on the table. It's important to understand though that none of these were elected as independents at the 2019 election. It's actually very difficult to get elected to the Commons as an independent though some may remember the ex-BBC journalist Martin Bell (the man in the white suit) doing just that at the 1997 election, after standing on an 'anti-sleaze' ticket. Dr Richard Taylor also won as an independent in both 2001 and 2005 having originally stood on the single issue of saving his local hospital from closure. But all of the six independents elected in 2019 were candidates of one of the main parties. The reason why they were sitting as independents in 2021 was because they had fallen out with their party for one reason or another and had 'had the whip withdrawn' which effectively meant they were no longer recognised as members of their parliamentary party. Of the six, one who became quite well known is Margaret Ferrier. Elected as an SNP MP she rather strangely travelled down from Scotland after taking a Covid test and then, having received a positive result whilst in London, travelled back to Scotland, each journey being made by public transport. Not only was she as a result thrown out of the SNP parliamentary party at Westminster, she was later arrested for her actions. The other of the six independents who is even more well-known is Jeremy Corbyn who, only a matter of months after stepping down as Labour's leader, was removed from the parliamentary party due to his reaction to the Equality and Human Rights Commission's report into alleged anti-Semitism in the party during his leadership.

Third: it is interesting to note that at the 2019 general election, for the first time one of the major political parties – Labour - had more women elected than men. The overall gender balance of the House of Commons is still though roughly 2:1 in favour of men and that's mainly because the gender split of Conservative MPs is roughly 3:1.

Fourth: if you were trying to work out exactly how many votes might be needed to win a vote in the Commons, you'd have to of course take into account the fact the seven Sinn Féin MPs don't vote. But there are four other MPs who also don't generally vote – the Speaker and his three deputies. In the figures above the Speaker is shown separately, but the three deputy speakers are included in the party figures – two in the Conservative Party and one Labour. This balance is due to the fact that the current Speaker himself – Sir Lindsay Hoyle – was originally elected to the Commons as a Labour MP. His three deputies may appear above as members of the Labour or Conservative party but in terms of their roles in the Commons it is similar to that played by the Speaker himself. Let's look at the Speaker's role.

The Speaker

In Figure 6 below, the Speaker's chair can be seen at the far end of the chamber at point 'A'. In the chamber, the Speaker's role is to preside over the House, keep order, decide who speaks when and make procedural decisions. He also plays a very significant role out of the public eye in the running of the Commons end of the Palace of Westminster. The current Speaker, Sir Lindsay Hoyle, is the MP for Chorley. In November 2019 Sir Lindsay was elected as Speaker by the House to replace John Bercow who had just resigned.

Historically the Speaker was the Commons' spokesperson in dealings with the Monarch. Because a number of Speakers in the past were executed by the Monarch, the office was seen as a dangerous one to hold. So even today, when a new Speaker is chosen by the House of Commons, he or she, feigning reluctance to take the office, has to be dragged to the chair by other MPs.

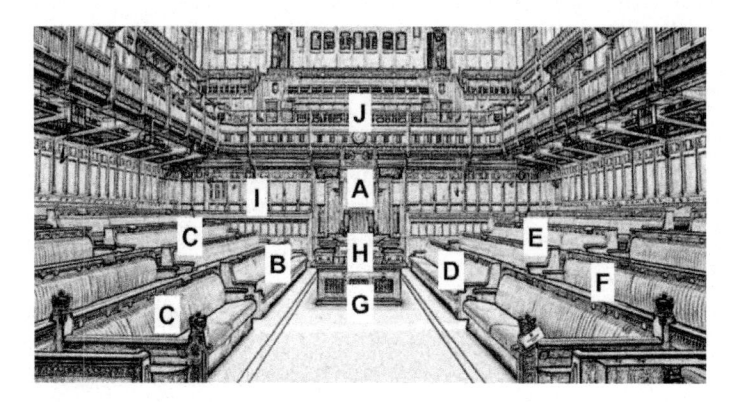

Figure 6

Most new Speakers take over in the middle, rather than at the start of a Parliament. Thus when Sir Lindsay was elected Speaker in the autumn of 2019 he was already sitting in the House as an MP (although, since 2010, as a non-voting one since he was a deputy Speaker), most recently having been elected at the 2017 election. He was therefore the Speaker when the 2019 general election was called. So Sir Lindsay first had to be re-elected to the House by his constituents in Chorley before he could be re-elected Speaker by MPs.

At a general election, if the Speaker is standing for re-election, by convention his seat will not be contested by the major UK-wide parties. However Speakers aren't always given a totally free run. At both the 2001 and 2005 elections Michael Martin was challenged in his Glasgow North-East seat by the SNP.[178] And John Bercow faced challenges in his seat of Buckingham at each of the 2010, 2015 and 2017 elections from the United Kingdom Independence Party (UKIP). In 2010 his UKIP challenger was Nigel Farage (who almost came to grief when the light aircraft flying a 'Vote UKIP' banner in which he was a passenger, crashed[179]). At the 2019 general election Sir Lindsay Hoyle, who had only been elected Speaker by the House a few weeks previously, faced a candidate from the Green Party and from an independent. He romped home with 67% of the vote.

A sitting Speaker's constituents are therefore usually faced with a limited choice when voting: either they can vote for the Speaker or for one of what are often fringe candidates. Certainly for many years it has been impossible to vote Labour, Conservative or Liberal Democrat in the Speaker's seat because those parties haven't put up candidates. This has often left voters in the Speaker's constituency feeling rather disenfranchised.

---

[178] In May 2009 Michael Martin resigned as Speaker following the furore over MPs' expenses. His resignation prevented his becoming the first Speaker to be forced from office since Sir John Trevor was removed in 1695 for the *high crime and misdemeanour* of taking bribes.

[179] https://www.theguardian.com/politics/2010/may/06/ukip-nigel-farage-plane-crash

The Speaker's constituents are put at a further disadvantage because their MP cannot vote in the House except when there is a tie. When this very occasionally occurs, Erskine May (the 'bible of parliamentary procedure' that was mentioned in chapter one) says that:

> *If the numbers in a division are equal, the Speaker must give the casting vote. In the performance of this duty to give a casting vote, the Speaker is at liberty to vote like any other Member, according to conscience, without assigning a reason; but, in order to avoid any imputation upon the Speaker's impartiality, it is usual for the Speaker, when practicable, to vote in such a manner as not to make the decision of the House final....*[180]

Because Speakers would always be expected to take the latter course rather than voting how they would personally prefer, even in this rare situation the Speaker's constituents won't really feel he is voting as a representative of them.

Although the Speaker cannot ask parliamentary questions or take part in debates, he can still write to and meet ministers and others on his constituents' behalf and, because of his office, is likely to have rather more influence than most MPs. In his autobiography, John Bercow is clear that he felt he had rather more influence over ministers than many other MPs did. And he particularly contrasts how much more he could do for his constituents than government ministers. He compares his position regarding the proposed building of the new high speed rail line HS2 with that of his parliamentary neighbour representing Aylesbury, David Lidington. Both faced having HS2 built through their constituencies against the wishes of many of their voters. (HS2 would bring about a lot of disruption without any of the obvious benefits like new stations.) John Bercow says that, although he was unable to speak about and vote on HS2, he wasn't completely barred from representing his constituents on the subject. On the other hand, David Lidington, as a government minister could do little. It was government policy to

---

[180] https://erskinemay.parliament.uk/section/4829/casting-vote-of-speaker/

build the railway line and therefore, under the rules of collective responsibility, he had to support, in public at least, its construction.[181]

The re-election by the House of a sitting Speaker is almost always a formality, with his re-election being voted through 'on the nod'. However, after the 2015 and 2017 general elections there was some speculation that someone – perhaps a Conservative MP – might stand against John Bercow. As he acknowledges in his auto-biography, Bercow was widely disliked on the Conservative benches.[182] This dislike was as great on the frontbench as it was on the backbenches and, right before the 2015 election there was an attempt by senior Conservative ministers to change the rules for the re-election of a sitting Speaker whereby in future the election would be carried out by secret rather than public ballot. Ministers clearly felt that this would help any potential challenger to Bercow after the election. This spectacularly backfired on the government, and in particular on the then Leader of the House of Commons William Hague, when enough Conservative MPs voted against the motion, which had been sprung on the House on its last sitting day before the election when most MPs had already left Westminster to start their campaigns, to defeat it.

Bercow's unpopularity amongst some Conservative MPs may partly have been due to his 'modernising agenda' for the Commons. As an example of this he decided not to wear the full Speaker's outfit – wig, knee-britches etc - when presiding over the House, reserving that clothing for major occasions like the State Opening of Parliament. Perhaps more though it was due to the personal political journey he had been on since first elected to the Commons in 1997. Back then he had been a member of what one might call the 'hard right' wing of the Conservative Party, but by the time he decided to run for the Speakership he had moved so far to the centre that he was being openly courted by senior members of the Labour Party in a bid to persuade

---

[181] John Bercow 'Unspeakable'. Published February 2020 by Weidenfeld & Nicolson ISBN: 9781474616621

[182] Ibid. John Bercow

him to switch parties.[183] In the end though, no challenge to him materialised after either election.

John Bercow was a controversial Speaker and many Conservative accused him of being biased against them. This was particularly so during the extraordinary events of the 2017-2019 Parliament which we discuss in chapter seven. Bercow always vigorously denies this. He would argue that he wasn't biased against the government or the Conservative Party but rather, he was biased *towards* the Commons and behaved as he did to help the House properly hold the government to account. He would say that this is the job of the Speaker. If that looked like bias against the government then so be it but it wasn't bias against the Conservative Party, he would say. Bercow was also a controversial figure because of accusations of harassment and bullying that were made against him in the period towards the end of his Speakership. He has always vigorously denied these allegations.

John Bercow's successor, Sir Lindsay Hoyle, is a rather different character. He's a much more understated person who doesn't court the controversy of his predecessor and he seems to be very widely liked across the Commons. He can still be tough though, in particular with ministers, the Prime Minister included. This can be seen by his regular lambasting of ministers, and Prime Minister Boris Johnson in particular, for their failure to make important announcements to Parliament prior to holding press conferences on the issue. This was a particular issue during the Covid pandemic. In June 2021 Sir Lindsay was notably scathing of Boris Johnson when he said:

> *It is entirely unacceptable that the Government did not make today's announcement to the House first. It was disrespectful to the House and to our constituents. The Government clearly planned that the media would be told information today not far from this chamber, and that this House would have to wait until tomorrow. I want to say very clearly to the Government that this*

---

[183] In the end, John Bercow did join Labour Party, but not for some 18 months after he had stepped down as Speaker: https://www.theguardian.com/politics/2021/jun/19/john-bercow-defects-to-labour-with-withering-attack-on-johnson

is not how this House should be treated....

I do not find it acceptable at all. Members of this House are elected to serve their constituents here, not via Sky or the BBC. Questions should be answered here. The Prime Minister should be here. I am sorry if his dinner would have been affected. I was told that he would be in Brussels—I think the nearest Brussels tonight were the sprouts in the dinner being served. I say now, Prime Minister, you are on my watch, and I want you to treat this House correctly.[184]

Who sits where?

By convention, the governing party or parties sit to the right of the Speaker. Ministers sit on the front bench above the gangway (B in Figure 6). Other governing party MPs sit behind the government front bench or below the gangway and are therefore known as 'backbenchers' (C). In the current Parliament, the spokespeople of the Official Opposition (the second largest party in the Commons) sit on the front bench to the Speaker's left (D). Its backbenchers sit behind them (E) and also on the benches below the gangway (F) which they share with the other political parties, of which the Scottish National Party is comfortably the largest.

Between the two front benches is the table of the House (G). Behind one end of the table, in front of the Speaker, sit the clerks (H) who advise the Speaker on points of procedure.

In Figure 7 we can see the Mace and the dispatch boxes on the table of the House.

---

[184] https://hansard.parliament.uk/Commons/2021-06-14/debates/C3A21764-726C-468F-9B89-A0DF45C2E640/Speaker%E2%80%99SStatement

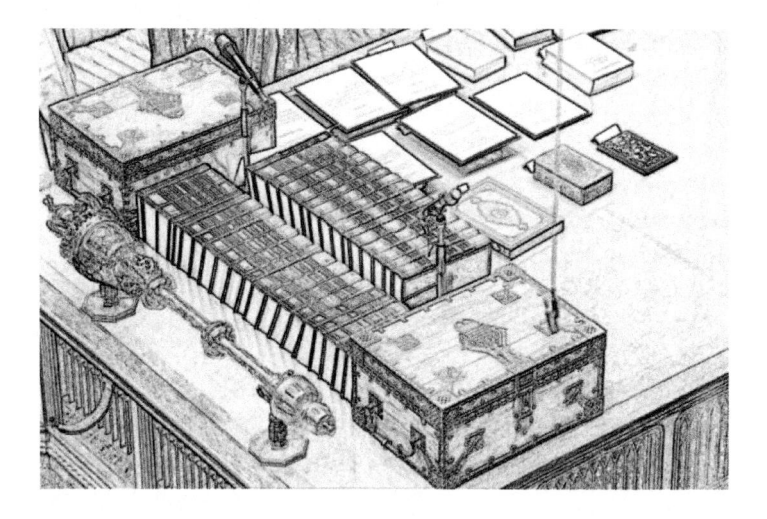

Figure 7

The Mace represents the Queen in Parliament. It is carried into the House every day by the Serjeant at Arms and laid so that its head is always on the government side of the table. The Mace is probably best known for the occasions that it has been interfered with by irate MPs. Probably the most famous of such occurrences was when in 1976 Michael Heseltine grabbed the Mace and waved it in anger at the government frontbench[185] but it has happened a number of times since then too.[186]

The dispatch boxes would have been once used to carry documents but are now used by ministers and their shadows to rest their papers on and to lean on when they are speaking. When speaking they are said to be 'at the dispatch box'.

---

[185] There is an interesting account of this event that appeared in The Guardian at the time. You can read it here:
https://www.theguardian.com/century/1970-1979/Story/0,,106906,00.html

[186] For example, Lloyd Russell-Moyle in 2018 https://www.bbc.co.uk/news/av/uk-politics-46531453 and Drew Hendry in 2020 https://www.bbc.co.uk/news/av/uk-politics-55336774

At the end of the government benches, set slightly back behind the Speaker's chair, is the officials' box (I in Figure 6). This is where civil servants sit in support of their ministers. The box is not strictly part of the chamber but it is in a position which allows civil servants to listen to what MPs, and in particular their ministers, are saying. If the minister makes a commitment to do something, a civil servant is there to make a note of it. Civil servants are also in the officials' box to help their minister should an issue arise on which the minister needs more briefing. If the minister is unable to answer a parliamentary question in the House, it is not possible to ask their officials for the answer, as the cut and thrust of Question Time doesn't allow for this. But when issues arise in a longer debate (for example the second reading of a bill), a civil servant will be able to pass a note to provide the minister with more information. If time permits, they may leave the box, collect the information that the minister needs and have it passed to the minister to use later in the debate. In the Commons a civil servant normally signals either to the minister's Parliamentary Private Secretary (PPS), usually sitting on the bench behind their minister, or to another backbench MP that they have a message they would like to be passed to the minister.

If a minister inadvertently says something wrong (for example committing the government to spend an extra £100bn on the NHS when it should have been £100m) a civil servant can quickly contact the Hansard Office to ask whether a correction can be made to the official report. Hansard records the content of all parliamentary debates, questions, statements etc. Although the transcript is these days written up from an audio recording, two or three Hansard writers are always present at the front of the media gallery (J in figure 6), at the opposite end of the chamber to the public gallery. Hansard is not a verbatim account but is nevertheless an accurate reflection of what has been said on the floor of both Houses and in its committees. Words spoken in either chamber usually appear in the digital version of Hansard on the parliamentary website a few hours after they have been spoken.[187]

Westminster Hall

Earlier in this chapter we mentioned Westminster Hall, part of the current Palace of Westminster that survives from the Norman era. Up the stairs in the south-west corner of Westminster Hall can be found what was formerly known as the 'Grand Committee Room'. In 1999 this was turned into the 'Westminster Hall Debating Chamber' (or, simply, 'Westminster Hall' as it is known in shorthand). The main purpose of creating this new chamber was to increase the amount of time available to backbench MPs to raise issues of concern, since on the floor of the House time is very limited. Westminster Hall usually sits from Monday to Thursday. (For more on the types of debate that take place in Westminster Hall, see the section on 'Debates' in chapter six.)

Voting

Located either side of the chamber of the House of Commons are the 'division lobbies'. Their name derives from votes in Parliament being known as 'divisions'. Behind the governing party benches is the 'aye' lobby and behind the opposition benches is the 'no' lobby. When a motion is put to the House, the Speaker (or one of his deputies) will call for an oral vote. Those in favour shout 'aye' and those against shout 'no'. If the Speaker thinks that many more have shouted for one side than the other he will state that 'the ayes (or the noes) have it'. If that is accepted, the motion will be carried (or rejected) with no formal vote taken. But often both sides will again shout aye or no rather more strongly, in which case the Speaker will call for a division by shouting 'clear the lobbies!' At this point the 'division bell' is rung to signify that a vote is taking place. It rings not only around the Palace of Westminster but also in surrounding parliamentary

---

[187] The House of Commons Hansard can be found here: https://hansard.parliament.uk/Commons and the Lords here: https://hansard.parliament.uk/lords

buildings such as Portcullis House, in nearby ministerial offices, and in other local establishments such as the Red Lion pub on Parliament Street. When the bell rings, MPs know that they have eight minutes to get into one or other of the division lobbies: the 'aye' lobby if they are voting in favour of the motion and the 'no' lobby if they are voting against. When the eight minutes are up, the Speaker will shout 'lock the doors!' at which point the doors going into the voting lobbies will be locked. Any MP who has not made it to the one of the lobbies within the eight minutes will be locked out and unable to vote. They will then find themselves in some difficulty with their whips (see below).[188]

As the division bell rings, so the voting lobbies begin to fill up with MPs. When the Covid pandemic struck, given that social distancing in the lobbies became impossible, new procedures for voting were brought in which are described below. But under the traditional system, MPs would crowd into the lobbies and, after the division bell had been ringing for a couple of minutes, would begin to file out at the far end of the lobby, first through one of three channels (alphabetically by surname) where a clerk would tick off their names, and then through a set of double doors, wedged open at 45 degrees to allow only one MP through at a time (see Figure 8 below). Whilst clerks no longer tick off the names of MPs, what has remained during and after the pandemic is the appointment of MPs as 'tellers' who stand on the far side of the double doors. In each lobby there will be one teller from the governing party side of the House and another from the opposition side. As MPs pass through the double doors the tellers count the numbers out loud. The tellers themselves are unable to vote, but they are recorded in Hansard as being 'tellers for the ayes' or 'tellers for the noes'. The four tellers (two from each lobby) then enter the House and advise the Speaker of the result of the vote. The Speaker then repeats the result to the House.

---

[188] It was to the embarrassment of two ministers in the Coalition Government that they failed to vote on the crucial Syria motion in August 2013. Apparently they hadn't heard the division bell ring despite being in a room in the Palace close to the Commons chamber.

Figure 8

There is no formal way of registering an abstention. An MP can of course simply stay in their seat and not vote but since this won't be registered in Hansard there is no way for people outside the House to know whether the MP is formally abstaining or simply hasn't turned up to vote. The only way for MP to formally abstain is, bizarrely, for them to vote in one lobby quickly and then cross over to the other lobby before the division bell has stopped ringing.

As one might imagine, voting in this way is rather time-consuming. Divisions rarely last less than ten minutes and are often much longer – especially when one party has a substantial majority. And when the House for example is voting on a series of amendments to a bill, MPs may spend a large part of the day simply voting.

In his entertaining book *Commons Knowledge: How to be a Backbencher*, the late Labour MP Paul Flynn describes what befell the former Conservative MP Toby Jessel. At a time when John Major had a very small majority, his government faced losing a vital vote in the Commons on VAT. When the division bell rang, Mr Jessel loyally voted with the government. Having voted he was then 'caught short', so he nipped into the 'Labour' lobby containing the gents' lavatory, only for the Speaker to shout 'lock the doors!' Paul Flynn describes Toby Jessel as *spread-eagling himself Garfield-like* against the glass-panelled doors, begging to be let out. But, because the rules demand that the doors remain locked, there was no way out of the lobby for Mr Jessel except by passing the clerks and the tellers, thereby casting a vote for the opposition and nullifying the one he had just cast for the government! Paul Flynn's tale continues:

> *Word spread round the chamber that Toby had retreated to the toilet and was refusing to leave. The Speaker's job then is to send in the Serjeant at Arms to prod the member out with his sword. The Government had lost by eight votes. Mercy was shown. The Serjeant at Arms put his pig sticker away and Toby was allowed to slink off.*[189]

Occasionally MPs may be physically unable to vote in a division because they are ill. In these circumstances, if whips from both sides of the House acknowledge that the MP is on the parliamentary estate, their votes, by convention, can be 'nodded through'. This was done on a number of occasions in the late 1970s when the Labour Government was operating without a parliamentary majority, most notably for the crucial 'No Confidence' vote in March 1979 when a number of sick MPs were brought in to vote. Between the 2017 and 2019 general elections the government was again operating without a majority. During this period there were a whole series of knife-edge votes on Brexit and on at least one occasion the parties' whips offices failed to agree to this convention operating. The then Labour MP Emma Dent-Coad described what happened in June 2018:

> *My colleague Naz Shah was forced to take a taxi from her Bradford constituency despite being in hospital since last Friday with serious nerve pain. She had to defy her doctor's advice to do so, and physically get through the*

---

[189] Paul Flynn 'How to be a Backbencher'. Poetry Wales Press Ltd ISBN 1-85411-206-6

voting lobby in a wheelchair, carrying a sick bucket and dosed up on morphine because the Conservative whips refused to honour the 'nodding through' process which normally allows ill MPs to miss votes if they can get themselves to the parliamentary estate.[190]

The Conservative whips' office would no doubt explain this rather differently but there was no doubt that Naz Shah was forced to go through the lobby in the way described. And during that same short Parliament there were examples of pregnant MPs and MPs who were very new parents being forced to be physically in Westminster to cast their vote in the lobbies. Negative reaction to this led to a system of 'proxy voting' being introduced to allow in these circumstances an MP's vote to be cast on their behalf by a colleague.

The voting system is not always 100% accurate. In the 18th century a member of the public managed to enter the No lobby and register a vote. This would be almost impossible today, but the system still relies on people being able to add up properly. In July 1993, on a crucial vote on an amendment to the government's policy on the Social Chapter of the Treaty on European Union (better known as the 'Maastricht Treaty'), the initial result announced by the Speaker Betty Boothroyd was a tie. The Speaker then cast her deciding vote against the amendment but it soon transpired that one too many aye votes had been recorded: the amendment had been lost by one vote anyway.

This rather archaic way of operating has prompted calls for electronic voting (which is used by most parliaments across the world and in the Scottish Parliament and Welsh Senedd). But many MPs have long resisted such a change because when they are locked in the voting lobby, they are provided with a valuable opportunity to speak to senior people in their party to whom they wouldn't otherwise have access. (Remember –

---

[190] https://www.theguardian.com/commentisfree/2018/jun/21/sick-mp-vote-wheelchair-commons-system-archaic

ministers have to vote just like any other MP.) If a backbench MP from the governing party wants to speak to the Prime Minister about an issue, he or she could of course contact Number 10 to ask for a meeting. But how quickly would that meeting happen? It may be much easier to speak to the Prime Minister when they are locked together in the voting lobby and when she is not surrounded by the usual gatekeepers. One of course can understand why MPs wouldn't want to lose this opportunity to speak to senior colleagues but one wonders whether there might not be a better way of allowing that to happen without a huge amount of time being taken up voting.

Voting During the Covid Pandemic

During the Covid pandemic it was of course impossible to operate divisions in the way described above, given that social distancing in the lobbies is practically impossible. For the first few weeks of the pandemic, important votes – particularly on legislation – were simply put on hold, but during the Easter 2020 recess a system of remote, electronic voting was developed. This was something of an innovation for the House of Commons whose procedures often look rather 19th century. Under the new system, MPs were able to cast their votes electronically on-line, from wherever they happened to be. They simply clicked on 'aye' or 'no' on their screen to cast a vote. This was a huge leap forward for the Commons which perhaps made it rather surprising that just a few weeks later, the House decided to discontinue with the new system. We can speculate as to the reasons why this happened. The House itself decides on its procedures and processes but, of course, when the government has a majority on the floor of the House in practice it means that the government is in control. The minister who has particular responsibility for Commons' procedures is the Leader of the House of Commons. Throughout the pandemic this position was held by Jacob Rees-Mogg. Rees-Mogg has the nickname 'the honourable member for the 18th century', mainly due to how he speaks and dresses, so it's easy to suggest that the scrapping of the electronic voting system was down, at least in part, to his innate conservatism. There might however be rather more to it than that. In particular, remote electronic voting takes away some of the powers of the whips (which are discussed below).

When the remote electronic system of voting wasn't renewed after the Whitsun 2020 recess, clearly there couldn't be a return to the old system of MPs crowding into the lobbies. So, for a brief period, physical voting took place in the chamber of the Commons itself. MPs queued up to enter the Commons, socially distanced, and would then pass by the dispatch box on the government side of the House to vote aye or the one on the opposition side to vote no. The problem with this system was that it was hugely time-consuming, with a long queue of MPs waiting to vote snaking its way around the parliamentary estate.

Voting in the chamber was therefore soon replaced by a system of 'semi-electronic' voting in the lobbies, not with MPs voting on-line but, instead, recording their participation in the division by tapping their security passes against a reader in whichever lobby they were voting. The readers only recorded the names of those voting. Tellers were still appointed in the traditional way to count the heads.

Whilst this improved things a little, what actually got rid of lengthy divisions was the extension of the proxy voting system which, as described above, had been introduced a couple of years previously to allow pregnant MPs and those who are new parents to have votes cast on their behalves by another MP. In the hybrid Commons proxy voting was initially extended to those MPs who were participating virtually (see below) and later extended to all MPs, including those who were physically at Westminster. By the end of 2020, the vast majority of MPs were having their votes cast on their behalves by another MP – often a party whip. One government whip was casting well over 300 votes on behalf of other members! This was a far from satisfactory situation given the role of the whips (see below), but since there was to be no return to full electronic remote voting, this widespread use of proxy voting remained in place for as long as the Commons operated in hybrid form.

When the Commons returned after the 2021 summer recess and hybrid proceedings were discontinued, proxy voting for Covid related reasons also came to an end. The use of pass readers to register the names of those voting however remained in place. Even the 'honourable member for the 18th century' seemed to support this degree of modernisation!

Before we leave the issue of how the Commons votes, it's worth emphasising that a lot of votes don't involve divisions. Many motions are passed 'on the nod' as there is no opposition to them. And on some less important business, where there nevertheless is opposition, there will be a 'deferred division'. For these votes MPs simply record on a voting slip whether they are voting for or against the motion. These votes are taken on a Wednesday afternoon and the results announced by the Speaker later in the day.

The Whips

On the large majority of motions tabled in both Houses of Parliament, each political party will hold a clear position that it expects its MPs to support in the voting lobbies. Most votes in Parliament are therefore 'whipped'. This hunting term derives from the 'whippers-in', who, at the rear of the pack, crack the whip to keep any straying hounds in line. Each party has a Chief Whip and a number of junior whips who together ensure that MPs from their party turn up and vote the 'right' way.

Each week the Chief Whip issues 'the whip', which lists the votes coming up during the following week. Figure 9 below shows an example of the whip. In this example most of the votes are underlined three times. 'Three line whips' are applied to the votes the party regards as most important. Other votes will be underlined once. These would be for less important business where the party does have a 'line' but voting for which isn't usually seen as obligatory. (Two line whips are very rarely used nowadays.) Votes of any real importance will be subject to a three line whip and the party will expect its MPs to attend and vote according to the party line. Occasionally there will be votes on the whip that aren't underlined at all. These are so-called 'free votes'. On these no whip is put on the vote and MPs can, in theory at least, vote how they please. Issues of conscience, such as abortion, are usually treated this way as were recent votes on the refurbishment of the Palace of Westminster.

THE BUSINESS FOR THE WEEK COMMENCING 6TH SEPTEMBER WILL BE:

MONDAY 6TH SEPTEMBER
The House meets at **2:30pm** for **Education Questions**
Remaining Stages of the Aviation Bill
Followed by
Motion relating to the appointment of Trustees to the House of Commons Pension Fund
Followed by
Motion relating to the Re-appointment of the Chair of the Boundary Commission for England
Followed by
Motion relating to the Re-appointment of an Electoral Commissioner
THERE WILL BE A RUNNING 3-LINE WHIP FROM 3:30PM AND UNTIL ALL GOVERNMENT BUSINESS HAS BEEN SECURED.

TUESDAY 7TH SEPTEMBER
Deadline for tabling: Work and Pensions
The House meets at **11:30am** for **Business, Energy and Industrial Strategy Questions**
Ten Minute Rule Motion: Football Supporters (Membership)
Remaining Stages of the Health (England) Bill [Lords]
THERE WILL BE A RUNNING 3-LINE WHIP FROM 12:30PM AND UNTIL ALL GOVERNMENT BUSINESS HAS BEEN SECURED.

WEDNESDAY 8TH SEPTEMBER
Deadline for tabling: Foreign, Commonwealth and Development Office
The House meets at **11:30am** for **Scotland Questions**
At **12noon: Prime Minister's Questions**
Ten Minute Rule Motion: Social Housing Provision
Opposition Day (12th Allotted Day) The Government's handling of the Covid pandemic
Followed by
A debate on Summer Exam Results
THERE WILL BE A 3-LINE WHIP AT 6PM FOR 7PM.

THURSDAY 9TH SEPTEMBER
Deadline for tabling: Prime Minister & Transport
The House meets at **9:30am** for **Environment, Food and Rural Affairs & Attorney General**
At **10:30am: Business Question**
General debate on Shipping
Followed by
General debate on Support for the Food and Drink Sector after the COVID – 19 Lockdown
The subjects for these debates were determined by the Backbench Business Committee
THERE WILL BE A 1-LINE WHIP.

FRIDAY 10TH SEPTEMBER
Private Members Bills
THERE WILL BE A 1-LINE WHIP.

Figure 9

On some votes, 'pairing' may be allowed: an MP from the governing party may 'pair' with an MP from one of the opposition parties, agreeing that neither will vote. Although pairing arrangements must be registered with the whips, they are not formally recognised by the rules of the House. If an MP reneged on a pairing arrangement and decided to vote, there would be nothing that his or her pair could do about it – except to withdraw from the pairing arrangement in future. One well-known former Labour MP proudly told the author and a group of civil servants how on first arriving in the Commons in 1970 he paired with a Conservative MP then turned up and voted anyway. When the author repeated this story to another Labour MP the latter said that actually his colleague had paired up with three different Conservative MPs and then voted anyway! More recently the pairing system was seen to break down in 2018 when the Liberal Democrat MP Jo Swinson was convinced that she was paired with Conservative MP Brandon Lewis for an important vote, only to note from her home in Scotland, where she was looking after her recently born child, that Lewis had voted anyway. Ministers said that it was an 'honest mistake' and a 'genuine mess up' but, whatever the rights and wrongs of the matter, there was nothing that could be done about it after the event.[191] It was this event in particular that led to proxy voting for MPs who are pregnant or are new parents finally being introduced.

Defying the whip, especially a three line whip, is something no MP does lightly. The whips have an array of sticks and carrots at their disposal to persuade MPs to vote according to the party line. Amongst the 'carrots' would be the influence the whips have over issues such as who gets which office on the parliamentary estate. Would you like a modern office on the fifth floor of Portcullis House with a beautiful view across the Thames or would you prefer one in the bowels of the Palace of Westminster that is a converted gents' toilet and regularly floods? But perhaps the most effective 'carrot' in the whips' armoury is their knowledge that most backbenchers want promotion to become

---

[191] https://www.bbc.co.uk/news/uk-politics-44867866

frontbenchers – whether as opposition spokespeople or government ministers. Whips are regularly feeding information to their party leader about how this or that MP is performing on the floor of the Commons or how loyal they have been during divisions. (There is always one whip from each of the main parties sitting on the end of the frontbench by the Speaker's chair keeping an eye on what's going on.) This is information that the party leader will use when considering a reshuffle of the frontbench team. Why would the party leader reward someone who is a poor parliamentary performer or, worse, a rebel? This is of course particularly important if the leader is also the Prime Minister. A new arrival on the backbenches of the governing party for a while will feel very pleased with themselves for managing to get elected to Parliament. It might not be long though before they realise that they really don't exercise much power. It's their colleagues on the frontbench who have the civil servants working for them, the money to spend and the powers in legislation to do things. If they want to be promoted to the frontbench themselves, they know that they will have to behave themselves.

As for the 'sticks', Chief Whips are famously said to record details of their MPs' private lives in a notebook to be used against them if they threaten rebellion. Whilst this sort of behaviour shouldn't be exaggerated, nor should we think it doesn't go on at all. Indeed we discovered in 2017 that the only inaccuracy in saying that the Chief Whip had such a notebook was that actually the information was now on a spreadsheet: the Chief Whip Gavin Williamson's spreadsheet being leaked and subsequently appearing on social media. (The author felt it best not to include it in this book.)

But the even bigger stick is the threat to 'withdraw the whip' from an MP. That literally means not giving them the whip each week but, much more importantly, it means the MP is no longer recognised as a member of the parliamentary party. You'll still be an MP of course, but you'll have to sit as an independent until the whip is restored, if indeed it ever is. This is what happened to each of the six independent MPs – including Jeremy Corbyn – that we discussed above. Whether the whip is restored is very much a matter for the party leader and the Chief Whip. While it might be surprising if the Labour whip were not restored to Jeremy Corbyn in the not too distant future, the SNP restoring the whip to Margaret Ferrier seems less likely.

Of crucial importance to the MP in question is whether the whip is restored in advance of the next general election. John Major famously withdrew the whip from nine of his backbenchers in 1994 for persistently rebelling on EU matters but all of them had it restored comfortably before the general election in 1997. However, in September 2019, Boris Johnson, who had only recently become Prime Minister, withdrew the whip from 21 of his backbenchers when they supported a bill that that would require him to seek an extension to the UK's departure from the EU in certain circumstances. There was quite an array of characters amongst that 21: Theresa May's former Chancellor of the Exchequer Philip Hammond, Father of the House Kenneth Clarke[192], seven other former Cabinet members (Greg Clark, David Gauke, Justine Greening, Dominic Grieve, Oliver Letwin, Caroline Nokes and Rory Stewart), and Winston Churchill's grandson Nicholas Soames. 10 of the 21 did have the whip restored in advance of the 2019 election, although of those, six decided not to contest the election. Of the 11 who didn't have the whip restored, six declined to stand at the election, while five stood as independents or as Liberal Democrats. All of them lost their seats. Thus having the whip withdrawn and not returned by the time of the general election probably marked the end of those six MPs' political careers. One of those six was the former Attorney General Dominic Grieve, a highly respected member of the House

---

[192] The *Father of the House* is the longest serving member of the House. So far this has always been a man but Harriet Harman is currently known as the *Mother of the House* as the longest serving female MP. Until the 2019 election, Ken Clarke had the title only because he was ahead of Denis Skinner in the queue to swear in after the 1970 election. Since the 2019 election the Father of the House has been Peter Bottomley who entered the Commons after winning a by-election in 1975.

but one who had incurred the wrath of both Theresa May and Boris Johnson for his, as they saw it, anti-Brexit views. Grieve had been the MP for the rock-solid Conservative seat of Beaconsfield since 1997. He was well-known, well-liked and widely regarded as extremely able. So he decided to stand in Beaconsfield as an independent. The Conservative Party put up a little known candidate to challenge him for the seat. In 2017 Grieve had won 65% of the vote. In 2019 he won just 29% to the Conservative candidate's 56%. This demonstrates just how difficult it is to get elected as an independent.

Backbench MPs are therefore all too aware of the dangers involved in defying the whips. But, as we have seen, that doesn't mean it never happens. When she was Prime Minister, Theresa May faced rebellions on Brexit day in day out from both 'remain' and 'leave' Conservative MPs. Boris Johnson has faced a number too, both before and after the 2019 election. During 2020 and early 2021 he faced significant rebellions on the issue of Covid regulations, but they were never large enough to defeat his government, even if on some occasions this was only because Labour and other MPs voted with the government. The biggest ever rebellion by governing party MPs in the history of the House of Commons took place in March 2003 when, as we have seen, 139 Labour MPs defied a three line whip to vote against going to war in Iraq. A government victory was never in doubt because the vast majority of Conservative MPs voted for Blair's motion but, nevertheless, it was a damaging rebellion for the Prime Minister to have faced.

Some backbench MPs will be more inclined than others to support their parties on important votes. It seems more than likely that, despite the huge rebellion, a good number of MPs from both of the two largest parties voted in favour of going to war in Iraq only because it was a whipped vote. But some MPs are less easily cajoled than others. There are some MPs who are never likely to be offered a frontbench job or who are unwilling to compromise their views in order to win one. This was particularly true of many MPs during the debates on Brexit. Such MPs are less likely to succumb to the whips' pressure than new MPs who are keen to get on. A good example was always Jeremy Corbyn who voted more times against the government than any other Labour MP after Labour came to power in 1997.[193] During the lifetime of the Labour Governments 1997-2010, Corbyn voted differently from the majority of Labour MPs in about 19% of all divisions. It was therefore somewhat ironic that he later became leader himself and faced a number of rebellions by MPs in his party who didn't exactly agree with all of the leadership's positions.

There used to be a commonly held view, notwithstanding votes like the one on Iraq and the voting records of MPs like Jeremy Corbyn, that MPs in the modern era have been much more supine – much less ready to rebel – than their predecessors. But the statistics actually show the opposite. In the 1950s there were two whole parliamentary sessions when not one government backbencher defied the party whip. This included the 1956-7 session when the Suez invasion took place. Labour backbenchers gradually became more rebellious during the Blair and Brown Governments and the 2010 Parliament proved to be one of the most rebellious ever, with newly elected Conservative MPs voting against the Coalition Government within weeks of being elected.[194] But this was as nothing compared to the rebellions faced by Theresa May when she was Prime Minister. Few would claim that MPs were supine during the 2017-19 Parliament. There is clear evidence too that rebellions tend to increase towards the end of a government's lifetime as more and more MPs fall into the category of 'has been' or 'never will be'. And once an MP has rebelled for the first time, it's clear that he or she is much more likely to do so again.

Before we leave this discussion about the whips', let's return to the issue of the changes made to the Commons' voting system during the Covid pandemic. MPs, as we have seen, have to

---

[193] Source: www.publicwhip.org.uk

[194] From Peter Riddell 'In Defence of Politicians' Biteback Publishing. 2011.

physically enter one lobby or other to vote. When they do that they have to pass by their whips who will be patrolling the entrance to the lobbies. This gives those whips one last chance to persuade their backbencher to vote the 'right way'. A friendly arm round the shoulder perhaps, or maybe a reminder of what's on the Chief Whip's spreadsheet, might just change their minds at the last minute. When the remote electronic voting system was briefly in operation in 2020 the whips lost the ability to make such last-minute interventions. This might then be one reason at least why the government wasn't happy with remote electronic voting and had it removed within a few weeks.

Virtual Participation during the Covid Pandemic

It wasn't just the method of voting in the Commons that had to change as a result of the Covid pandemic. Clearly the House could no longer operate with, at times, over 600 MPs squeezed into the handful of square metres that make up the Commons chamber. So a series of innovations were rapidly introduced including, most importantly, a system of virtual participation using 'Zoom'. The changes introduced have been described as *some of the greatest procedural innovations in 750 years of the House of Commons.*[195]

A maximum of 50 MPs was allowed in the chamber with all other MPs, if they wished to participate, appearing on screens that were hastily put up around the chamber.[196] This became known as the 'hybrid' Commons. Initially, MPs that were unable to attend Westminster due to the pandemic could participate

---

[195] "The House of Commons and the pandemic: How the House kept on functioning in the face of Covid-19"
https://www.parliament.uk/globalassets/mps-lords--offices/offices/15705_hoc_year-of-pandemic-proceedings_digital_aw.pdf

[196] The maximum number of MPs in the chamber was later increased to 64.

virtually in all proceedings. However, around the same time as the Commons scrapped the remote electronic voting system (after the Whitsun 2020 recess) the government announced that these hybrid provisions would also come to an end. This has been described by the highly respected Constitution Unit at University College London as *a particularly appalling moment for parliamentary accountability*.[197] Under pressure, the government did then backtrack by allowing virtual participation for MPs deemed to be 'clinically vulnerable' or 'clinically extremely vulnerable'. But virtual participation was only restored for what the Leader of the House of Commons, Jacob Rees-Mogg, likes to describe as 'interrogative proceedings', in other words, the parliamentary questions asked, and ministerial statements made, at the start of the day. The most vulnerable of MPs would therefore be barred from participating in key Commons' processes such as debating legislation. They could vote – by proxy – but they couldn't actually speak in debate. Needless to say, a lot of MPs were very unhappy about this situation.

Things came to a head towards the end of 2020 with two events in particular putting pressure on the government. The first of these was Boris Johnson's need to participate virtually at a Prime Minister's Questions (PMQs) in November 2020 when he was forced to isolate after an MP he'd had a meeting with had tested positive for Covid. The Prime Minister appearing virtually was totally within the rules – PMQs taking place during that early part of the Commons' day when virtual participation was allowed – but it nevertheless prompted people to ask why it was alright for Boris Johnson to appear virtually when, at other times at least, other MPs couldn't. The second concerned a debate that took place in Westminster Hall concerning breast cancer. One particular MP – Tracey Crouch – would very much have liked to participate in the debate as she was at the time suffering from breast cancer herself. But she

---

[197] https://constitution-unit.com/2021/04/21/covid-and-parliament-one-year-on/

was unable to do so because she was understandably sheltering at home and it wasn't possible to participate virtually in Westminster Hall debates. (After Christmas 2020 'Westminster Hall debates' were moved to one of the large select committee rooms across the road in Portcullis House where virtual participation was possible.)

When London was moved into the highest Covid tier in December 2020 it became impossible for the government to maintain its stance on limiting virtual participation and the House returned to operating virtually for the whole Commons' day. On 19 July 2021, most social restrictions in England were lifted. This day was the beginning of Parliament's last sitting week before the summer recess. Most of the restrictions in the chamber concerning, for example, on which benches members could sit, were lifted but virtual participation remained in place for the final four Commons sitting days prior to the recess. With the limits on the number of MPs able to sit in the chamber lifted, Boris Johnson therefore had the expectation that his final Prime Minister's Questions prior to the summer recess, due to take place on the Wednesday, would be his first since Easter 2020 at which he would be able to have large numbers of Conservative MPs behind him cheering him on. But things didn't quite work out as he had planned. A few days previously his new Health Secretary, Sajid Javid, had tested positive for Covid leading not only to Javid being required to self-isolate but those with whom he'd been in contact too, including Johnson and the Chancellor Rishi Sunak. Thus Johnson had to appear at this Prime Minister's Questions virtually.

The operation of the Commons in hybrid form came completely to an end when the House returned after the 2021 summer recess. Virtual participation had not been entirely satisfactory - in particular because it took away much of the spontaneity of Commons' debates, with the Speaker being much less able to call MPs 'on the hoof' to speak. But it did represent a huge technological leap forward for the House of Commons. So while virtual participation might have been discontinued, its relatively successful operation during the pandemic does suggest that that it could easily be reintroduced if required.

The Parliamentary Timetable

The State Opening of Parliament and Parliamentary Sessions

A 'Parliament' is the period between two general elections. Within that period, Parliament will sit for a number of 'sessions' until it is dissolved prior to the next general election. A session begins with the State Opening of Parliament.[198]

The State Opening is a very grand state occasion. The Queen arrives in the House of Lords and despatches Black Rod[199] to command members of the House of Commons to come to the Lords to hear the 'gracious speech'. By tradition, when Black Rod arrives at the front of the House of Commons, the heavy doors are slammed in her face. She bangs three times on the door with her staff, at which point she is allowed to enter the Commons to command the MPs to come to the Lords. Many, led by the Speaker, Prime Minister and Leader of the Opposition, follow Black Rod to the Lords to hear the Monarch deliver the speech. But some MPs refuse to follow and even those that do follow deliberately feign a lack of interest in the proceedings.

This feigned hostility shown towards Black Rod dates from 1642, when King Charles I entered the House of Commons in an attempt to arrest five MPs. When it emerged that the five MPs had

---

[198] It's potentially confusing that there was both a 2017-19 session and a 2017-19 Parliament. Both started following the general election of 2017. Parliament was finally prorogued in the autumn of 2019, thereby bringing to an end the 2017-2019 session. There then followed an extremely short session which lasted up until the dissolution of Parliament prior to the 2019 election. There is more on the 2017-19 Parliament in Chapter 7.

[199] The full name of Black Rod, traditionally, is 'the Gentleman Usher of the Black Rod'. However, the full title of the current and first ever female Black Rod is 'Lady Usher of the Black Rod'.

already escaped, Charles demanded that Speaker Lenthall should reveal their whereabouts. The Speaker replied: *May it please your Majesty, I have neither eyes to see, nor tongue to speak in this place, but as this House is pleased to direct me, whose servant I am.* The King left the chamber empty-handed, with MPs' shouts of *Privilege! Privilege!* ringing in his ears. Since that time no Monarch has been allowed to enter the House of Commons. This seminal event is depicted in a painting that hangs in the corridor connecting the House of Lords to the Central Lobby of Parliament, and it was referred to several times when the House authorities allowed the Metropolitan Police to raid the offices of Conservative MP Damian Green in 2008.[200]

While the Queen is giving her speech in the Lords, a government minister (usually a junior whip) stays in Buckingham Palace as a 'hostage' to ensure the Queen's safe return from Parliament. The Queen's Speech catalogues the government's legislative proposals for the coming session. The Commons and the Lords then spend a number of days debating the contents of the Queen's Speech.

Parliamentary sessions start with the Queen's Speech and run through until Parliament is prorogued. Until 2011 the parliamentary session usually ran for a year starting in November. An exception was in an election year when the session would begin after the general election and continue through to the autumn of the following year, regardless of when in the year the election had taken place. This timetable, however, changed once the Fixed-term Parliaments Act (FTPA) came into force (see above). Under the FTPA the norm would be for general elections to take place in the May of every fifth year (although, as we have seen, elections can take place at other times). The parliamentary session has therefore shifted from the previous cycle to one that usually starts and finishes in the spring. However, as we discussed in reference to the unlawful prorogation of September 2019, the decision to end a parliamentary session rests with ministers, not

---

[200] https://www.theguardian.com/global/2008/nov/28/damian-green-arrest-conservatives

with Parliament. If the government therefore wishes for a particular session to run for longer than the usual year it is at liberty to allow that to happen. So, for example, the session that began after the 2010 election ran for two years and the one that started after the 2017 election ran, in the end, for almost two and a half years.

A key issue for governments about prorogation is that, in most circumstances, legislation has to complete all its stages before the end of a session. The couple of weeks before prorogation can therefore be a frantic period in Parliament, with bills rattling to and fro between the Commons and the Lords. This is something we explore further in the section on Legislation in chapter six.

The session is currently divided into four 'terms' – autumn, winter, spring and summer – separated by recesses of varying length. These recesses can be interrupted if Parliament is recalled. Only the government can request a recall and the Speaker of the Commons has the final say. This is a fairly rare event, though Parliament was recalled four times between late 2020 and the summer of 2021: first, in late December 2020, to debate the European Union (Future Relationship) Bill which concerned the implementation of the deal just made between the government and the EU on the UK's departure from the transitional arrangements that had been in place since the UK's departure from the EU just under a year previously; second, in January 2021, to debate and vote on the government's latest Covid regulations; third, in April 2021, following the death of the Duke of Edinburgh and fourth, in August 2021, to debate the situation in Afghanistan. The latter may have been the fourth recall in just a few months but it was only the 34th to take place since 1948.[201]

The long recess has always been in the summer, which used to run from late July to early/mid-October. In recent years

---

[201] https://www.parliament.uk/business/news/2021/january/house-of-commons-recalled-on-6-january-2021/

however, the House of Commons has returned for a two week sitting in September. The length of the summer recess – even when there has been a September sitting - has often been criticised by people claiming that MPs have excessively long 'holidays'. The reality for MPs is rather different: most of them are working hard in their constituencies during much of the summer recess.

The Parliamentary Week in the Commons

The Commons sits at varying times during the week. On Mondays it sits at 2.30pm and usually rises at 10.30pm. On Tuesdays and Wednesdays it sits from 11.30am to 7.30pm, and on Thursdays from 9.30am to 5.30pm, although on any day a vote in the House can put back the finishing time or 'adjournment'. The House usually sits on 13 Fridays during a session, from 9.30am to 3pm. When it does sit on a Friday, it is usually considering less contentious business, allowing most MPs to return to their constituencies on a Thursday evening.

Among MPs, sitting times are a contentious issue. Traditionally the Commons sat only in the afternoon and evening as MPs had work in other professions which they carried out in the morning. But recent years have seen a shift towards earlier sittings. Sitting times on Mondays have not changed because on Monday mornings MPs travel back to Westminster from their constituencies. But the sitting times on Tuesdays, Wednesdays and Thursdays are now much earlier than they used to be. MPs' opinions are sharply divided about whether the House should sit more 'family friendly' hours. An aspect of this that inevitably influences their views is how close to London their constituency is. For an MP from the north of England or Scotland, finishing at 7pm rather than 10pm doesn't help them return to their families. Sitting hours are also an issue for ministers, who have to attend to their ministerial as well as parliamentary duties during 'working hours'.

The Parliamentary Day in the Commons

The pattern of the parliamentary day is similar from Monday to Thursday. The day in the Commons starts with prayers led by the Chaplain of the House, followed by an hour of oral parliamentary questions. If there are any 'urgent parliamentary questions' they will be dealt with immediately after the main Question Time. (For more on parliamentary questions, including urgent questions, see chapter six.) Sometimes there will then be an oral statement from a minister.[202] Routine announcements are made via a written ministerial statement but important announcements should be made orally by the minister.

After any urgent questions or ministerial statements there follows the main business of the day. This might be legislation (for example the second reading of a bill), a debate on government policy, or some 'domestic' business (perhaps a debate on modernising procedures or changing sitting hours). On some days there is more than one main item of business.

The main business usually comes to an end at 10pm on Mondays, 7pm on Tuesdays and Wednesdays and 5pm on Thursdays. On Fridays, if the House is sitting, the main business will usually finish at 2.30pm. Following the main business, for the last half hour of the day, there will be the 'adjournment debate' when a backbench MP can raise an issue of concern in the House. These are often on constituency issues and therefore not well attended. However, other MPs are able to intervene in the debate if allowed to do so and a minister will always reply on behalf of the government.

---

[202] Occasionally there may be more than one oral statement.

5

The House of Lords

Membership

For reasons explained below, the membership of the House of Lords changes all the time. However as of mid-July 2021 it was as follows:

Party	Men	Women	Total
Conservative	194	67	261
Crossbench	141	47	188
Labour	113	59	172
Liberal Democrat	54	32	86
Non-Affiliated	36	8	44
Bishops	19	7[1]	26
Democratic Unionist Party	5	0	5
Green	0	2	2
Ulster Unionist Party	2	0	2
Conservative Independent	1	0	1
Independent Social Democrat	1	0	1
Labour Independent	0	1	1
Plaid Cymru	1	0	1
Lord Speaker	1	0	1

1. One of these seven is awaiting introduction

Figure 10

A number of points stand out from these figures, in particular the presence of Church of England bishops. These are discussed in more detail below. Also notable is the large group of 'Crossbenchers' or independent members of the Lords. Although independents, its members have decided to join this grouping as by doing so they gain more influence for example over the timetabling of business in the Lords. Because the government doesn't have a majority in the Lords it needs to negotiate the timetable not only with the other major political parties in the House – Labour and Liberal Democrat - but also with the Crossbenchers. There is also a substantial group of 'Non-Affiliated' members who are not part of that Crossbench group. These tend to be either members who hold some official position in the House which makes membership of a group – even the Crossbenchers – inappropriate, or they are peers who have fallen foul of their former parties like the independents in the Commons. As can be seen, some such peers decide formally to sit as 'Labour Independent' or 'Conservative Independent' but most just designate themselves as Non-Affiliated. Also, note the complete absence of members from the Scottish National Party. The SNP has refused to nominate people for the House of Lords for as long as the party has existed, regarding the Lords to be undemocratic and unrepresentative. Finally, it's notable that the Liberal Democrats have a large number of Lords' members, particularly when compared to their current numbers in the Commons. This is in part due to the number of peerages created under the Coalition Government which is discussed below. The Liberal Democrats would of course argue that having around an eighth of the seats in the Lords better reflects their support in the country than the small number of MPs they have in the Commons.

There are three main categories of member of the House of Lords (or 'peers' as they are often called): Hereditary Peers, who have inherited their titles and voting rights in the Lords through their families (members of the aristocracy); Life Peers, who have been given their title and sitting rights in the Lords for their lifetime only and so cannot pass these on to their children or other members of their families; and the Church of England bishops (or

'Lords Spiritual' as they are properly known).[203] Not all Church of England bishops have seats in the Lords. The five most senior bishops always do: the Archbishops of Canterbury and York and the bishops of London, Durham and Winchester. 21 other bishops are also members of the Lords. Traditionally, who these are has been based on a bishop's length of service but, following the Church of England's decision in 2014 to allow women to become bishops, the rules were temporarily changed so that whenever there is now a vacancy amongst the Lords Spiritual following the retirement of a bishop, he is replaced by female bishop.[204]

To have senior clerics from one branch of one religion guaranteed seats in the Parliament of a democracy in the 21st century might to many seem a little odd.[205] (The only other country to do something similar is Iran). But its origins come from the almost complete lack of separation of Church and State in the United Kingdom – something that is clearly demonstrated by the Monarch's role not only as Head of State but also as Supreme Governor of the Church of England. It's important to emphasise that the bishops are full members of the House of Lords who attend debates and, most importantly, vote on legislation that comes before the Upper House.

Until 1958 the House of Lords was dominated by the Hereditary

---

[203] Until October 2009 there was a fourth category – the Law Lords (or 'Lords of Appeal in Ordinary' to give them their proper title) who acted as the highest Court of Appeal.

[204] This temporary change was introduced by the Lords Spiritual (Women) Act 2015. The act has effect until 2025. The elevation of a woman to be a Lord Spiritual obviously requires there to be a qualifying female bishop in post. Only diocesan bishops – as opposed to suffragan bishops - can be elevated to the Lords. When the bishops of Salisbury and Rochester retired in 2021 there were no female diocesan bishops other than those who were already in the Lords. Thus the two bishops elevated to the Lords as replacements - the bishops of Exeter and Liverpool – were both men.

[205] You might find, for example, a Roman Catholic bishop, a Rabbi or an Imam in the House of Lords but that would be only because they have been given a Life Peerage.

Peers. In effect the House of Lords was the British aristocracy sitting in Parliament, its only other members being the Law Lords (who've now departed) and the bishops. Any person who inherited an aristocratic title on the death of their father (usually) automatically also inherited the seat in the Lords. Because most Hereditary Peers are at least 'small c' conservative, the House was therefore very unbalanced politically. In 1955, for example, there were only 55 Labour peers and 42 Liberals compared with 507 Conservatives and 238 Independents.

House of Lords Reform

The first major step to reform the composition of the House of Lords was the Life Peerages Act of 1958, which allowed the appointment of Life Peers. Unlike Hereditary Peers, the new Life Peers would not be able to pass on their titles and seats in the Lords to their eldest sons. The act enabled a better political balance to be established in the House. In 1963, the Peerages Act allowed women Hereditary Peers to sit in the Lords – women Life Peers having been allowed to sit following the passing of the 1958 Act. But because of the rule of male primogeniture in the aristocracy it is unusual for many female Hereditary Peers to be in the Lords. Where it has happened, it's usually because the peer is Scottish since, in the Scottish aristocracy, titles can be passed down to a female. For example, at the time of her retirement in 2020, there was one female Hereditary Peer in the Lords: the Countess of Mar. She is a Scottish peer who inherited the title on the death of her father, the Earl of Mar. Following her retirement from the Lords there were no female Hereditary Peers in the Upper House. (It's worth noting here that for some time now the rules of succession for the Royal Family have been different to those for the aristocracy. If the rules of succession that currently apply to the English aristocracy had applied to the Royal Family in 1952, the present Queen wouldn't have become Monarch.)

The 1963 Act also permitted peers to renounce their titles. As we discussed earlier, this was the act used by both Viscount Stansgate (Tony Benn) and Lord Home to renounce their hereditary peerages thereby allowing them to sit in the Commons.

Any further attempts over the following 35 years to reform the composition of the House of Lords foundered in a storm of opposition from all sides of the political divide. In the late 1960s Harold Wilson's Labour Government planned to legislate to remove Hereditary Peers from the Lords, but its proposals were defeated in the Commons. One of the concerns that led to the defeat of these proposals was the issue of patronage. While it might have been possible to get a majority in favour of removing Hereditary Peers from the Lords, the more controversial question of who should have the power to appoint Life Peers remained. That power rested largely with the Prime Minister, as it continues to. Although, by convention, the Prime Minister puts forward names of politicians from other parties as well as her own for elevation to the Lords, she has the sole right to nominate people to the Monarch. This remains an issue that dominates and complicates reform of the House of Lords. It is surely a constitutional quirk that the head of a government that is accountable to Parliament also has the power to appoint people to that Parliament.

Although by the early 1980s Labour's policy on the House of Lords had moved to outright abolition, by the time the party produced its manifesto for the 1997 general election its policy was less radical:

> *The House of Lords must be reformed. As an initial, self-contained reform, not dependent on further reform in the future, the right of Hereditary Peers to sit and vote in the House of Lords will be ended by statute. This will be the first stage in a process of reform to make the House of Lords more democratic and representative. The legislative powers of the House of Lords will remain unaltered. The system of appointment of Life Peers to the House of Lords will be reviewed. Our objective will be to ensure that over time party appointees as Life Peers more accurately reflect the proportion of votes cast at the previous general election. We are committed to maintaining an independent cross-bench presence of Life*

> Peers. No one political party should seek a majority in the House of Lords.[206]

What followed was a bill to enact the first stage of these proposals – the removal of the Hereditary Peers – but the act eventually passed did not fully implement this commitment. The commitment was unfulfilled because the act allowed 92 Hereditary Peers to remain in the Lords. The inevitable problem facing the government's House of Lords Bill was that it would have to be passed by the Lords itself – and turkeys seldom vote for Christmas! The government could have resorted to the Parliament Acts to override the Lords' opposition but there were two potential problems with this approach. The first was that this time-consuming piece of legislation would devour still more parliamentary time if it had to be considered twice. The second was that, although the letter of the law expressed in the Parliament Acts might allow the government to force legislation through against the wishes of the Lords, using the acts to make major constitutional change would not universally have been seen as being within the spirit of the law. It would certainly have raised some judicial eyebrows.[207]

Instead, the government decided to agree a compromise with the House of Lords and specifically with the Conservative Leader in the House of Lords, Viscount Cranborne. The final agreement allowed 92 Hereditary Peers to remain. Because the deal was never officially sanctioned by the leadership of the Conservative Party, it led to the sacking of Viscount Cranborne as Shadow Leader of the Lords by the Conservative leader William Hague. But the necessary amendment to the bill was tabled by Lord Weatherill, a former Speaker of the House of Commons and by then 'Convenor' of the Crossbenchers in the House of Lords. This amendment was duly accepted by both Lords

---

[206] Labour Party Manifesto 1997. http://www.labour-party.org.uk/manifestos/1997/1997-labour-manifesto.shtml

[207] As mentioned above, when the Lords announced their judgment in July 2005 on the validity of the Hunting Act they questioned whether a government should be able to use the Parliament Acts to force through major constitutional change.

and Commons and so appeared in the act. Thus the UK would remain one of only two countries in the world that reserves seats in its Parliament for hereditary chiefs, the other being Lesotho.

Which 92 Hereditary Peers would be allowed to keep their seats would be decided by votes of members of the House of Lords themselves. 75 were elected by their own party or crossbench groups (42 Conservatives, 28 Crossbenchers, three Liberal Democrats and two Labour); 15 were elected by the whole House as deputy speakers or committee chairs; and two hereditary royal appointments, the Earl Marshal and the Lord Great Chamberlain, were retained without election. The Hereditary Peers who wished to stand for election were allowed to write a 75 word personal manifesto about why they wished to remain in the Upper House.

On the death of one of the 92, their hereditary title would be passed on to a member of their family in the usual way. However, their seat in the Lords would not be inherited by a family member. Rather, to keep the total number of Hereditary Peers in the Lords at 92, provision was made in the 1999 Act to replace any of the 92 who died (or, since a change to the rules in 2014, retired) with a Hereditary Peer currently outside the Lords. In the early years following the 1999 Act, the Hereditary Peer elected to fill a vacancy in the Lords was usually a peer who had been removed from the Lords by the 1999 Act but more recently, given the advancing age of those removed in 1999, this has not always been the case. Increasingly, rather than return a former member, the Lords chooses to elect the eldest son (or whoever has inherited the title) of a Hereditary Peer removed in 1999 who has subsequently died.

On the death of one of the 15 elected by the whole House, the act allows all members to vote in the by-election. In the event of one of the 75 peers elected by their party leaving the Lords, the remaining Hereditary Peers from that party would hold a by-election to fill the vacancy. If a Labour or Liberal Democrat Hereditary Peer dies, the electorate is therefore very small. When the Liberal Democrat peer Lord Avebury died in 2016 and was replaced by the Viscount Thurso, the electorate consisted of the three surviving Liberal Democrat Hereditary Peers. The election of Viscount Thurso to the Lords was noteworthy not only because of the tiny size of the electorate. What was also of interest what the fact that after having been thrown out of Lords following the passing of the 1999 Act, Thurso, now being able to stand for election to the Commons, successfully won the Caithness, Sutherland and Easter Ross constituency for the Liberal Democrats at the 2001 general election. He lost the seat in 2015 to the SNP but was soon able to return to Parliament – this time back in the Lords - courtesy of his winning the hereditary by-election.

An interesting example of the son of a former member of the Lords entering the House via a by-election occurred when Viscount Stansgate, also known as Stephen Benn, was elected in 2021. He had inherited the viscountcy on the death of his father Tony some years previously. As mentioned earlier, Tony Benn had used the 1963 Peerages Act to renounce his hereditary title; however, that act allowed for a hereditary peerage only to be renounced for oneself, not for one's successors. Thus when Tony Benn died, his eldest son Stephen inherited the title. When the vacancy occurred in the Lords, Stephen Benn put his name forward as a candidate and was elected unopposed.

Few people in 1999 would have believed that by the third decade of the 21st century this structure of the House of Lords, with its 680 or so Life Peers, 26 bishops and 92 Hereditary Peers, would be largely unchanged, but the progress of further Lords' reform has been very slow.

After the 1999 Act there were some moves towards further Lords reform, but by the time of the 2010 general election only a few changes had resulted. One concerned the appointment of Life Peers. Although the Prime Minister remains the sole person who can make nominations to the Queen, there is now an Appointments Commission which nominates crossbench Life Peers (though by convention the Prime Minister retains the right to nominate up to 10 crossbench peers of her own choice per

Parliament.). Individuals can have their name put forward to the Commission for nomination as what have become known as 'People's Peers'. When the first 'People's Peers' were announced in April 2001, there was some disappointment that, among the eleven men and four women selected, there were seven knights, the wife of a peer and three professors. Lord Stevenson, the chair of the Appointments Commission, also raised a few eyebrows when he said, at the time of the announcement: *You haven't got your hairdresser in this list, but if you go back to our criteria one of them is that the human being will be comfortable operating in the House of Lords.* The Appointments Commission also vets the political nominations of all parties to ensure the highest standards of propriety before the Prime Minister puts them forward to the Queen.

The key issue of debate concerning the House of Lords has always been whether it should be chosen by election, appointment or a combination of the two, although there are other issues to be resolved, such as the continuing presence of Church of England bishops.[208] The argument in favour of electing the Upper House is simply the democratic argument which says that the people should choose those who represent their interests in Parliament. And this, after all, is the principle that dictates what happens in the vast majority of democratic countries. There are, however, a number of counter-arguments. One is that an elected Lords, even without any formal strengthening of its powers, would challenge the supremacy of the Commons, which might on occasion lead to parliamentary gridlock. Another is that the country would lose the enormous amount of expertise that simply wouldn't be present in the Lords if it were elected. A further argument is that an elected Lords would not demonstrate the independence of the present chamber and would therefore lose some of its effectiveness as a check on government. From 1983 to 1992 and again from 1997 to 2010, the Lords acted as a check on governments, one Tory, one Labour, that enjoyed large majorities in the Commons, and it has

---

[208] The issue of the Law Lords was however resolved, as discussed, by the passing of the Constitutional Reform Act 2005.

been doing so again since the 2019 election. It is a therefore a paradox that the House of Lords, which might be indefensible from a democratic viewpoint, should several times have acted as the defender of democratic freedoms. However, the Lord's lack of democratic legitimacy will always limit its effectiveness as a parliamentary chamber. Yes it can and does regularly challenge and often defeat the government and we can point to plenty of examples of where the Lords have, for example, successfully amended important bills. But when there is a complete stand-off between the Lords and the Commons, because the Lords is an unelected chamber, there is only going to be one winner.

Both the Labour and Coalition Governments did try to further reform the Lords after the passing of the 1999 Act. In 2007 the House of Commons voted on a series of options for the composition of the Lords, ranging from wholly elected through to wholly appointed but no progress was made. In 2009 the Labour Government included in its Constitutional Reform and Governance Bill proposals to phase out the hereditary principle in the House of Lords by ending by-elections for Hereditary Peers. The bill also provided for the disqualification of peers convicted of a serious crime and, in certain circumstances, the expulsion or suspension of peers. The bill would also have allowed Life Peers to resign and renounce their peerages. But these parts of the bill were withdrawn to ease the passage of the rest of the bill in advance of the 2010 general election. Gordon Brown's government also promised further comprehensive reform of the Lords if it won the 2010 general election.

That, as we know, didn't happen, but that election did bring to power a party that had long been committed to reform of the Upper House: the Liberal Democrats. When the Conservative and Liberal Democrat parties agreed their Programme for Government in May 2010 they had this to say about House of Lords Reform:

> *We will establish a committee to bring forward proposals for a wholly or mainly elected upper chamber*

on the basis of proportional representation.[209]

The Programme for Government went on to describe how, as an interim measure, appointments would be made to the Lords to make it reflective of the votes cast at the 2010 general election. This was clearly designed to be a precursor to wholesale reform of the Upper House. In 2012 the Coalition Government presented its House of Lords Reform Bill to Parliament.[210] The bill proposed that 80% of the reformed House should be elected with 20% nominated. The total membership would be 450 (an increase from the 300 suggested in a draft bill), including 12 bishops sitting as ex-officio members.

Elections to the new House would take place at the same time as general elections, subject to a caveat where a general election to the House of Commons took place within two years of the last election to the reformed House of Lords. Members of the new House would sit for a single non-renewable membership term of three normal election cycles which in practice, given that Parliaments had been set at five years by the Fixed-term Parliaments Act, would be 15 years. Elections to the House would be staggered so that a third of the seats were contested at each election. There would therefore be a transitional period of ten years during which existing members of the Lords would retain their seats. The 20% appointed, independent, members would be nominated by a statutory Appointments Commission and, as now, recommended by the Prime Minister to the Queen for appointment.

The powers and functions of the reformed Upper House would be the same as those of the current House.

Even before the bill had been published it was clear that it would face problems in Parliament, particularly from a substantial number of Conservative backbenchers in the Commons and from

---

[209] Ibid. p.27
[210] www.publications.parliament.uk/pa/Bills/cBill/2012-2013/0052/cBill_2012-20130052_en_1.htm

a large proportion of the House of Lords too. When in July 2012 the bill had its second reading on the floor of the House of Commons, it was passed by a substantial majority: 462 to 124. That might suggest that all would be plain sailing for the bill, in the Commons at least. But the reality was very different. Of the 124 who had voted against the bill at second reading, 93 were Conservative MPs. As it was the policy of the Labour Opposition to support the bill, there was never any real doubt that the bill would pass at second reading. The problems lay with the remaining stages of the bill in the Commons. Under the conventions of the House of Commons, because the bill had constitutional implications, it had to have its detailed committee scrutiny take place on the floor of the House rather than, as is the case for most bills, in a small public bill committee. (For more on this see the section on Legislation in chapter six).

Most government bills are subjected to a 'Programme Motion' which, if passed, limits debate on the bill to the time specified in the motion. It was clear that the passing of this bill's Programme Motion would be crucial to its future progress in the Commons: without it, the bill could get tied up on the floor of the House for a long time, thereby potentially wrecking the rest of the government's legislative programme. Whilst the government could have faced down a rebellion if it had once again received the support of the Official Opposition, that support was not forthcoming. (Arguably, Labour's desire to split the Coalition outweighed its desire to reform the Lords.) So faced with imminent defeat on the Programme Motion, the government withdrew the bill. Whilst it initially said that it would attempt to revive the bill in the autumn, on the first day that the Commons returned in September 2012, the Deputy Prime Minister, Nick Clegg, announced that: *the government have decided not to proceed with the House of Lords Reform Bill during this Parliament, and I can confirm that the Government have today withdrawn that bill.*[211] Some might find it surprising that a bill

---

[211] https://hansard.parliament.uk/Commons/2012-09-03/debates/1209038000001/HouseOfLordsReformBill

could pass by a majority of 338 in the Commons at second reading and yet still fail to make progress!

So once again, serious Lords reform was off the agenda, until the following general election at least. One important act was however passed in 2014: the House of Lords Reform (No. 2) Act.[212] This legislation was introduced as a Private Members' Bill (for more on these see chapter six) by the Conservative MP Dan Byles and it focused more on how members might exit, as opposed to enter, the House of Lords. The bill contained three reforms: first, the removal of peers convicted of a criminal offence that carries a prison sentence of one year or more; second, the introduction of a voluntary retirement scheme and third, the expulsion of peers who fail to attend the Lords at least once during a full parliamentary session without taking a leave of absence. With the backing of the government this bill became law.

Other attempts at reform have been made, in particular to remove the 92 Hereditary Peers from the Lords. One member of the Lords, Lord Grocott, has three times introduced legislation to do just that but on each occasion he has been thwarted by the filibustering of a very small number of Conservative Hereditary Peers – Lords Trefgarne and Caithness in particular.[213]

Since 2014 no further substantial Lords reform has even appeared on the horizon. With the 2015, 2017 and 2019 elections all producing single-party Conservative governments (who have always been less inclined than other governments to make constitutional reforms) and with the recent political agenda being hijacked almost entirely by Brexit and Covid, for a number of years now progress has seemed unlikely.

---

[212] https://www.legislation.gov.uk/ukpga/2014/24/contents/enacted

[213] It's noteworthy that the new Lord Speaker, Lord McFall, said soon after his appointment in April 2021 that he would press for government legislation to scrap the 'absurd' system of Hereditary Peer by-elections: https://www.telegraph.co.uk/politics/2021/05/02/hereditary-peers-must-prove-worth-remain-says-new-lord-speaker/.

Prime Ministerial Patronage

One of the arguments sometimes put forward for not removing the 92 hereditaries is that this shouldn't be done in isolation but rather as part of a wider package of constitutional reform. Another argument is that by simply removing the remaining Hereditary Peers, what would be left is a chamber that is almost entirely a creature of the Prime Minister's patronage. Whether that is a sufficient reason for keeping the 92, the extent of prime ministerial patronage over Lords' appointments is quite worrying for some. To make the point again: can it really be right in a modern democracy that the Head of Government simply appoints people to Parliament? Would the American or French people be happy with their Presidents simply appointing people to their Senates? Almost certainly not. But that is what happens in the UK.

As with other prime ministerial powers, appointing people to the House of Lords is one of those where the expectation is that it will be carried out in a principled way. There is no limit to the number of people that a Prime Minister can put in the Lords and there is no law stopping her only appointing people from her own party. But the expectation is that a Prime Minister won't 'go mad' in the number of appointments she makes and that she will also appoint people from other parties and as independents.

Peerages are usually given to some people almost automatically when they retire from a senior job. Such people would include Cabinet Secretaries, Heads of the Diplomatic Service, Chiefs of the Defence Staff, Queen's Private Secretaries, senior bishops and Speakers of the House of Commons. John Bercow, however, was not given a peerage on his retirement as Boris Johnson refused to put his name forward to the Queen. This was the first time in two centuries that a retiring Speaker had not been given a seat in the House of Lords. The official reason given for this concerned the allegations of bullying that had been made against Bercow, but it is hard to imagine that the difficulties Bercow caused the May and Johnson Governments in respect of

Brexit didn't play a part in this decision. When Bercow wasn't nominated for a peerage by Boris Johnson, the Leader of the Opposition, Jeremy Corbyn, instead nominated him but Johnson again refused to put Bercow's name forward to the Queen.

When it comes to appointing people to the Lords, different Prime Ministers behave in different ways. The controversy that surrounds appointments to the Lords is not usually just about the numbers or even the political make up; it's also about the type of people who are appointed. An advantage of an appointed chamber is that you can put people in it who are very experienced in their fields – business, medicine, diplomacy etc - and this experience is very useful when, for example, the Lords are scrutinising legislation. Such people would rarely want to stand for election and would therefore be lost to Parliament if the Upper House were ever to be elected. But, on the other hand, it means the Lords lacks any real legitimacy. The British people have no say over their arrival in Parliament; nor can they do anything to have them removed. Additionally, not all Lords will be appointed for their experience. It's important to realise that being given a peerage is part of the honours system in the UK and some people are rewarded with a seat in the Lords in the way that others might be rewarded with a CBE, damehood or knighthood. These are sometimes well deserved rewards but, as is well known, honours are also given to people who, for example, have made donations to the governing party or who have publicly supported the government on some important issue.

Appointments to the House of Lords by PM

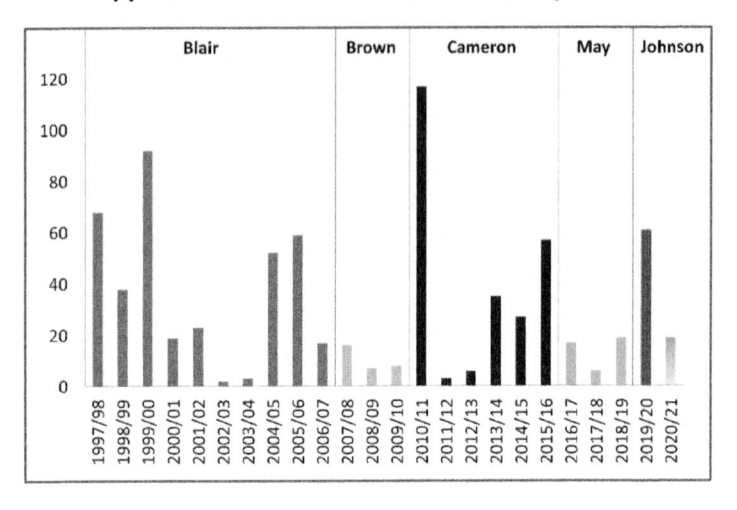

Figure 11 Source: *https://lordslibrary.parliament.uk/new-lords-appointments-december-2020/ The figures for 2020/21 are to end the of 2020 only*

Figure 11 shows us that Tony Blair made a considerable number of appointments to the Lords, for which he was criticised. (He might have argued that he was simply making up for hundreds of years of Conservative domination of the Lords.) He was also criticised for putting personal friends and allies in the Lords (sometimes rather disparagingly described as 'Tony's Cronies'.) And it was the vetting process carried out by the House of Lords Appointments Commission which first shone light on the issue of 'loans for peerages' or 'cash for honours' which dogged Tony Blair in his last year as Prime Minister.

Gordon Brown had a rather different approach. As can be seen, not only did he appoint fewer peers per year than his predecessor, he also put people into the Lords from different walks of life who he wanted to bring into his government. As we have seen earlier, it's not unusual for Prime Ministers to put people into the Lords because they want to make them a minister. But what was more unusual in this case was that some of the people Brown brought into his government weren't members of or even perhaps natural allies of the Labour Party. The retired admiral Alan West, eminent surgeon Ara Darzi, former head of the CBI Digby Jones and former Deputy Secretary-General of the United Nations Mark Malloch-Brown all joined the government without having any obvious ties to the Labour Party. As ministers they were part of what became known as Brown's GOATS (government of all the talents).

When the Coalition Government came to power in 2010 it announced plans to make the Lords "reflective of the vote" at the general election (the number of Life Peers in the Lords having swung significantly towards the Labour Party during the Blair years). To do that, given that Labour peers couldn't be removed, would require the appointment of over 150 Conservative or Liberal Democrat peers, not to mention numerous peers from UKIP, the BNP and other parties. (Some have suggested that the Lords, as a result, would have ended up with a membership of around 1200.) While this aspiration was never achieved, as can be seen from Figure 11, a very significant number of new Peers joined the House of Lords during the time of David Cameron's premiership, in particular during its first year. 60 new peerages were created between the general election and the summer recess in 2010 with another 58 announced in November 2010. About three-quarters of these were Conservatives. By the summer of 2013 the membership of the House of Lords was well over 800, with parity restored between the number of Labour and Conservative Life Peers. Life Peerages were now being created in record numbers. Cameron would claim that he was only 'rebalancing' the Lords in advance of proposed substantial reform, but the increase in the size of the Lords was nevertheless exceptional.

Rather like when Gordon Brown replaced Tony Blair, so when Theresa May replaced David Cameron as Prime Minister the creation of Life Peerages began to slow down only once again to speed up when Boris Johnson became Prime Minister. Johnson has been widely criticised for the way in which he has made appointments to the Lords, not just for the number of peerages created but for who those peers have been. One of those he appointed to the Lords was his own brother. Others have been rewarded with seats in the Lords for no obvious reason other than the fact they supported Brexit. (The former cricketer Ian Botham's elevation to the Lords was not to allow him to explain the 'Leg Before Wicket' rule to their Lordships but rather because of his public support for Brexit.) The numbers of Life Peers by party have now skewed once again significantly towards the Conservative Party as they did under David Cameron. And in December 2020, Boris Johnson became the first Prime Minister to give a peerage to someone against the advice of the independent House of Lords Appointments Commission. The Commission wrote to Boris Johnson concerning his proposed appointment to the Lords of Peter Cruddas who had been one of the founders of the Vote Leave campaign and had donated millions of pounds to the Conservative party. The Commission said that it couldn't support the nomination due to concerns about allegations made during Mr Cruddas' term as treasurer of the Conservative party.[214] Peter Cruddas formally joined the House of Lords on 2 February 2021. On 8 February he made a donation of £500,000 to the Conservative Party.[215] In June 2021, the 'Good Law Project' announced that they thought Cruddas' appointment was unlawful and that they would be challenging it in the courts.[216]

Around the same time Johnson was criticised by the then Speaker of the House of Lords itself, Lord Fowler, for the number of peerages now being created. Lord Fowler said:

I regret very much that we've now added another 17 peers to

---

[214] Boris Johnson's reasons for rejecting the Commission's advice can be found in his reply to the commission here:
https://assets.publishing.service.gov.uk/government/uploads/system/uploads/attachment_data/file/947211/Lord_Bew_signed_letter_001.pdf

215
http://search.electoralcommission.org.uk/English/Donations/C0545244

[216] https://goodlawproject.org/news/handing-out-peerages/?utm_source=Twitter&utm_medium=social%20media&utm_campaign=cruddas%20tw%201206

the list ... 53 new peers in the past 12 months. "It means that all the retirements that have just taken place have now been nullified and it stands on its head the previous policy of Theresa May that appointments were going to be pursued moderately. I don't regard this as being the definition of moderation." [217]

Of the 79 appointments Johnson made up to the end of 2020, 41 were Conservatives, 13 were Labour and 14 were Crossbenchers.

The irony though is that despite this prime ministerial control over appointments to the Lords, since 1997 the Lords have been ever more ready to defeat whatever government has been in power. What prime ministerial control hasn't delivered is a majority for any government in the Lords. (Even those Prime Ministers who have been inclined to appoint large numbers to the Lords haven't gone as far as giving their party a majority of the seats.) And given, since the passing of the 1999 Act, that the Lords perhaps feel they have a greater legitimacy since the hereditary principle has largely been removed, governments have found themselves time after time defeated in the Lords. In the House of Commons, governments with reasonable majorities rarely lose votes whereas in more recent times they have found themselves losing as many as 50% of all the votes cast in the Lords. Whilst, as we shall see in the chapter six, many of these defeats will be overturned in the Commons, not all will be. The reality is that many Acts of Parliament reflect changes made to them as bills by the Lords, against the wishes of the government of the day.

Powers of the House of Lords

In chapter one we saw how the powers of the House of Lords were limited by the Parliament Acts of 1911 and 1949. These acts allow the Commons to override a Lords' 'veto' on bills if, following its rejection by the House of Lords, a bill is reintroduced to

---

[217] https://www.politico.eu/article/boris-johnson-house-of-lords-nominations-peter-cruddas-dan-hannan/

Parliament in the following session. We saw also that this power is rarely used because governments are reluctant to put their legislation through Parliament twice in order to override the Lords. But there is another reason why the Parliament Acts have been used rarely: because of the practice that the House of Lords does not normally block government bills. This is particularly true in the case of government bills that have been clearly foreshadowed in the governing party's most recent election manifesto – a principle that is set out in the 'Salisbury Convention'.

Salisbury Convention

The Salisbury Convention dates from 1945 when Lord Salisbury, the leader of the Conservatives in the House of Lords, reached an understanding with Lord Addison, the Leader of the House of Lords in what was the first ever majority Labour Government.[218] This understanding recognised the democratic right of the government not to have legislation that was clearly foreshadowed in its general election manifesto rejected by the unelected House of Lords. The convention has meant that successive governments have not had bills that would enact manifesto commitments rejected outright by the House of Lords. Not rejecting bills outright is quite different, of course, from not amending bills: the House of Lords is certainly not restricted in amending bills that enact manifesto commitments, although inserting a 'wrecking amendment' into a bill would normally be considered as being contrary to the convention.

In recent times the Salisbury Convention has begun to be questioned because the House of Lords of today is very different to the House which adopted the convention in the 1940s: most of the Hereditary Peers are long gone and with them went much of the large 'anti-Labour bias' in the Lords.

Whether the Salisbury Convention still applied following the

---

[218] For this reason, the convention is sometimes referred to as the 'Salisbury-Addison Doctrine'. Labour had come to power in the general election held in the summer of 1945.

creation of the Coalition Government was a rather interesting constitutional point. Can a coalition government be said to have a manifesto on which it was elected? Not really, as the parties that make it up have distinct manifestos. Could the Coalition Government's Programme for Government be treated as a manifesto for the purposes of the Salisbury Convention? Again, not really, as the Programme was never put before the electorate at a general election. However, in its 2014 report on *The Constitutional Implications of Coalition Government*, the House of Lords Constitution Committee said of the Salisbury Convention:

> *We do not consider that a coalition agreement has the status of a manifesto, or that the commitments it contains are subject to the Salisbury-Addison convention. However, commitments in such an agreement that had previously appeared in the manifestos of parties making up the coalition should be treated as subject to the convention.*[219]

In reality, the Salisbury Convention is mentioned less often than one might think in discussions about the power of the Lords. The reason for this is that, in practice, the Lords vote down or wreck very few bills, whether or not they are enacting manifesto commitments. This is because the Lords recognise they lack the legitimacy to do this, in particular to bills that come to them having already been passed by the Commons. They certainly make many amendments to bills, some of them important ones, but blocking a bill outright is usually seen as a step too far. Consider for example the various bills Parliament had to consider that concerned the UK's departure from the EU. It was common knowledge that the Lords contained a majority of peers who were anti-Brexit, but it was unthinkable for them to vote down such bills. (Imagine the reaction in some parts of the media to the unelected Lords not only defying the will of the elected House but

---

[219] Quoted from the report's summary.
www.publications.parliament.uk/pa/ld201314/ldselect/ldconst/130/13003.htm

also of, as they would have seen it, the will of the people as expressed in the 2016 referendum.)

The future of the Salisbury Convention and the powers of the House of Lords more generally form part of the wider debate about Lords reform. But in the years since Labour's election in 1997, the debate has been focused very much on the composition of the House of Lords. The issue of its power has been discussed much less. The Labour Government's 2008 White Paper on Lords' Reform proposed no changes to the powers of the reformed second chamber and the Coalition Government adopted the same position in its House of Lords Reform Bill. There is no reason why the formal powers of the Upper House would need to change following reform of its membership. In practice though, an Upper House that was elected, particularly if it were elected by proportional representation, would feel it had much greater legitimacy and might therefore be prepared to challenge the Commons much more readily.

Who Sits Where?

The House of Lords is dominated by the throne (A in Figure 12) and its surrounding 'Cloth of Estate' at one end of the chamber. The throne, which is used only by the Queen at the State Opening of Parliament, is raised up from the rest of the House and on the steps leading up to it people who are not members of the House can sit and listen to the business of the House. In the days when all Hereditary Peers were eligible to sit in the Lords, their eldest sons were allowed to sit on the steps of the throne to watch the chamber at work, in preparation for their own elevation to the House. Nowadays this right is given to the eldest child of any peer. Privy Counsellors, who we discussed in chapter two, are also allowed to sit on the steps of the throne.

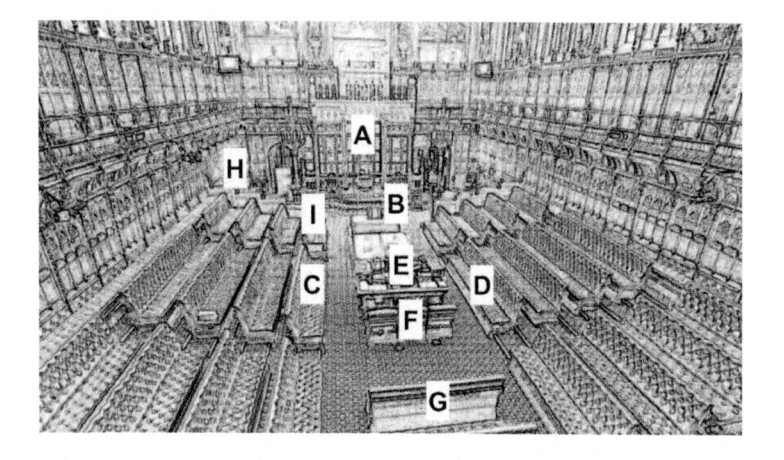

Figure 12

The Lord Speaker

Seated on the Woolsack (B), the Speaker of the House of Lords presides over the chamber. The Woolsack is a large, wool-stuffed cushion covered with red cloth. It originally contained English wool as a symbol of the nation's prosperity, but when it was remade after being damaged during the Second World War, wool from the various nations of the Commonwealth was used, to symbolise the Commonwealth's unity. The Mace, representing as in the Commons the Queen in Parliament, lies on the Woolsack behind the Speaker.

As we have seen, until July 2006 the Lord Chancellor, who was also a government minister, was the Speaker of the House of Lords. This may seem rather strange when one considers the role played by the Speaker in the House of Commons, where the need to act with absolute impartiality is crucial. But this is to misunderstand the role of the Speaker of the Lords, whose job is to preside over, rather than to control, the chamber. The House of Lords is often described as a 'self-regulating' chamber where the Speaker plays no role in choosing who speaks when or in enforcing good behaviour. In debates, lists of contributors are agreed behind the scenes via the 'usual channels', in other words, in discussion by the whips and other party managers. (The 'usual channels' are used in both Houses rather more than many might think. Due to the confrontational nature of the British parliamentary system, one might assume that there wouldn't be a lot of co-operation behind the scenes between party managers. The reality is that there is quite a lot, and both Houses rely on it considerably for their smooth running. But, although co-operation via the 'usual channels' might be thought to be a good thing, it didn't stop them being referred to as 'the most polluted waterway' in Britain. This description is attributed by some to Tony Benn and by others to Enoch Powell. But one can believe either of them saying it. Both would have seen the 'usual channels' as being a frontbench stitch up against backbenchers.)

Another difference to the Commons Speaker is that his counterpart in the Lords doesn't cast a deciding vote in the event of a tie. In this situation, Standing Order 54 is invoked. For votes on legislation, this in effect says that legislation cannot be rejected or amended unless there is a majority in favour. For other motions, a tied vote is treated as a vote against the motion.

Since 2006, when Baroness Hayman became the first female Speaker of the House of Lords, the Lords have elected their own Speaker. Baroness D'Souza was elected as Baroness Hayman's successor in 2011 and she in turn was succeeded by Lord Fowler in 2016 (prompting some jokes about him breaking through a 'glass ceiling' having become the first man ever to be elected as Lord Speaker!) When Lord Fowler retired in April 2021 he was replaced as Lord Speaker by Lord McFall who had previously been a Labour peer.

As in the Commons, the governing party or parties sit on the Speaker's right, with its ministers sitting on the front bench in the middle section of benches (C) and its backbenchers sitting elsewhere on the same side. Peers from the opposition parties sit on the Speaker's left with the spokespeople of the Official Opposition sitting on the front bench in the middle section of benches (D). The frontbenchers from the governing and main opposition parties debate with each other across the table of the

House (E), behind which sit the clerks (F). The crossbenches (G) run at right angles to the other benches. This is where the independent Crossbenchers traditionally sit, although (because of their numbers) they will also be found sitting on the end of the benches on both the government and opposition sides. Civil servants in support of ministers or other government spokespeople sit in the officials' box (H), close to the throne.

The bishops' bench is the front bench on the government side nearest to the Speaker (I). As the bishops are known as the 'Lords Spiritual', this is known as the 'spiritual side' of the House. At the start of the parliamentary day the 'duty bishop' says a prayer. The bishops' bench is the only bench in the House to have an armrest at each end. Why these armrests are there is a matter of some debate. Some hold that it is to distinguish the Lords Spiritual from the Lords Temporal. Others maintain that the armrests date from an incident many years ago when a sleeping bishop rolled off the bench!

House of Lords Parliamentary Processes

The Lords follow a calendar similar to that of the Commons, with recesses for Christmas, Easter, Whitsun and summer. It sits at 1pm on Mondays and at 12 noon on Tuesdays, Wednesdays and Thursdays. It sometimes sits on a Friday, at 11am. On a typical day the business starts with 40 minutes of oral parliamentary questions. Unless there is a ministerial statement (some oral ministerial statements made in the Commons are repeated in the Lords), the main business of the day follows – perhaps the second reading of a bill or a debate on an issue of government policy.

In many respects the House of Lords operates in a similar way to the House of Commons. It, too, is organised on a party basis, but it has a very different atmosphere from the Commons. Its members are less rigidly partisan and are likely to be less sensitive to party political interests than MPs. And, of course, they have no constituency interests to consider. Political members of the Lords are whipped like their colleagues in the Commons but, although party discipline in the Lords has become stricter in recent years, the whips in the Lords are not in such a strong position as their counterparts in the Commons. MPs' reliance on the membership and patronage of their party places the Commons whips in a powerful position. In the Lords the whips usually have to rely on persuasion, rather than threats.

Like MPs, members of the Lords vote in divisions, using voting lobbies located either side of the chamber. One procedural difference, however, is that the Lords do not vote 'aye' or 'no' as in the Commons, but rather they cast their votes in the 'content' or 'not content' lobbies.

The House of Lords is far less adversarial than the Commons with its members much politer to each other than in the 'other place' (as each House likes to call the other). The House of Lords is therefore sometimes less entertaining to observe. (There is, for example, no Lords parallel to Prime Minister's Questions.) But admirers of the Lords argue that, while it might lack the cut and thrust of the House of Commons, the quality of debate is often higher, partly because its members are less overtly partisan and partly because of the immense experience and knowledge of the members sitting on its red benches. Former Prime Ministers, Foreign Secretaries and Cabinet Secretaries, archbishops, senior business and trade union leaders, Chief Rabbis and others bring immense expertise to the Upper House. But whether or not these benefits compensate for its lack of democratic legitimacy, as we have seen, remains a fundamental question in the debate on Lords reform that has ebbed and flowed for more than a century.

Procedures during the Covid Pandemic

Earlier we discussed how the House of Commons had adapted following the onset of the Covid pandemic. The House of Lords introduced much the same processes to deal with the new situation – in particular, virtual participation and remote electronic voting. Its difference to the Commons however was that once the Lords had introduced these new processes, it stuck with them. In particular, the

Lords used remote electronic voting throughout the pandemic unlike the Commons which voted to scrap it just a few weeks after it had been introduced. In this respect then, members of the Lords have perhaps been rather more modern and forward looking than their colleagues at the other end of the building. Shortly before the summer recess of 2021 the Lords considered whether any of the procedures brought in during the pandemic should continue in the long-term. They decided, in particular, that virtual participation should continue to be available for sick or disabled members who were unable to come to Westminster. And regarding voting, they agreed to keep using remote electronic voting until a system of voting in the lobbies using pass readers, similar to that in the Commons, could be introduced.

The Highest Court of Appeal (until October 2009)

In front of the Speaker's Woolsack is the 'Judges' Woolsack', so called because this is where the Law Lords, and now their successors in the Supreme Court, sit at the State Opening of Parliament. This is a reminder that the House of Lords until recently was also a court – the highest Court of Appeal in the UK for all cases except Scottish criminal cases. Usually five Law Lords would hear a particular case, but occasionally more. Appeals used to be heard in the chamber of the House of Lords itself but, after 1948, the Law Lords sat in one of the Lords' committee rooms. The Law Lords were formally known as the Appellate Committee of the House of Lords.

Judgments were always given on the floor of the House itself, at 9.45am on Wednesdays a few weeks after a particular hearing. By convention, although they could attend, members of the House who were not Law Lords took no part in judicial proceedings. When the judgments were given, each Law Lord who had heard the appeal, starting with the most senior, would rise to give his or her 'opinion' which was the equivalent of a judgment in lower courts. Once all of the Law Lords on the Appellate Committee had given their opinion, the Law Lord sitting on the Woolsack as Speaker (i.e. the senior Law Lord present) put the question to the House: *That the report from the Appellate Committee be agreed to*. The judgment was given to the relevant parties, counsel for whom would be present at the Bar of the House when the judgment was delivered. All this of course, since the creation of the Supreme Court in 2009, is now part of Britain's constitutional history.

6

The Functions of Parliament

Producing a Government

The United Kingdom is a parliamentary democracy. A primary function of Parliament in a parliamentary democracy is to produce a government. A government is in power not because it was directly elected but because, usually, it has won a majority of the seats in the House of Commons at the previous general election. Contrast this with the presidential system of the United States where every four years the American people are not only voting for people to represent them in Congress (ie the legislature) but also for who they wish to be the Head of Government (i.e. the President).[220] In a parliamentary democracy Parliament can also, as we have seen, remove a government from power, which is what happened to the Labour Government in 1979 (although this became a little more difficult following the passing of the Fixed-term Parliaments Act in 2011).

---

[220] Americans actually elect people to the House of Representatives every two years, so every other one of these elections coincides with a presidential election. In the USA the President is the Head of State as well as the Head of Government.

Representing Constituents

While the House of Commons will be packed to the rafters during Prime Minister's Questions, for most of the time the chamber will seem rather empty. Even for a relatively important event such as questions to the Home Office, there may be no more than 100 MPs in the House. MPs are often criticised in the media for their 'non-attendance' in Parliament (they were once particularly criticised in the media for their lack of attendance at a debate on truancy!) but much of the time this is unfair. Much else is going on at Westminster to demand MPs' attention – perhaps working on a select committee or serving on a committee scrutinising a bill. But a substantial part of an MP's job involves dealing with issues and problems brought to them by their constituents. Whilst they are at Westminster, MPs and their staff will be dealing with the emails, letters and phone calls from constituents seeking their help. But the main focus on this aspect of their work will take place in the constituency over the long weekend.

Most MPs will have a home in the constituency to which they will travel from Westminster, usually on Thursday evening. They would then typically return to Westminster on Monday morning. If they choose to have their home in London then they might travel to the constituency on Thursday evening or Friday morning, returning to London perhaps on Sunday. (During times when Parliament is in recess, MPs will spend rather more time in the constituency.) MPs whose diaries might look a little different to this are those who have constituencies within easy travelling distance from Westminster. They may well be commuting to Westminster from the constituency on each day that Parliament is sitting. And for those whose seats are very close to Westminster, they might find themselves travelling backward and forward between their constituency and Parliament more than once a day. (I have often heard Jeremy Corbyn, the MP for Islington North, describe his frequent cycle rides between the constituency and Westminster.) Whether having a constituency close to London is advantageous is a 'swings and roundabouts' question. One might think life is rather easier for Jane Aiken, the MP who actually has the Palace of Westminster in her constituency, than it is, say, for Jamie Stone, the MP for Caithness, Sutherland and Easter Ross in the far north of Scotland. But Jane Aiken's constituents will know that she's rarely going to be far away from the constituency and they therefore might expect her to attend events in the constituency on days that the Commons is sitting whereas Jamie Stone's constituents will know that once he's departed (probably very early!) on a Monday morning, they won't see him in the constituency again until late Thursday night.

Many MPs hold a weekly surgery in their constituency on a Friday or Saturday to which constituents will bring along their many and varied concerns. They may also visit various workplaces in the constituency and attend other events. The array of problems that constituents bring before MPs is vast – housing, immigration, benefit payments, asylum, planning etc – and over many of these, being local government matters, MPs have virtually no power. Having the letters 'MP' after their name does, however, give them some influence, which is what their constituents are hoping they will bring to bear. MPs will spend a lot of time telephoning and emailing various agencies about their constituents' concerns. Sometimes MPs will contact ministers themselves about constituents' problems, either in writing or in face-to-face meetings. It's relatively rare, however, for the concerns of individual constituents to be aired on the floor of the House. It's fair to say that the large majority of MPs take this side of their job very seriously. It's tempting for people to assume it's just 'grubbing up votes' but that is, perhaps, unfair. Yes, the size of an MP's majority may have some influence on how hard they work for their constituents but perhaps less than one might think.

Before leaving this discussion of an MP's constituency work, it's worth remembering that most ministers (those in the Commons) have to do this too. Although being a minister is a full-time job in itself, most ministers will be in their constituencies over the long weekend working for their constituents. Ministers will be all too aware that spending too much time on ministerial work, at the expense of their constituents, may come back to bite them. There's little point being a brilliant minister if you manage that only by spending very little time on the concerns of your constituents. Additionally, being a minister, you have to follow the 'government line'. But what if the large majority of your constituents don't agree with the government position, for example, on building a new railway line through the constituency? Publicly supporting the government line might keep you in a job as a minister but that won't count for much if your constituents turf you out at the next general election. At the 2001 general election, David Lock was one of very few Labour MPs to lose their seat. Lock had been a minister in Tony Blair's government and, as such, had to support the government's decision to close his local hospital in Kidderminster. An independent, Dr Richard Taylor, decided to stand against him as a candidate fighting on a single issue: the saving of Kidderminster hospital. Dr Taylor won the seat with a substantial majority; but one has to assume that David Lock would have retained his seat comfortably if he had been a backbench MP and therefore able to oppose the closure of the hospital.

Holding the Government to Account

In the parliamentary democracy that is the UK, as we have seen, ministers are almost always a member of one of the two Houses of Parliament. They can therefore be held to account by Parliament on a day-to-day basis. Parliament's theoretical powers may be considerable (the doctrine of parliamentary sovereignty acknowledges no higher power) but in practice they are limited, often by conventions or even Parliament's own Standing Orders which tend to favour the will of the executive. In times of single-party majority government in the UK, the reality is that a government, particularly one with a large majority in the House of Commons, ought to be able to get its legislation through Parliament, most of the time, largely unscathed. Defeats in the Commons for the governments of Tony Blair, Gordon Brown and David Cameron were rare (although the defeat for Cameron on the Syria motion of 2013 was hugely important.) For Theresa May, as we have seen, things were very different, particularly so after she lost her majority at the 2017 election. Boris Johnson inherited this difficult situation from Theresa May in the summer of 2019 and similarly found himself often defeated in the Commons – but only until the December general election at which he won a healthy majority and the more normal balance of power between the executive and the legislature was thereby restored. The 2017-19 Parliament, which is discussed in more detail in the next chapter, was an exceptional one. For those of us who are 'Westminster watchers' it was an extremely interesting, even entertaining, one. But it was highly unusual.

So in practice, the powers of the British legislature vis-à-vis the government's often seem rather weak. But for ministers and the civil servants who work for them, it feels very different. Parliament looms large in their daily work. Parliamentary work takes up a substantial proportion of the ministerial diary and how individual ministers perform on the floor of the House is still a very important determinant of their future careers in politics.

Debates

The word 'Parliament' is derived from the old French for 'speaking' and debates are fundamental to any parliament's purpose. In the Westminster Parliament they take many forms. A government with a clear majority is going to have control over most of the agenda of the House of Commons and will therefore usually be deciding the topics for debate. Debates in 'government time' vary in type. There may be a debate on a substantive motion concerning the government's policy on a particular issue or perhaps a debate on an issue to do with the internal workings of the Commons such as those in 2020 and 2021 on the operation of the Commons during the Covid pandemic. On some debates the Speaker will impose limits on the length of speeches, with frontbench speakers usually being given more time than those on the backbenches. Members may intervene on another MP's speech, but only if the latter gives way.

Because a government with a majority has control over most of the agenda of the House of Commons, it will usually be deciding the topic for debate. However the rules of the Commons do allow some time for debate on issues where the subject matter is not decided by ministers but at which they will nevertheless be required to attend in order to speak for the government. These times are as follows:

Backbench Business Committee Debates

The Backbench Business Committee is a relatively recent creation, having come into being after the 2010 general election following a recommendation of the House of Commons Reform Committee (often referred to the 'Wright Committee' after its chair, the then Labour MP Tony Wright).[221] The Committee, which is a cross-party select committee of the Commons, can grant 90-minute, three-hour or full-day debates in the main chamber. Such debates usually take place on Thursdays. The Committee can also grant 90-minute or three-hour debates in Westminster Hall (see below). Sometimes such debates will be ones which the government might prefer not to be having. For example, not that long after the creation of the committee there was a Backbench Business Committee debate on whether a referendum should be held on the UK's membership of the European Union which led to a rebellion of 81 Conservative MPs.[222] This was probably the first sign for David Cameron of the serious problems he faced with his own party on the issue of holding a referendum on leaving the EU.

Opposition Day Debates

Under the rules of the House of Commons, on a minimum of 20 days in each session, the opposition parties are allowed to choose the topics for debate. Of these, 17 will be under the control of the Official Opposition. On the remaining three days it is for

---

[221] www.publications.parliament.uk/pa/cm200809/cmselect/cmrefhoc/1117/1117.pdf

[222] https://hansard.parliament.uk/Commons/2011-10-24/debates/11102470 00001/NationalReferendumOnTheEuropeanUnion

the other opposition parties to choose the topics for debate. There will often be more than one debate on the day in question.

Adjournment Debates

At the end of every day in the Commons backbench MPs have an opportunity, either through a ballot or by being chosen by the Speaker, to hold an adjournment debate. The Speaker chooses the topic for debate on a Thursday and on other days it is chosen by ballot. These debates usually last for 30 minutes and often just consist of the backbench MP speaking for around 15 minutes with a minister responding for a similar length of time. Adjournment debates, particularly those on constituency issues, are often very poorly attended. But for the MP who has chosen the topic it provides an opportunity to raise an issue with the government and what is said in the debate is, of course, recorded in Hansard. So the MP may receive some coverage of the debate, if not in the national media then perhaps locally, which may not always mention how few MPs actually attended it!

Petitions Committee Debates

The House of Commons has a Petitions Committee which looks, in particular, at the e-petitions to which members of the public can sign up.[223] Once 100,000 people have signed an e-petition, the Petitions Committee considers whether the issue should be debated in the Commons or, more commonly, in Westminster Hall. A high profile example of such a debate was the one in 2011 on whether there should be a full disclosure of documents concerning the 1989 Hillsborough disaster.[224] More recently there have been debates, for example, on preventing

---

[223] https://petition.parliament.uk/

[224] https://hansard.parliament.uk/Commons/2011-10-17/debates/11101715 000001/HillsboroughDisaster

Donald Trump from making a state visit to the UK [225] and on holding a second referendum before leaving the EU [226]

Westminster Hall Debates

As well as Petitions Committee and Backbench Business Committee debates, the Westminster Hall debating chamber also hosts general debates which allow backbench MPs to raise issues of importance to them. These debates usually take place on Tuesdays and Wednesdays and last either 30 or 90 minutes. They are quite similar to the end-of-day adjournment debates that occur in the main chamber with constituency issues predominating. They also therefore tend to be fairly sparsely attended.

Emergency Debates

Very occasionally the Speaker will grant an emergency debate when requested to do so by a member. The MP is given three minutes to make a speech about why the issue is of such importance and the Speaker then decides whether to submit the application to the House. If MPs, by standing up, indicate their assent to the request, the emergency debate will usually take place the next sitting day.

Debates in the Lords

As we have seen, the government has less control over the Lords than it does the Commons due to it not having a majority in the Upper House. Governments therefore have to negotiate the Lords' timetable with the other parties and the Crossbenchers through the 'usual channels'. Debates in the name of ministers are often held in the House of Lords but many will be on motions in the name of backbench members.

---

[225] https://hansard.parliament.uk/Commons/2017-02-20/debates/34847E5C-8B14-46E6-8251-AE99526CC011/PresidentTrumpStateVisit

[226] https://hansard.parliament.uk/Commons/2019-01-14/debates/694BA27D-566E-4F52-BC4B-8FC1ACA3F109/LeavingTheEU

The equivalent in the House of Lords of the adjournment debates that are held at the end of the day in the Commons are 'Questions for Short Debate' (QSDs). The peer in whose name the question appears is allotted ten minutes to speak and the minister has twelve minutes in which to reply. Any other time is shared amongst other speakers. 90 minute QSDs are held at the end of the day and one hour ones during the 'dinner break'. (Does any other legislative chamber in the world have a dinner break? According to one member of the Lords, dinner breaks *give those peers who have been heavily engaged in discussing the legislation, especially frontbenchers, an opportunity to have a break and get something to eat.*[227])

The Authorisation of Tax and Expenditure

In theory, government can collect no taxes nor spend any money without the prior authorisation of Parliament. Given, as we saw in chapter one, the limits placed on the House of Lords over issues to do with the raising and spending of money, it's not surprising that the Upper House plays next to no role in these matters. But, given the complexity of government finance, in practice, the role of the Commons is extremely limited too.

The most important and well-known aspect of the Commons' scrutiny of the government's financial plans is the annual budget speech. At this important event in the parliamentary calendar, the Chancellor of the Exchequer sets out the government's taxation proposals and provides an overview of the health of the nation's economy.[228] Following the budget speech, a series of votes takes

---

[227] http://lordsoftheblog.net/2009/10/21/dinner-break-business/

[228] By convention, it is the Leader of the Opposition, not the Shadow Chancellor who responds to the Chancellor's speech. According to a rather less important convention, the budget speech is the one occasion when alcohol may be drunk in the chamber – by, and only by, the Chancellor. This exception to the rules is made due to the length of the speech. According to Parliament's website: 'Former Chancellor George Osborne chose to drink mineral water. Other Chancellors have chosen

place in the Commons to allow the government provisionally to make taxation changes. Later, Parliament debates and votes on the Finance Bill which translates the budget into law.

As far as government spending is concerned, each year the government puts its proposals before the Commons in what are known as the 'estimates'. The main estimates are published around the start of the financial year to which they relate. In reality, detailed scrutiny of the estimates by the Commons is minimal. Rather, what happens is that on three days of the parliamentary session the Commons debates particular aspects of government spending, often based on recent reports of Commons' select committees.[229] The government's public expenditure plans are then presented to Parliament in the form of 'Supply and Appropriation Bills'. These bills are passed by Parliament usually with the bare minimum of scrutiny.

Legislating

A central function of Parliament is to debate, scrutinise and vote on legislation. The vast bulk of legislation debated in Parliament is brought to it by ministers. Less legislation that actually becomes law will have been introduced by backbench members of the Commons or Lords.

Two main types of legislation may come before Parliament: primary and secondary. Primary legislation consists of bills scrutinised by the two Houses of Parliament

---

mineral water (Gordon Brown and Alastair Darling), whisky (Kenneth Clarke), spritzer (Nigel Lawson), gin and tonic (Geoffrey Howe), brandy and water (Benjamin Disraeli) and sherry and beaten egg (William Ewart Gladstone)'. https://www.parliament.uk/about/how/role/check-and-approve-government-spending-and-taxation/the-budget-and-parliament/

[229] For more information on select committees, see below in this chapter. Perhaps the best scrutiny of the budget takes place not on the floor of the House of Commons but by the Treasury Select Committee. You can find information on its inquiry into the 2020 budget here: https://committees.parliament.uk/work/139/spring-budget-2020/

that, if passed, are sent to the Queen for Royal Assent, after which they become Acts of Parliament.[230] Secondary legislation consists of the regulations, rules, orders etc which are made, usually by ministers, using powers given to them in an act. The Health and Safety at Work Act 1974 is a good example of an act that gives ministers extensive powers to make secondary legislation. The act itself lays down broad obligations on employers to provide safe work places but the large volume of detailed health and safety legislation – for example the *Control of Substances Hazardous to Health (COSHH) Regulations* – has been made by ministers using powers given to them by the parent act. Secondary legislation also comes in a number of other forms such as schemes, byelaws, directions and statutory codes of practice. The *Highway Code* is a good example of the last of these.[231]

Public Bills and Private Bills (Primary Legislation)

Primary legislation falls into two main types: Public Bills and Private Bills. Private Bills are bills promoted by individuals or organisations outside Parliament. For example, a local authority or a private company may be seeking to obtain powers specific to itself. Public Bills, on the other hand, when they become acts, apply to everyone in the country in the same way.[232] Private Bills are much rarer than they once were because such powers can now often be granted via secondary legislation. The process by which such bills go through Parliament is much more complex and time-consuming than that which applies to Public Bills. An example of a Private Bill going through Parliament at the time of writing is the 'Highgate Cemetery Bill' which *authorise(s) the (Highgate Cemetery) Trust to extinguish rights of burial in grave spaces,*

---

[230] The only other form of primary legislation are Orders-in-Council made under the Royal Prerogative.

[231] The original Highway Code was made by ministers using powers given to them in the Road Traffic Act 1930.

[232] Although they may specify to which of the four constituent parts of the UK they apply.

and to disturb and reinter human remains in graves in order to increase the space for further interments in such graves and improve Highgate Cemetery....[233]

Some bills have characteristics of both Public and Private Bills. These are known as 'Hybrid Bills'. Hybrid Bills are those which affect the general interest but which have an impact upon certain individuals or organisations in a significantly greater way than upon others. Their parliamentary process is more like that of a Public Bill than a Private Bill but there is additional scrutiny than there would be for a Public Bill. They tend to be used in respect of major transport building projects such as Crossrail and High Speed 2. Because Private Bills and Hybrid Bills have fewer restrictions placed on them in terms of how long they can spend going through Parliament, for some such bills this can take many years.

Most bills that come before Parliament are however Public Bills. The majority of Public Bills that are passed by Parliament are part of the government's legislative programme. At the State Opening of Parliament the Queen announces the major bills that the government is planning to bring before Parliament in the coming session. The government is not then obliged to bring forward any particular bill, nor is it restricted only to presenting bills that were mentioned in the Queen's Speech, but the Speech is a helpful guide to what bills are likely to go through Parliament in the coming session.

Bills – the Pre-Parliamentary Process

It's important to realise that a government bill's initial introduction to Parliament doesn't mark the beginning of that bill's life since for a considerable time before it is introduced to Parliament it will have undergone a gestation period in government.[234] We might refer to this as the 'pre-parliamentary'

---

[233] https://bills.parliament.uk/bills/2518

[234] Some bills, such as the Coronavirus Bill 2020, are introduced at very short notice in response to unforeseen events taking place.

stage of a bill's life. During this time the bill will be put together by civil servants, including departmental lawyers and those who work in the Office of the Parliamentary Counsel who carry out the actual drafting. When developing and drafting the bill, ministers and officials will have to consider many issues – for example, the bill's impact on business and other sectors, whether there are any devolution or human rights issues, and whether the bill has any impact on the personal interests and prerogatives of the Queen. (We discussed Queen's Consent in chapter one.)

Although a particular bill may be the exclusive product of one department's ministers and civil servants, it won't be allowed to proceed to Parliament without the consent of ministers from other departments. In particular those on the 'Parliamentary Business and Legislation' Cabinet Committee will have to agree for the bill to be included in the Queen's Speech (although the final decision on this is the Cabinet's) and will also have to agree the final draft of the bill before it is brought to Parliament. There will also be a Cabinet Committee whose remit covers the policy area from which the bill emanates and this committee will have to clear the bill before it is introduced in Parliament. This is all part of the collective decision-making processes of government.

There may be opportunities during this pre-parliamentary period for people outside of government to make comments on and therefore, potentially, have some influence on the content of the bill. The government might publish a Green Paper or a White Paper on a proposed piece of legislation. The former is a consultation document in which the government invites people to comment on a proposed bill. A White Paper is a clearer statement about the contents of a bill. These days, fewer Green Papers are published than was once the case, in part because White Papers also now often invite comments on government proposals.[235] Additionally, the government may publish a bill in draft, prior to the publication of the actual bill itself. In this case, a select committee of Parliament will examine the contents of the bill. As part

---

[235] An example of a pre-legislative White Paper in which comments were invited would be the 'Online Harms White Paper 2019'.
https://www.gov.uk/government/consultations/online-harms-white-paper

of its scrutiny of the bill the committee will invite people to provide written and oral evidence on the bill, in much the same way as they would on any other inquiry they hold. (This is described in some detail in the section below on select committees.) At the end of the process the committee will make some recommendations about the content of the bill, which ministers may or may not take on board.[236]

Those who wish to influence the content of legislation should certainly consider the opportunities that this pre-parliamentary process might offer. As we describe below, bills can be amended as they progress through the two Houses of Parliament, but the reality is that it is going to be difficult to get changes made to a bill which ministers aren't happy to accept. Thus trying to influence them, and the officials who work for them, during the pre-parliamentary stage might prove to be more fruitful.

Private Members' Bills

Those bills that are not the government's are called Private Members' Bills. (These are Public Bills and shouldn't be confused with Private Bills which were mentioned above.) As their name suggests, these are bills brought before Parliament by individual MPs or peers who are backbenchers. The substantial majority of bills that are presented to Parliament are Private Members' Bills (283 of the 334 Public Bills in the 2020-21 session of Parliament) but few of them become law (seven of the 283 in 2020-21).[237] There are various forms of Private Members' Bills – three that start their lives in the Commons and one in the Lords: Ballot Bills, Ten Minute Rule Bills, Presentation Bills and House of Lords Private Members' Bills. MPs and peers who propose them know that it is relatively unusual for such bills to become acts and often introduce them more to gain

---

[236] An example of a draft bill would be the 'Draft Building Safety Bill 2020'. https://www.gov.uk/government/publications/draft-building-safety-bill

[237] The number of successful Private Members' Bills during the 2019-21 session was lower than usual because the Covid pandemic limited the amount of time available for consideration of such legislation.

publicity for a particular issue than as a genuine attempt to change the law. When either House is sitting on a Friday, it is almost always Private Members' Bills that it will be considering. Such bills would not normally be considered on other days of the week.

The majority of successful Private Members' Bills are 'Ballot Bills'. Soon after the start of the new parliamentary session, a ballot is held of those MPs who would like to introduce a Ballot Bill. The 20 MPs whose names are drawn 'out of the hat' then have the opportunity to pilot a bill through Parliament.[238] As most MPs won't have given much thought to the issue that they would like their bill to tackle (given that there's only about a one in twenty chance of their name being pulled out of the hat), there will be plenty of lobby and pressure groups on hand to make helpful suggestions. Each of the first seven on the list will be guaranteed debate time on a particular sitting Friday.

In 2019-21, all of the seven Private Members' Bills that became law were Ballot Bills. That two of these bills came eleventh and fifteenth on the list demonstrates that how high up in the ballot a particular bill is drawn is not the only factor in determining its chances of success. Because so little time is given to Private Members' Bills, if a particular bill is not near the top of the list it is less likely that there will be time for it to be considered. But just as important are two other factors: the degree of opposition to the bill and whether the government is supportive. If the government agrees with what the bill is trying to achieve then it may give up some of its own time on the floor of the House to allow the bill to be considered. But, if there is organised opposition to the bill, it will be difficult for it to proceed. There are a large number of parliamentary devices at the disposal of the opponents of a Private Members' Bill which can be used to frustrate its passage through

---

[238] Rather than actually being drawn out of a hat, the draw is more like a tombola at a village fair. You can see the June 2017 draw being made here: https://www.bbc.co.uk/news/av/uk-politics-40441539

Parliament. Under the slightly arcane rules for Private Members' Bills, debate does not end until everyone who wishes to speak has spoken. And given that there are no time limits on speeches, opponents of the bill can keep on talking till time runs out, unless 100 or more MPs support a closure motion to end the debate.

Ten Minute Rule Bills, Presentation Bills and Private Members' Bills that start their parliamentary passage in the Lords are normally very unlikely to pass unless there is almost no opposition to them in either House. Because they can only be considered in the Commons once the Ballot Bills have been dealt with on any particular Friday, it means that they can only pass if there is no debate i.e. if there is no opposition at all to the bill. All it takes is for one MP to shout 'object' when a bill's title is read out in advance of the second reading for the bill to fall – and there are a handful of MPs who, for whatever reason, regularly object to bills in this way. There was particular controversy in June 2018 when the Conservative MP Christopher Chope objected to the 'Upskirting Bill' (properly known as the 'Voyeurism (Offences) Bill'). Chope robustly defended his actions along the lines of the bill not being properly scrutinised if it went through 'on the nod' but that explanation didn't satisfy many – including, the then Prime Minister Theresa May, whose government then introduced its own similar legislation which rapidly became law. As it's by no means certain that the Private Members' Bill would have had time to pass, by objecting to it Chope perhaps helped bring about the change in the law.

So, successful Private Members' Bills usually need to be fairly non-controversial. But this has not always been the case. In the 1960s some important social legislation was passed which had been introduced to Parliament in the form of Private Members' Bills. The most famous example is the 1967 Abortion Act which, if it didn't technically legalise abortions, provided for the first time a legal defence for those carrying them out.[239] This was a

---

[239] The act applied to England, Scotland and Wales but not to Northern Ireland.

Private Members' Bill brought before Parliament by a young Liberal MP, David Steel. Other Private Members' Bills around this time were the 1965 Murder (Abolition of Death Penalty) Act which abolished the death penalty for murder (but left it in place for some other crimes such as high treason) and the 1969 Divorce Reform Act, which made obtaining a divorce easier. In all of these examples, however, it is fair to say that they would probably not have become law without the support of Harold Wilson's Labour Government.

In contrast, it is very unusual for a government bill to be defeated in the House of Commons. The last example was in 1986 when the Shops Bill, which would have deregulated Sunday trading to some degree, was defeated by an 'unholy alliance' of 'Keep Sunday Special' Conservatives and Labour MPs who wanted to protect workers' rights.[240] It is more common, but still unusual, for a bill to be rejected by the House of Lords, it most recently happening during the 2006-7 session when the Lords rejected the Fraud (Trials Without a Jury) Bill. Thus the large majority of government bills are passed by Parliament. If a government bill doesn't successfully pass during a particular session it's likely to be because it ran out of time. But given that determining when a particular session should come to an end is, as we have seen, largely a matter for the government, it is a government choice to let such bills fall. For example, when Parliament was prorogued at the end of the 2017-19 session, nine government bills fell. But it was the government's decision to prorogue Parliament at that point. Where government will have less control however is when a Parliament is coming to end before a general election. Given that the maximum length of a Parliament is, as we have seen, set in law at five years, governments are often under some pressure to get their legislation through Parliament in the days prior to the dissolution of Parliament. This is often referred to as the 'wash up' period.

---

[240] Although the Shops Bill was the last government bill actually to be defeated in the Commons, a number of bills since then have been withdrawn by government to avoid either an obvious defeat or, in the example of the House of Lords Bill 2012, a long drawn out battle.

During this time deals may need to be done with opposition parties in both Houses if the legislation is to pass.

Whilst it's true that the Commons and the Lords rarely reject government bills outright, that doesn't mean that the parliamentary passage of a bill is a mere formality. This is because either House may try to make amendments to the bill. When the government has a majority in the Commons, successful amendments to government bills (other than those which the government itself is making) are rare but in the Lords they are much more likely to pass.

Let's look at how a bill proceeds through Parliament.

The Passage of a Public Bill through Parliament

Bills may be introduced in the Commons or the Lords. More controversial legislation and all financial legislation starts in the Commons and it is worth remembering that the Parliament Acts cannot be used on bills that start in the House of Lords. But a good number of bills do start their parliamentary passage in the Lords if only to even out the legislative workload of both Houses across the session. Let's assume here that a particular bill is starting its parliamentary passage in the Commons.

The Commons

The first reading of the bill is a formality. All that happens is that the short title[241] of the bill is read out by one of the clerks, the

---

[241] Bills have both short titles and long titles. For example the short title of a bill introduced in 2020 was the Environment Bill. Its long title was: "A Bill to make provision about targets, plans and policies for improving the natural environment; for statements and reports about environmental protection; for the Office for Environmental Protection; about waste and resource efficiency; about air quality; for the recall of products that fail to meet environmental standards; about water; about nature and biodiversity; for conservation covenants; about the regulation of chemicals; and for connected purposes." The long title is also called the 'scope' and any amendments to the bill that aren't 'in scope' will almost certainly be ruled out by the clerks or, ultimately, by the Speaker.

Speaker asks a minister for a date for the bill's second reading and that's it. Indeed the bill hasn't even usually been published at this point. The next stage is the second reading, usually a couple of weeks later, before which the bill will have been published. This is the first time that MPs will have had an opportunity to debate the contents of the bill. The second reading debate will be a wide-ranging one on the principles of the bill. The House is not discussing the details at this stage but rather whether it agrees to the broad principles behind the bill. On a major bill the second reading will be the main item of business on any particular day. One of the ministers in the department leading on the bill will open the debate in the Commons, proposing that *the bill be now read a second time*. A number of MPs will be invited to speak on the bill, including from the opposition frontbench, before another minister in the department makes the closing speech. The House will then vote on the bill. Following the second reading, the Commons may have to vote on a Money Resolution specifically to authorise those parts of the bill that make a significant charge on public funds, or on a Ways and Means Resolution which is needed to authorise the raising of taxes or other charges.

Following the passing of a government bill at second reading there will very often be a Programme Motion put before the Commons. This will set out a strict timetable for consideration of the remaining stages of the bill in the Commons. This stops MPs filibustering a government bill in the way they can, as we have seen, with a Private Members' Bill.[242] Whilst the programming of bills may help ministers get their bills through Parliament in the quickest possible time, it does very much limit the scrutiny of bills by MPs and often means that substantial parts of government bills are never properly scrutinised by the House of Commons.

Next the bill proceeds to its committee stage, which will usually take one of two forms. Where the bill has been deemed by the government, in consultation with the opposition, to be a

---

[242] We saw earlier how the failure to secure a Programme Motion on the House of Lords Reform Bill led, in effect, to the scuppering of that bill in July 2012.

'constitutional bill' (like for example the 2017 EU Withdrawal Bill), the committee stage would normally take place on the floor of the House of Commons. The government also agrees with the opposition which parts of the annual Finance Bill should have their committee stage on the floor of the House. When the House is sitting in this way it is known as 'Committee of the Whole House'.[243] In other words, all MPs are members of the committee, or, strictly speaking, all but the Speaker are members as the Speaker doesn't preside over the House when it's in committee. His role in committee is played by the Chairman of Ways and Means who is the senior deputy Speaker. She doesn't sit in the Speaker's chair when the House is in committee but in one of the clerks' seats just in front of the Speaker's chair.[244] The other sign that the House is in committee is that the Mace, representing the Monarch, will now be hanging under the table of the House rather than lying on top of it. Prior to the House going into committee the Serjeant at Arms will have entered the House and moved the Mace from above to below the table.

Most bills however will be referred to a 'public bill committee' made up of, typically, 18 members drawn from both sides of the House according to the balance of the parties on the floor of the House.[245] The committee will usually include a couple of ministers and a whip. The first stage of the public bill committee process is for the committee to undertake a scrutiny of the bill not unlike a select committee hearing. Witnesses will be called before the committee to give evidence on the bill. These will include people from within and

---

[243] There are other reasons why a bill might be considered by Committee of the Whole House, for example if the bill is being rushed through very quickly.

[244] During the Covid pandemic, for social distancing reasons, the Deputy Speaker did sit in the Speaker's chair during Committee of the Whole House.

[245] Although, following the 2017 election at which Theresa May's government lost its majority, it managed to hold onto its majorities on public bill committees by the simple method of putting a motion down before the House suggesting that this be the case. With the support of the DUP, the motion was passed.

from outside government. Written evidence will also be called for. At some point in the proceedings, the minister, who up to this point will have been scrutinising the witnesses with the other committee members, will give evidence him- or herself. These evidence-taking sessions inform the committee for the second part of the committee stage process which is to follow. Before the introduction of public bill committees during the 2006-7 session, these legislative committees were known as 'standing committees' (a confusing title given that, as with public bill committees, they were created and disbanded for specific bills). Standing committees undertook what has now become the second stage of the public bill process: a line-by-line scrutiny of the bill.

All bills, whether or not they have been subject to the 'stage one' scrutiny, have their clauses (which are renamed 'sections' when the bill becomes an act) debated and voted on by the committee.[246] These debates are known as 'stand part' debates as MPs are deciding whether any particular clause should stand part of the bill. Committee members will also table amendments which, if accepted for debate by the committee chair (who is a backbench MP playing in the committee a role similar to that played by the Speaker on the floor of the House), will also be voted on. 'Divisions' take place in committees though, unlike on the floor of the House, MPs simply say 'aye' or 'no' when their name is called out. This is the stage of the bill most likely to be severely truncated as a result of the programme motion. On many government bills a large proportion of the clauses will not have been discussed at all. Given that the government has a majority on the committee (assuming it has one on the floor of the House), defeats for the government in committee will be rare. That doesn't mean, however, that government bills are rarely amended in committee because it's not at all unusual for ministers to want to amend their own legislation, for whatever reason, whilst it's progressing through Parliament.

---

[246] There is no 'part one' of the public bill process for Private Members' Bills, nor for bills that have come to the Commons from the Lords, nor for bills that have their committee stage on the floor of the House of Commons.

When the bill has finished its committee stage it returns to the floor of the House of Commons for the report (or consideration) stage. This is a further opportunity for the House to amend the bill. There may be many amendments tabled and it's up to the Speaker to decide which are debated. As at the committee stage the government may wish to amend its own legislation and, if so, the expectation will be that the Speaker will select those amendments in the name of a minister. He will also likely accept for debate an amendment in the name of the Leader of the Opposition but many will be rejected. At the end of the day, this is the Speaker's decision and he doesn't have to give his reasons as to why he selected this rather than that amendment.

Report stage is followed, usually immediately, by the bill's third reading. This is the final review of the bill as, potentially, amended in committee or at report. There will be a short debate and a vote, after which the bill, if passed, will be sent to the House of Lords. However, until recently, there was for some bills an extra stage in the parliamentary process between report and third reading: English Votes for English Laws

English Votes for English Laws

Following the Scottish independence referendum 2014, Prime Minister David Cameron soon announced a change to the legislative process that his government wished to make. This concerned how the UK Parliament dealt with legislation that only affected England. As an example, because education is a policy matter that is almost entirely devolved to Scotland, Wales and Northern Ireland (about which more in chapter eight), when the UK Parliament is considering legislation to do with education, it's highly likely that the legislation will affect schools or other education establishments in England only. However, as bills pass through the House of Commons, all MPs vote on them – including those from Scotland, Wales and Northern Ireland. This, it could be argued, was 'unfair' on the English who had no say over education policy in those other parts of the UK. Thus an extra stage, known as 'English Votes for English Laws' (EVEL), was added to the legislative process for such bills in the Commons. Under this system, after the report stage, only MPs representing English constituencies had a vote on the bill (or on those parts of the bill that were specific to England). When they were discussing the bill at this stage they were known as the 'English Grand Committee'.

The committee met in the Commons chamber, and MPs from Scotland, Wales and Northern Ireland had the right to be present, but not to vote. MPs from English constituencies had the right at this stage to vote the bill down. Assuming that didn't happen, then the bill would still need to be passed at the final stage of the parliamentary process i.e. third reading. It's no great surprise that the English Grand Committee actually never voted down a bill that the House as a whole had passed at second reading. Why is that not surprising? Because, ever since EVEL was introduced in 2015, UK Governments had for most of the time enjoyed not only a majority of seats across the UK but also in England.[247] Only if the UK ever again had a government reliant on, say, seats in Scotland and Wales for its majority at Westminster, might EVEL have become more important. In the past there had been Labour governments who were only in power because of the seats the party won in Scotland and Wales but this seemed unlikely to occur again in the immediate future given the collapse of support for the Labour Party in Scotland. This may then have been part of the reason why EVEL was abolished in July 2021. EVEL had actually been suspended during the Covid pandemic in order to simplify the legislative process and, given what little effect it had had on the legislative process prior to the pandemic, Boris Johnson's government felt that it wouldn't be missed. And at a time when the union was coming under threat from the growth of support for independence in Scotland, getting rid of it might actually help the government promote the idea of the UK Parliament working *for*

---

[247] With the exception of Theresa May's government after the 2017 election which had a majority of English seats but not a majority of UK seats.

every part of the UK and every party in the UK. [248]

As an aside, it's worth considering for a moment how simple it was to create and then to abolish the EVEL procedure. All it took was a simple majority vote in the House of Commons to amend the relevant standing orders of the Commons. The procedure wasn't even introduced and repealed by an Act of Parliament. But EVEL was an important constitutional change denying, as it did, the right of some MPs (the non-English ones) to vote at a particular stage of a bill's passage through the House of Commons. Can you imagine something similar happening, for example, in the United States? Almost certainly the view on the other side of the Atlantic would be that to deny the vote to some members of Congress would, as a minimum, require an Act of Congress and more likely a change to the US Constitution. But here in the UK this important constitutional change was made after a one hour debate in the Commons on a motion that went through 'on the nod' i.e. without a formal division.[249]

The Lords

Having been passed by the Commons, the bill will move to the House of Lords for consideration. The passage of a bill through the Lords is similar in many respects but differs from the Commons process in three main ways.

First, at the second reading the Lords will debate, but will rarely vote on, the bill. This is particularly likely if the bill is enacting a manifesto commitment.[250] Second, at the committee stage all members of the Lords are technically members of the committee. Sometimes the committee stage will be taken on the

---

[248] Michael Gove, quoted in the Daily Record.
https://www.dailyrecord.co.uk/news/politics/support-union-fraying-warns-expert-24330199

[249] https://hansard.parliament.uk/Commons/2021-07-13/debates/97CC04FD-5886-4C37-8877-F6A599A0C7CF/EnglishVotesForEnglishLaws

[250] This is due to the Salisbury Convention described above.

floor of the House, but often the bill will be considered by a Grand Committee meeting in the Moses Room, which is just off the lobby at the entrance to the Lords (so called due to the large painting hanging on one of its walls of Moses being handed the 10 commandments on Mount Sinai.) But even if the committee stage takes place in the Moses Room, every peer can table amendments and has a vote. At the Lords committee stage, given that any proposed amendment can be considered and that debate on amendments is unrestricted, this stage can be considerably longer than its counterpart in the Commons. But if the committee is meeting in the Moses Room (Grand Committee), the only amendments that can be made are those accepted unanimously. Any that are contested would have to be retabled for consideration at the report stage. Third, at the third reading, unlike in the Commons, the Lords can amend a bill provided the issue has not already been voted on at an earlier stage. Amendments at this stage in the Lords are often used to clarify certain aspects of the bill or to give the government an opportunity to make amendments to the bill that it has promised earlier in the parliamentary process. But as at second reading, a vote on the bill in its entirety is rare.

Ping Pong

Once a bill has completed its stages in the second House, it's highly likely that it will be different to how it looked when it left the first House. For a bill to be presented to the Monarch for Royal Assent it needs to have been agreed in the same form by both Houses. So, if a bill that started its parliamentary passage in the Commons is amended by the Lords, it must go back to the Commons for their Lordships' amendments to be considered. The Commons may agree with the amendments, in which case the bill can go to the Monarch for Royal Assent. But if the Commons either reject any of the amendments, or further amend the Lords' amendments, they will then send the bill back to the Lords for the Lords to consider why the Commons has not accepted their amendments and whether or not to insist on them again. If they do insist on them, then once again the bill will return to the

Commons. This shuttling of a bill between the two Houses has become known as parliamentary 'ping pong'.

Ping pong will continue until agreement is reached and the bill can be sent to the Monarch for Royal Assent. If this is impossible, it may be that 'double insistence' is reached, in which case the bill is lost. Double insistence is when one House twice insists on an amendment which the other House twice insists it disagrees with it. If this happens, which is very unusual, the whole bill is lost. But if the bill keeps being amended in both Houses, ping pong can go on until the end of the parliamentary session when, in normal circumstances, it would be lost. This would be very unusual though because the Lords ping ponging a bill all the way to the end of the session, thereby killing it off, is not constitutionally really any different to them voting a bill down in its entirety at second or third reading which, as we've seen, the Lords will very rarely do. This did, however, happen to the Hunting Bill which eventually became an act in 2004. This bill was never rejected outright by the Lords. Rather, they removed from the bill the crucial words that a person *commits an offence if he hunts a wild mammal with a dog* and replaced them with wording that would allow hunting with dogs to continue under a licensing scheme. For two successive sessions the bill ping ponged between the two Houses until, eventually, the government was able to use the Parliament Acts to override what would otherwise have been a Lords' veto. It is therefore a fact that the Lords never actually voted down the Hunting Bill. Rather, they twice passed the bill, albeit a version of it which was unacceptable to the Commons.

Financial Privilege

The 1911 Parliament Act removed the power of the House of Lords to reject or even amend a money bill. But what is the power of the Lords over the financial aspects of legislation which has not been designated by the Speaker of the Commons as a money bill? As we saw earlier, the Commons' supremacy over financial matters dates back to resolutions passed in the 17th century and occasionally the Commons will invoke this supremacy, in effect to ignore amendments to legislation made by the Lords which have financial implications. The Commons often choose to waive their financial privileges, but not always.

Carry Over

Parliament's ability to amend bills is strengthened by the fact that a bill usually has to complete its parliamentary passage in both Houses before the end of the parliamentary session. However, in 2002 the parliamentary process changed in this respect to allow government bills that were first introduced in the House of Commons, with the approval of Parliament, to be carried over from one session to the next.[251] This was a controversial change as it removed the power of Parliament (and especially the Lords) to delay such bills until the end of the session, when traditionally they would have fallen. However, the passage of a bill is still time limited: usually to twelve months after its first reading in the Commons. So whilst the bill won't fall at the end of the session, it would fall 12 months after its first reading if it hadn't completed its parliamentary passage by then. However, the standing orders of the House of Commons do allow for the 'carry over motion' put before the House to extend the lifetime of a bill for a period longer than 12 months after its first reading, so long as the bill is passed by the end of the session into which it has been carried over. As an example, the carry over motion concerning the Environment Bill that was introduced in January 2020 required the bill to be passed within two years, rather than the usual one year after its first reading.[252] Thus the bill, having been carried over into the 2021-22 session, didn't complete its parliamentary passage until the autumn of 2021.

Royal Assent and Commencement

An act does not usually become the law of the land as soon as

---

[251] Although 'carry over' had been used before on an ad hoc basis, for example with the Financial Services and Markets Bill 1998-99.
[252] https://hansard.parliament.uk/Commons/2021-01-26/debates/8723DE1E-7E99-45D0-99DE-E97BD9C1E013/BusinessOfTheHouse(EnvironmentBillCarry-Over)

the bill is given Royal Assent. Rather, it comes into effect either on the time and date stated in the act (and different parts of the act could come into force at different times), or when a minister lays before Parliament the 'Commencement Order'. For this reason, some acts have never come into force. For example the Easter Act 1928, which would have fixed the date of Easter Sunday as the day after the second Saturday in April, has yet to come into force. (And it's unlikely that it ever will.)

Secondary Legislation

Secondary legislation may not be the most exciting part of the parliamentary process; however given that during the Covid pandemic most of the rules governing the various 'lockdowns' etc were based in secondary legislation, its importance has become apparent to many.

Secondary legislation consists of the regulations, rules and orders that are made, usually by ministers, using powers given to them in acts. It is also sometimes referred to as 'delegated legislation' or 'subordinate legislation'. These are all the same thing. Sometimes secondary legislation is in the form of 'Statutory Instruments' where the Statutory Instruments Act 1946 established certain procedural requirements. Although it is a general 'rule' that primary legislation should be amended only by primary legislation, secondary legislation can also be used to amend primary legislation. It is not that unusual or controversial to find an act that contains powers to make secondary legislation to amend the same act. What is more controversial, however, is where primary legislation contains powers to make secondary legislation to amend other acts. Such powers are sometimes referred to as 'Henry VIII powers'.[253] The EU (Withdrawal) Act 2018 for example gives considerable powers to ministers to make significant changes to acts following the UK's departure from the

---

[253] These powers derive their name from The Statute of Proclamations of 1539, which gave Henry VIII the right to pass laws directly, bypassing Parliament.

EU.[254]

It is important to emphasise that it is ministers, not Parliament, who make secondary legislation. Ministers can make secondary legislation only insofar as the parent act gives them the powers to do so. If ministers make secondary legislation outside the scope of the powers given in the act, they are acting *ultra vires* (beyond their powers) and risk the courts deciding that the legislation is unlawful. As well as having to be *intra vires* (in other words *within the powers* set out in the act), all secondary legislation must also be compatible with the European Convention on Human Rights (ECHR). (It's perhaps worth mentioning again that the UK's adherence to the ECHR continues following its departure from the EU.) If secondary legislation is incompatible with the ECHR, it again risks being struck down in the courts (unlike primary legislation where, as we have seen, all the judges can do is make a 'declaration of incompatibility').

Parliamentary Scrutiny

Secondary legislation may be scrutinised in Parliament by the Joint Committee on Statutory Instruments, the Select Committee on Statutory Instruments and the Secondary Legislation Scrutiny Committee. The first committee is a joint committee of the Commons and Lords, which looks specifically at drafting issues and whether the instrument is *intra vires*. The second is a committee of the House of Commons only, which considers instruments that do not require House of Lords approval: usually financial instruments. The third is a House of Lords committee, which considers the merits of all secondary legislation laid before either House where parliamentary approval is required before the legislation can become law.

Parliamentary Approval

Not all secondary legislation requires parliamentary approval. Whether or not it does depends on what the parent act says. Well

---

[254] https://www.legislation.gov.uk/ukpga/2018/16/contents/enacted

over 2000 pieces of secondary legislation become law every year, the large majority of which don't require any parliamentary approval. Many orders made by ministers are fairly uncontroversial – for example Traffic Orders to make changes to vehicular access to certain roads to allow for roadworks etc. Few would argue that there ought to be a vote in Parliament before such an order is made.

However, if parliamentary approval is required, then the legislation (or 'instrument') will be subject to either the 'negative resolution procedure' or the 'affirmative resolution procedure'. In the former case, which represent about 80% of those instruments where the act does require a parliamentary procedure, the instrument is 'made' by the minister signing it, after which it is laid before Parliament for a particular period of time (usually three weeks) at the end of which it becomes law unless it has been successfully 'prayed against' in either House of Parliament. To pray against an instrument means that a member has put down a resolution before the House for the instrument to be 'annulled'. It is quite rare for this to happen and it is almost unheard of for an instrument to be successfully prayed against. This is because (a) the government is largely in control of the timetable in the Commons and therefore time will rarely be found to hold such a debate and vote; (b) because if such a vote does take place in the Commons, the government usually has sufficient votes to defeat the motion and (c) in the House of Lords, peers will be very cautious about voting down secondary legislation for the same reasons as to why they rarely vote down primary legislation which we discussed earlier. If either House did however vote the instrument down after it had come into force, it would immediately be annulled. In normal circumstances each House has up to 40 days to vote the legislation down. The 40 day period does not run when Parliament is dissolved, prorogued, or during a period when both Houses are adjourned for more than four days.

In the case of affirmative resolution, which represents about 20% of those instruments where the act requires a parliamentary procedure, the instrument will usually be laid before Parliament *in draft* and cannot normally become law until both Houses have voted on it. In the Commons, debates on annulling or approving secondary legislation usually take place in one of the Delegated Legislation Committees, although any votes to annul or approve are taken on the floor of the House. In the Lords, debates usually take place on the floor of the House.

Some acts do however allow an exception to the requirement that both Houses vote in favour of a regulation before it comes into force. This was relevant to the regulations made by ministers during the Covid pandemic. The majority of the regulations concerning lockdowns, curfews, tiers, roadmaps etc were made by ministers using powers given to them by the 'Public Health (Control of Disease) Act 1984' which allows for regulations to be made under what's called the 'made affirmative' procedure.[255] Sometimes ministers need to act quickly: if they announced new regulations that would only come into force following a debate and vote in both Houses of Parliament, that would delay their implementation. In the case of Covid, such delays could of course be problematic if people behaved in unsafe ways prior to the new regulations coming into force. So on many occasions during the pandemic ministers introduced 'made affirmative' regulations. In other words, the regulations were still subject to a vote in both Houses but they came into force *before* those votes took place. This was the case for example with the lockdown regulations of January 2021.[256] It is quite controversial for ministers to use the 'made affirmative' procedure and they are required formally to notify the Speakers of both Houses of their use and explain to them why there is a need for such urgency. In response to the number of MPs, in particular on the government's own backbenches, who were unhappy about the use of this procedure, ministers did say that where possible they would hold votes prior to new regulations coming into force and this did happen before

---

[255] https://www.legislation.gov.uk/ukpga/1984/22

[256] https://www.legislation.gov.uk/uksi/2021/8/made

the 'roadmap' regulations came into force in March 2021.[257]

An issue for parliamentary control of secondary legislation is that, unlike with bills, such legislation can't be amended. Parliament has no power other than to accept or reject the legislation outright. The reality however is that Parliament very rarely votes down secondary legislation. The last time that a negative resolution instrument was annulled by the Lords was in 2000 and by the Commons in 1979. The most recent example of the Lords voting down an affirmative instrument was in 2012 whilst in the Commons it was in 1978. Given that thousands of such instruments become law each year, the percentage that are voted down is almost infinitesimally small.

For many years there has been some debate about whether there is a convention that the Lords should not, in normal circumstances, defeat secondary legislation. This debate came to a head in 2015 when the Lords passed a motion to delay, rather than to reject outright, a reform to the tax credits system which the then Chancellor, George Osborne, was attempting to bring in via secondary legislation. When the Lords voted to delay the legislation there were complaints from within government about this being 'unconstitutional' and even suggestions that the Lords should have had nothing to do with such legislation because it concerned 'money'. None of these were particularly convincing arguments but the issue did prompt the government to set up a review under the former Conservative Leader of the House of Lords, Lord Strathclyde, to look at whether the Lords' powers over secondary legislation ought to be formally limited. The review concluded that the Lords should be limited to being able to do no more than ask the Commons to *think again* about secondary legislation of which it disapproved.[258] But, rather than accept the recommendation, the government decided instead to let the issue drop.

---

[257] https://www.legislation.gov.uk/uksi/2021/364/pdfs/uksi_20210364_en.pdf

[258] https://www.gov.uk/government/publications/strathclyde-review-secondary-legislation-and-the-primacy-of-the-house-of-commons

One last point about secondary legislation: we discussed above the now-abandoned procedure known as 'English Votes for English Laws' (EVEL) in respect of bills that only affected England. EVEL also applied to secondary legislation, with MPs from English constituencies having the opportunity to block affirmative resolution instruments that only affected England. There wasn't a separate vote, as with primary legislation, but when the vote on the instrument took place, to pass, the instrument had to gain majorities of the votes of both MPs from English constituencies and all MPs. As with primary legislation, this process was discontinued in July 2021.

Parliamentary Questions

Parliamentary questions (PQs) are short questions that MPs and peers ask of government ministers. The questions and the answers given to them all appear in the official record of Parliament. The first recorded parliamentary question appears to have been asked in the House of Lords in 1721 with the first parliamentary question being asked in the Commons in 1835. Over time, the number of parliamentary questions asked by parliamentarians has increased substantially.

There are two main types of parliamentary question: oral questions, which ministers answer in each House during Question Time, and written questions, which are not asked in the House but the answers to which are printed in Hansard.

MPs and peers may ask a parliamentary question for several reasons. They may be trying to obtain information or to get information placed 'on the record'. They may be trying to demonstrate a personal interest in a particular matter or in an area of government business, or to keep up to date in an area of specialist interest. They may be raising a matter of concern to an interest or pressure group or a matter relevant to their constituency. Some parliamentary questions are part of a wider campaign to draw attention to a particular cause or to press for action. It is not unheard of for the person asking the question already to know the answer – they are just trying to get the minister to admit to it!

Some MPs and peers ask a lot of parliamentary questions; others ask few. Whilst it is tempting to use the numbers any particular MP or peer asks as a yardstick with which to measure how hard they work, this can be a little unfair. Those asking few parliamentary questions may be using other methods of holding government to account. And of course one group of parliamentarians – ministers – can't ask any parliamentary questions at all. Their job is to answer them!

MPs can ask questions only to ministers who have seats in the Commons and peers can ask questions only to those with seats in the Lords. A member may raise anything in a parliamentary question for which a minister is ministerially responsible. Although an MP is more likely to deal with an individual constituent's problem privately by writing to the minister concerned, individual cases are occasionally the subject of parliamentary questions – particularly if a member thinks a department has been slow or inefficient in dealing with the issue via correspondence. But, whatever may have prompted the question, the process involved requires ministers personally to account to Parliament for the work and conduct of their officials, and for the exercise of their own powers and responsibilities. So parliamentary questions are democratic accountability in action. Although most ministers will want to answer parliamentary questions in a timely and open way, there are some circumstances in which a minister may decline to give a full answer. The most common of these is where the cost of answering the parliamentary question would be above the 'disproportionate cost threshold'.

All questions in the House of Commons are asked of the most senior minister in the department concerned although they may be answered by any one of the ministers in the department.

Written Questions in the Commons

MPs send written questions electronically to the clerks in the

Table Office of the House of Commons. There are two types of written parliamentary question in the Commons – ordinary written questions and 'Named Day' questions. Although ordinary written questions have a date for earliest answer, the convention is that ministers should reply within a working week of that date. A Named Day question is one where the MP has specified the date for answer. This date may be no more than two days after the question has been published. These questions must receive an answer on the date specified, even if it is only a 'holding answer'.[259] While there is no limit to the number of parliamentary questions an MP may put down for ordinary written answer, MPs are restricted to asking a maximum of five Named Day questions per day.

Oral Questions in the Commons

Question Time is the first item on the agenda of the House of Commons from Monday to Thursday. It ends about an hour later irrespective of how many questions on the Order Paper have been reached. When Parliament is sitting, departmental ministers have to answer questions once every five weeks. On most days, one department will be answering questions for the full hour. But on Wednesdays, when the Prime Minister answers questions, the department preceding her has just half an hour of questions. Smaller departments and other bodies who answer questions (such as the House of Commons Commission) answer for shorter periods of time every fifth week.

When just one department is answering questions for the full hour, the first 45 minutes of the Question Time are taken up by the answering of parliamentary questions that MPs have asked in advance. Each MP is restricted to two such questions per day, and one oral question to any individual department per day. They may table oral questions to a department any time after the day when

---

[259] The usual 'holding answer' is: '*The department has indicated that it will not be possible to answer this question within the usual time period. An answer is being prepared and will be provided as soon as it is available*'.

that department's ministers last answered questions in the House. Although oral questions may therefore be tabled some weeks in advance of the actual Question Time, they will not be published until after 12.30, three sitting days before the Question Time, excluding Fridays. Because many more questions are tabled than are published, a computer 'shuffle' each day of all the oral parliamentary questions tabled produces a random list, usually of 25. It is therefore a matter of chance both whether an MP's question gets on to the Order Paper at all and, if it does, how high it appears in the order of questions.

The Speaker calls successively each MP in whose name a question appears on the Order Paper. The MP rises and asks the question by stating its number on the Order Paper. (The MP doesn't read out the text of the question because it is printed on the Order Paper, and time is saved by calling the number only.) MPs who are not present when their question is reached, and those whose questions are not reached, receive a written reply. It is unusual for all the questions in a particular Question Time to be answered, although when John Bercow became Speaker he made considerable efforts to have more questions answered than was the case under his predecessors. Sir Lindsay Hoyle has continued in the same vein.

After the minister has read out the prepared answer, the Speaker allows the MP who asked the question, and normally others from both sides of the House, to put supplementary (follow-up) questions to the minister. The scope of supplementary questions is limited only by the rule that they have to be linked to the original question. How many are asked, and who asks them, is entirely at the discretion of the Speaker. The Speaker will be conscious of the number of MPs who have approached him prior to the Question Time to ask whether he might perhaps call them to ask a supplementary question. He will also be noting how many members are bobbing up and down on the day, trying to catch his eye. (Remember - if the House is busy and an MP can't find a place to sit, they will not be called to speak.) In deciding who should actually be called to ask a 'supplementary', the Speaker will be taking into account a number of factors such as political balance, the constituency interests of MPs etc. These supplementary questions are then answered impromptu by the minister on the basis of briefing provided by his or her civil servants.

Topical Questions

For departments that answer for the full hour of Question Time, the last fifteen minutes are reserved for what are called topical questions. For those departments answering for shorter periods, topical questions will be asked and answered in a proportionately shorter period of time. This type of parliamentary question was introduced in 2007 to allow MPs to ask questions that are right up-to-date (the problem being that those questions asked in the first 45 minutes of the Question Time are, by definition, at least four days old by the time they are actually asked).

There is a separate shuffle for topical questions carried out at the same time as the shuffle for the questions asked in the first part of the Question Time. This produces a list of ten MPs. The crucial difference with 'topicals' though is that there is no actual question on the order paper – just the name of the MP.[260] Thus the MP can decide at the very last moment exactly what they want to ask. Whilst MPs who are members of the governing party will be unlikely to wish to catch out a minister and will therefore have usually told the minister in advance what their question is going to be, this is certainly not true of MPs sitting on the other side of the House.[261] And given that ministers in a department share out the

---

[260] The opening question is actually *to ask the Secretary of State if he/she will make a statement on his/her departmental responsibilities*. The Secretary of State briefly answers this question, addressing the major issues of the day. The MP who has this question will then ask a question on any area of the Secretary of State's departmental responsibilities.

[261] The author recalls one occasion when an opposition MP had clearly read something on their smartphone after the Question Time had actually started and decided to ask the minister about it. The minister, who wouldn't have been able to look at his own phone because he had been

answering of all the questions according to the portfolios that they hold in the department, sometimes a last second decision has to be made as to which minister will answer the question.[262]

Considerable care has to be taken by civil servants to provide their ministers with sufficient briefing to cover any topic that might come up without giving them so much that it becomes unusable. And whilst it may be very helpful knowing who is going to be asking the ten questions on the list, there will usually be some time for the Speaker to allow further topical questions to be asked by MPs who are not on the list. Thus ministers can potentially be asked by anyone about anything for which they are responsible.

Prime Minister's Questions

The first session of Prime Minister's Questions (PMQs) took place in July 1961 when Prime Minister Harold Macmillan faced questions from the Leader of the Opposition, Hugh Gaitskell and from other MPs. The Prime Minister now answers oral questions every Wednesday between 12 noon and 12.30. (Until Tony Blair became Prime Minister, PMQs had occurred twice a week, on Tuesdays and Thursdays, from 3.15 to 3.30.) A shuffle produces a list of 15 questions. Nearly always all of these will ask her to list her engagements for the day (only the first of which is printed).[263] Such questions allow the MP's supplementary question to be about any subject at all. And when, as usual, further supplementary questions are allowed by the Speaker, there is not

---

too busy answering earlier questions, not surprisingly struggled to provide a coherent answer.

[262] Consider topical questions to Foreign Office ministers who have portfolios based on different parts of the world. If the questioner decides to leave the name of the country to which they are referring to the very end of the question, the ministerial team will have no time at all to decide who is the correct minister to answer.

[263] The reason why these 'engagement' questions were first asked was to stop the Prime Minister, in advance of the Question Time, passing on a specific question to the relevant Cabinet minister to answer.

even a requirement for those questions to be on the same topic as the previous one. Thus the Prime Minister has to field a series of questions on any number of subjects, many of which she will have had no notice. The reason why it is 'many', rather than 'all', is because MPs asking questions to the Prime Minister from her own side of the House will very often have already informed her what their question is going to be. (This is also true of supplementary and, as mentioned, topical questions to ministers at departmental Question Times.) As John Bercow says in his autobiography:

> *Over recent decades there has been a growing and, to me, regrettable tendency for MPs to ask 'toady' questions, often supplied by the government whips' office, known to the Prime Minister in advance, and allowing the Member to reel off a list of achievements real or imagined.*[264]

The Prime Minister doesn't actually answer the engagement question, except for the first time that it is asked. Subsequently, MPs come straight in with their actual question. Those MPs whose names appear on the order paper are allowed one question, as are other MPs who, if there is time, the Speaker selects to ask a question. Additionally, the Leader of the Opposition is allowed to intervene six times and the leader of the 'third party' (currently the SNP) twice. In the past, Leaders of the Opposition tended to split their allocation of questions, perhaps with three near the start on one topic and three nearer the end on a different topic, but when Leader of the Opposition, David Cameron very often used all of his six questions at once, near the start of the Question Time, and this is a pattern that has generally continued ever since. In addition to the party leaders, the Speaker will also invite further questions from other MPs who are not on the list. John Bercow provides an interesting insight into how he decided who he would invite to ask supplementary questions when he explains that, as well as being successful in the shuffle:

---

[264] John Bercow. Unspeakable: The Autobiography p. 245. Orion.

there is a second method to 'get called' to ask a question. That is to 'bob'. In other words, Members not selected in the ballot can and do stand, usually at the start of the session and, if necessary, throughout it in order to try to 'catch the Speaker's eye' and be called to ask their question of the Prime Minister.

The established process is for the Speaker to alternate between the two sides of the House, so if there are two Opposition Members drawn immediately after each other in the ballot, I would look to call a government backbencher in between them. This is the concept of a 'free hit' – not an allotted space or booked spot, but a spontaneous opportunity to take part. Some weeks there are several such opportunities and other weeks there is none. How did I decide to whom to give a free hit? There is an internal arrangement whereby leaders of the smaller parties, namely the Liberal Democrats, DUP, Plaid Cymru and the Greens, are given a rotating slot because it is important to ensure that minority parties get a hearing. Once every four weeks, if there is time, one of them had the chance to put a question. Beyond that, the Speaker's office has a complete record of exactly how many times someone 'bobbing' has asked a question. As Speaker, I tried to ensure that everyone who 'bobbed' regularly had an opportunity and naturally I looked to call people who had a lower score. That was a big, but not the only, factor. If I knew that a Member wished to ask a question topical only for that week, I might call her or him. Similarly, a Member in whose constituency an atrocity, a tragedy or some other unwanted event had occurred and had tipped me off might find favour. I worked to achieve gender balance. If there were half a dozen free hits, there was no way on earth that I would call half a dozen men, unless no female Members were standing; likewise I sought to achieve an ethnic balance. It was important to try to accommodate Members from different parts of the country and from different intakes.

> *Just as importantly, I set out to ensure that dissident or maverick voices were heard. Often… I saw backbenchers standing whom I knew to be independent-minded, fearless and certain to ask a question of their own choosing – no one else's. Often such a question was critical of the government and unhelpful to the Prime Minister. So be it, was my attitude. It was no part of my role to seek to shield the PM from challenging enquiries and, if anything, it was my duty to give free-spirited backbenchers the best opportunity to raise their concerns with the leader of our country. I could not control the answers but I could at least give the free-spirited Members their chance…. My instinct was to give the blunt-speaking fraternity their say because, frankly, that should be what Parliament is about.*[265]

For some, PMQs is the highlight of the parliamentary week. For others it's a rather tedious Punch and Judy show that sheds little light on what the Prime Minister and her government are actually up to. It may be cult viewing in some countries but for many people in Britain it's a little embarrassing to watch their elected representatives behaving in the way they sometimes do at PMQs. But the party leaders themselves certainly take it very seriously. Their performances on a Wednesday certainly affect how they are perceived by other MPs, in particular those on the same benches as themselves. Whether their performances have any great effect on how the public perceive them is more debatable however. William Hague, who for four years sparred against Tony Blair at PMQs, provides a good illustration. Most people would say he regularly bested Tony Blair at PMQs after the 1997 election – often through his deft use of humour. But did it do him and his party any good? A net gain of one seat and another crushing defeat in 2001 suggests not. (One of Hague's particularly good jokes at Blair's expense was when the left wing Labour MP Ken Livingstone was battling with Blair's preferred choice, the former Secretary of State for Health, Frank Dobson, to be Labour's candidate for London Mayor in 2000. During the debate on the Queen's Speech in 1999, Hague amusingly

---

[265] Ibid. John Bercow p. 244

suggested a solution for Tony Blair's problems with Livingstone:

> *Why does he not split the job of mayor of London? The former Health Secretary can run as his 'day-mayor' and the hon. Member for Brent, East (Mr. Livingstone) can run as his 'night-mayor.)* [266]

Urgent Questions

Because the minimum period of notice for an oral question may not be appropriate in the case of an emergency or important unexpected development, any MP may apply to the Speaker for permission to ask an 'urgent question' of the responsible minister. An urgent question is therefore one which has not appeared on the Order Paper but which, in the Speaker's opinion, raises an urgent matter of public importance. Urgent questions can be asked of any department on any sitting day, usually being answered immediately after the normal Question Time or at 11am on Fridays. As well as urgent questions being asked about emergencies that have just arisen, the Speaker will sometimes grant an urgent question to an opposition spokesperson who thinks a minister is reluctant to come to the House to discuss an important current issue.

The number of urgent questions asked in the Commons increased dramatically after John Bercow became Speaker. In the last full session before he became Speaker, his predecessor had accepted just four.[267] By contrast, in the 10 years that he was Speaker, John Bercow accepted no fewer than 685.[268] His successor, whilst not accepting requests at quite the same rate, is still granting far more than Bercow's predecessors. The growth in number of urgent questions has added to the burden on ministers –

---

[266] https://hansard.parliament.uk/Commons/1999-11-17/debates/2f9db323-e1cd-46c2-a163-cce24cc5b19d/DebateOnTheAddress

[267] https://commonslibrary.parliament.uk/research-briefings/cbp-8344/

[268] Ibid John Bercow p.164

and therefore on the officials who work for them. But John Bercow defends his approach to this very robustly:

> *I was keen to grant decent applications from MPs to put Urgent Questions to ministers. Standing Orders of the House had long permitted such questions, but few applications appeared to have been made in recent years and, in the twelve months before my election to the Chair, only two had been granted by the Speaker. The urgency, the relevance, the topicality of our proceedings were gravely undermined by the absence of such questions. MPs who had such matters to raise were blogging, writing for newspapers or giving radio or TV interviews instead, sucking the life out of the chamber. Meanwhile, ministers were getting off scot-free. Instead of being questioned and held to account by the people's elected representatives, they were free either to say nothing at times of controversy or to take to the airwaves. Whichever they did, they were not answering to the House of Commons.*
>
> *I was determined to restore the basic and inviolable principle that government ministers – members of what we call the executive branch of our political system – must be accountable to the legislative branch, namely Parliament. By granting an Urgent Question, I was not saying that the government was wrong on an issue, though in some cases there was an implicit criticism of them for not volunteering to account to the House by offering an oral statement. It is not for the Speaker to pronounce whether the government or Opposition is right or wrong on a policy issue. Rather, I was simply ruling that the issue warranted the presence of a minister and the attention of the House that day.*[269]

---

[269] Ibid. John Bercow pp.145-146

Parliamentary Questions in the Hybrid Commons

The operation of the hybrid Commons during the Covid pandemic arguably affected parliamentary questions more than any other part of the parliamentary process. With the majority of MPs participating via Zoom it was impossible for the Speaker to call members to ask supplementary questions 'on the hoof'. Instead, 'call lists' of MPs who would be asking questions were drawn up ahead of any Question Time, urgent question or questions on a ministerial statement. At oral questions, lists of parliamentary questions would be drawn via the shuffle process as normal, but only the MP whose question had been selected would be able to ask a supplementary question. The only exception to this was that supplementary questions from the opposition frontbench and from the chairs of those select committees that scrutinise the departmental ministers who were being questioned, would also be allowed. But these wouldn't be spontaneous – they had to be added to the call list in advance of the Question Time. This all made life rather easier for ministers. Knowing who would be asking the questions and when made it easier to prepare the answers. It also made Question Times rather stilted compared to how they are in more normal times.

Parliamentary Questions in the House of Lords

Procedures for dealing with questions in the House of Lords are similar to those in the Commons, although there are differences in their form and in the way in which they are answered. Overall there are fewer questions asked in the House of Lords than in the House of Commons. However, while the number of oral questions is fixed (currently at sixteen a week), the number of questions for written answer, as in the Commons, has risen substantially in recent years.

Questions tabled in the Lords are asked of Her Majesty's Government rather than addressed to a particular minister or department. This is essentially because the most senior minister in a department isn't normally a member of the Lords – he or she is usually in the Commons. The process of written questions asked in the Lords is similar to that in the Commons, the main differences being that (i) there are no 'named day' questions in the Lords, (ii) by convention, ministers have two weeks to answer the question as opposed to one week in the Commons and (iii) peers are limited to asking six written questions per day.

Because questions in the Lords are asked of Her Majesty's Government, rather than of, say, a Secretary of State, there is no departmental rota for answering oral questions in the Lords. Instead four oral questions are asked on Mondays, Tuesdays, Wednesdays and Thursdays for 40 minutes at the start of each day.[270] The majority of these questions are chosen by a ballot held four weeks prior to the date for answer.[271] However there is also one topical question asked in the Lords on each Tuesday, Wednesday and Thursday. For these a separate ballot is held two working days previously.

There is an exception to the rule that questions in the Lords are asked of Her Majesty's Government and therefore there is no departmental rota of oral questions. Because in the latter part of the 2005 Parliament there were two Secretaries of State in the Lords, (Lord Adonis at Transport and Lord Mandelson at Business, Innovation and Skills), arrangements were introduced to allow them to have their own specific Question Time in the Lords. Questions were put down in a way similar to other oral questions in the Lords but were answered by each Secretary of State once a month during a fifteen minute Question Time.

---

[270] Oral questions in the Lords had traditionally lasted for 30 minutes; however the duration was increased to 40 minutes when the Lords was operating in hybrid form during the Covid pandemic. The Lords decided to stick with the 40 minute duration of oral questions after the proceedings of the House had largely returned to normal after the summer recess of 2021.

[271] Prior to the introduction of the hybrid Lords during the Covid pandemic, these four questions were selected on a first-come-first-served basis. In the hybrid Lords this process was abandoned and the balloting system introduced instead. Members later voted to keep the balloting system in the post-hybrid Lords.

When Labour lost office at the 2010 election these arrangements were no longer required. But they were restored, very briefly, after the 2019 general election when, as we have seen, Nicky Morgan, who had stepped down as an MP at the election, was nevertheless given a seat in the Lords and kept in her post as Secretary of State for Digital, Culture, Media and Sport. So the special departmental Question Time process in the Lords was reinstated for her. She made only a single appearance at one of these before her sacking but the process was reinstated once again, a year or so later, when Boris Johnson appointed Lord (David) Frost to his Cabinet to lead on the UK's post-Brexit negotiations with the EU. Frost only holds Minister of State rank, but because Frost is a full Cabinet minister, he has his own Question Time in the Lords like Morgan, Adonis and Mandelson before him.[272]

At Question Time each member who has put down an oral question rises when called upon by the clerk and *begs leave of the House to ask the question standing in my name on the Order Paper*. The minister (or government spokesperson) gives the prepared answer. Supplementary questions are then asked as they are in the Commons. As we have seen, the Lords is a 'self-regulating' chamber and therefore peers aren't called to ask supplementary questions by the Speaker. In the past, if two or more peers stood up to ask a 'supplementary' at the same time, the hope was that members would give way, leaving just one member standing. Whilst that may have happened most of the time, peers could sometimes rather stubbornly stay on their feet, trying to over-talk other members who were perhaps trying to do the same thing. In this situation it still wasn't the Speaker who intervened, but, rather, someone on the government frontbench – perhaps the Leader of the House of Lords.

This changed when, as in the Commons, the parliamentary

---

[272] These were increased to 30 minutes when the Lords was operating in hybrid form during the Covid pandemic. Again, the Lords decided to stick with this extended duration after the Lords had largely returned to normal.

questions procedure in the Lords had to adapt to the hybrid processes that were used during the Covid pandemic. Members would no longer spontaneously stand up to ask supplementary questions but rather, they would apply in advance to ask a supplementary question. This process was managed by the office of the government's Chief Whip in the Lords who, in discussion with the other parties and the Crossbenchers through the 'usual channels', would produce a 'Speaker's list' of 10 supplementary questions for each question put down in advance, similar to the call lists used in the Commons. Just before the summer recess of 2021, the Lords voted to maintain the use of Speaker's lists in the future, thereby bringing to an end the rather odd situation of members over-talking each other in a bid to ask a supplementary question.

Supplementary questions in the Lords tend to be longer and may range more widely than is usual in the Commons. Again though, the Lord Speaker wouldn't intervene to cut off a peer who has perhaps been going on too long. Rather, it will be the disapproving murmurs going round the red benches that will indicate to a noble member that they should probably stop talking.

Ten minutes are allowed for each question and, when this time is up, the Lord Speaker will move the House onto the next question. Thus all four oral questions on any particular day will be answered and there is therefore no need for an equivalent in the Lords of the Commons' practice where an oral question receives a written reply if it is not reached or called.

Private Notice Questions (PNQs) in the Lords are the equivalent of urgent questions in the Commons, allowing peers the opportunity to raise pressing matters on any sitting day. Whether a request to ask a PNQ is accepted is at the discretion of the Lord Speaker, whose decision is final. As in the Commons, PNQs are taken immediately after oral questions and supplementary questions can be asked. Very often, urgent questions that have been answered in the Commons will be answered again in the Lords later in the day.

Select Committees

Like parliamentary questions, select committees are a prominent part of the process by which Parliament scrutinises the work of government. This scrutiny doesn't take place on the floor of the House of Commons or the Lords but in the committee rooms in the Palace of Westminster or across the road in Portcullis House. Not all select committees are involved in the day-to-day scrutiny of government. Some concern themselves with 'domestic' parliamentary matters (Standards, Privileges, Finance and Services etc) or legislation (for example the Joint Committee on Statutory Instruments). Most of those in the House of Commons, however, are involved in the scrutiny of the work of government departments. These departmental select committees, as they are known, scrutinise the work not only of government departments, including their executive agencies, but also of the various non-ministerial departments, non-departmental public bodies and other public bodies for which that department is responsible. As the Standing Orders of the Commons say, the task of departmental select committees is to *examine the expenditure, administration and policy of the principal government departments ... and associated public bodies.*[273] As they were only created after the 1979 election, they are still a relatively recent innovation. But after their introduction select committees rapidly became an established feature of the parliamentary process.

There is broadly one Commons select committee for each government department although there are exceptions to this. There is no select committee that specifically scrutinises the work of the Cabinet Office. This is surprising considering this department now manages the UK's relations with the EU in the post-Brexit era. When Theresa May created the Department for Exiting the European Union (DexEU) after the 2016 referendum, a select committee was set up to scrutinise its work. When,

---

[273] Standing Order of the House of Commons No 152. https://publications.parliament.uk/pa/cm201919/cmstords/341/so_341_05 1119_web.pdf

following the UK's exit from the EU, this department was abolished, the 'Exiting the European Union' select committee was replaced by the 'Future Relations with the EU' select committee, carrying on in much the same way as its predecessor. However, when in January 2021 the UK exited from the post-Brexit transition period, this select committee was abolished. There is now therefore no select committee looking at this specific issue.[274] The government would argue that such work can be carried out by individual select committees such as those that look at agriculture, transport, international trade etc but this argument may not be entirely convincing. This development demonstrated clearly the government's control over the process of creating and abolishing select committees. In theory, it's down to the House as a whole to determine what select committees it has. But as we have seen in many other areas, if the government has a majority on the floor of the House it will usually get its own way on issues concerning the remits of select committees.

There are other exceptions to the rule of there being one select committee for each government department. First, there is a separate Science & Technology select committee. This committee, which had quite a high profile during the Covid pandemic, scrutinises the work of the Government Office for Science (GOS) and its current head, Sir Patrick Vallance, even though the GOS sits within the wider Department of Business, Energy, Innovation and Skills (BEIS). Second, there continue to be separate Foreign Affairs and International Development select committees despite the merger of the Foreign & Commonwealth Office and the Department for International Development in the autumn of 2020.[275] Additionally there are select committees that have a more cross-cutting remit. One of these is the Public Accounts Committee which is discussed in

---

[274] Although the European Scrutiny Committee, which, when the UK was a member of the EU used to examine legislation emanating from Brussels, does now play an important role in scrutinising the working of the Withdrawal Agreement, the Northern Ireland Protocol etc

[275] They merged into what is now known as the Foreign, Commonwealth & Development Office

more detail below. Two others are the Environmental Audit Committee, which has a remit to consider environmental protection and sustainable development across government and the Public Administration and Constitutional Affairs Committee which looks at constitutional issues and standards of administration across government.[276]

Membership

A large percentage of backbench MPs will sit on a select committee. A few will sit on more than one. Being a select committee member adds significantly to the workload of an MP, given that there will be one or two meetings of the committee a week to attend and considerable paperwork to read. This is particularly true if they are the chair of the committee. But many MPs regard this as a very worthwhile part of the job, allowing them to quiz ministers and others on topics in a manner that just isn't possible on the floor of the House of Commons. And whilst most MPs might see the ultimate prize as a place on the frontbench, there are others who decide to pursue an 'alternative career' through the select committee system.

Most select committees in the 2019 Parliament have eleven members divided up between the political parties in the ratio six Conservative, four Labour, and one SNP. This is the ratio which best reflected the balance of the parties on the floor of the Commons after the 2019 general election.[277] Other committees will have a different number of members and on some there will be representatives of the smaller parties. (As examples, the Education Committee currently has only two parties represented on it – seven Conservative and four Labour – and the Defence Committee has a DUP member and only five from the Conservative Party.)

---

[276] All the committees of both Houses can be found here: https://committees.parliament.uk/committees/

[277] In the 2017 Parliament, the balance had been 5 Conservative, 5 Labour and 1 SNP

How the members, and in particular the chairs, of these committees are chosen underwent substantial reform as a result of recommendations made in 2010 by the aforementioned Wright Committee. Prior to the 2010 election, select committee chairs and members had been chosen via the murky waters of the 'usual channels' in which the party whips and leaders exercised their influence. It may seem extraordinary that government ministers, in effect, decided who should be chairing the committees that held them to account but this was often the case. In his entertaining diaries, the former Labour MP Chris Mullin describes how he let it be known that he would be interested in chairing the Commons Home Affairs select committee in the 1997 Parliament. That this post was in the gift of the Home Secretary, Jack Straw, and the Prime Minister, Tony Blair, is apparent from this short extract:

> *At the 10 o'clock division Jack Straw took me aside and said that The Man (Tony Blair) had agreed that I should chair the Home Affairs Committee.*[278]

After the 2010 general election this all changed. The chairs of select committees are now elected by MPs. Elections to these posts take place in secret, using the Alternative Vote system of election. The number of committees that each party chairs is related to the balance of the parties on the floor of the House, with the Conservatives currently chairing 16, Labour nine and the SNP two. (The Conservatives gained three chairs and Labour lost three after the 2019 election.) The one part of the process that is still rather opaque is the decision as to which political party should chair which committee. This is agreed through the 'usual channels' although there are some conventions in operation here: for example you would usually find MPs from the governing party chairing the Foreign Affairs and Treasury Committees whereas an MP from the Official Opposition party normally chairs the Home Affairs Committee. And although it may not yet be a convention that the SNP chairs the Scottish Affairs Committee, there will be every expectation – amongst SNP

---

[278] Ibid. Chris Mullin p.383

members at least! – that someone from that party will be in the chair.

Once the committees have been divided up in this way, MPs from the relevant parties put their names forward to stand for the chair. This means that each committee will have candidates for chair from only one party, with MPs being obliged to vote across party boundaries. And remember, this is a secret vote. This is important as it limits whips and other party managers leaning on their members to vote for one particular candidate or other. Any MP who wishes to be elected chair of a select committee will know that they will need to win votes beyond those from their own party. Thus those MPs from the governing party who are well-known to be the type of member who sees his or her role simply in terms of ingratiating themselves with ministers in the hope that one day they too might end up sitting on the frontbench, are unlikely to be elected. One important effect therefore of the changes introduced in 2010 was that committee chairs were more likely in future to be independently-minded MPs than 'friends of the whips'.

Some elections to be select committee chairs have been quite fiercely contested. For example, in the elections held at the start of the 2019 Parliament, five Conservative MPs fought to be chair of the Defence Committee and four Labour MPs stood to be chair of the Work & Pensions Committee. On other committees there was a less competitive election, with a number of chairs being elected unopposed. (To some degree this was because they had been elected only two and a half years previously - after the 2017 election - and many of their colleagues felt it was only fair to allow them to remain as chair.)

The other members of a select committee are chosen by their parliamentary party. How this happens will depend to some degree on the popularity of any particular committee. If the supply of potential members outstrips demand, there may be an election held. But on less popular committees there may need to be a bit of 'strong-arming' by the whips to ensure their party's slots are all filled.

The chair and other members of select committees are appointed to serve for a Parliament, i.e. until the next general election. There will however be changes to the membership of select committees during a Parliament. This is because select committees are made up of backbench MPs (you won't find ministers or their shadows on them) and backbenchers sometimes become frontbenchers. So if a committee member is appointed to be a minister or a frontbench spokesperson they will have to leave the committee. If it's an ordinary member of the committee who's promoted, their party will fill the vacancy. But if it is the chair who is elevated to the frontbench, there will need to be an election to select a new chair. This happened for example in 2020 when the newly elected Labour leader Sir Kier Starmer wished to give a position in his Shadow Cabinet to Rachel Reeves. She therefore had to step down as chair of the Business, Energy and Industrial Strategy Select Committee. In the election that followed to fill the vacant chair, only Labour MPs could stand, with the winner being Darren Jones.

Many MPs sitting on the backbenches will be very keen for promotion to their party's frontbench and this will include some who are select committee chairs. So it's not unusual to see members, and even chairs, of committees step down to take up a place on the frontbench, as Rachel Reeves did. But there will always be some MPs – a smallish minority perhaps – who see their role more as legislators and as scrutineers of government rather than simply as frontbenchers-in-waiting. Some MPs may be tempted to stand for election as a select committee chair because of the enhanced salary that comes with the job, but it would be unfair to suggest that this is the sole motivation. Some will consider being the chair of, for example, the Treasury, Foreign Affairs or Defence Committee as a rather more interesting and, perhaps even, more influential job than being a junior minister. (It's certainly true that the current chairs of these three committees have a higher profile than the most junior ministers in the departments that their committees hold to account.)

Inquiries and Reports

What inquiries select committees hold is entirely a matter for them. Some will be long, others much shorter. Initially the committee will call for written evidence. Whilst there will be some people and organisations from which the committee would particularly like to receive written evidence, anyone with an interest in the topic of inquiry can submit evidence via the relevant committee's webpage on the Parliament website.[279] Having collected together the written evidence, the committee will decide from whom it wishes to receive oral evidence. Whilst, again, there will be some people that the committee specifically wishes to see, to some degree they will be influenced in their choice of witness by the written evidence that they have received. Once all the evidence, written and oral, has been received and discussed, the committee will write its report. The first draft of this will normally be written by the committee clerks. Once the report has been agreed, it will be sent to the ministers to whom it is addressed. Ministers are usually required to respond to the report within 60 days.

Most select committee reports are agreed unanimously. This may come as a surprise to many, particularly if one's view of MPs at work is overly influenced by watching, for example, Prime Minister's Questions. MPs on select committees generally behave in a much more co-operative way than they normally do on the floor of the House, with committee chairs working hard to agree unanimous reports. Committee members will be all too conscious of the fact that a unanimous report will carry rather more weight with ministers than one that is passed only on a majority vote. Any minister who receives a report from a committee of MPs who are unanimously recommending a particular course of action would be foolish to completely ignore it, if for no other reason that it means that probably six MPs from their own party have signed up to the report. So select committees work much more co-operatively than an observer of the behaviour of MPs on the floor of the House might expect. This behaviour is encouraged by the

---

[279] www.parliament.uk

fact that members sit around a horseshoe shaped table, which is rather less confrontational than the layout of the House of Commons.

Whilst there may be no obligation on ministers to do what any report recommends, nor to accept what it is saying, ministers do take select committee reports seriously - arguably more seriously than much of what is said on the floor of the House of Commons. Compare the select committee process to the answering of parliamentary questions on the floor of the House. No-one should suggest that the latter is easy, but ministers are much more in control of the process than they are of a select committee hearing. At Question Time, most of the time an MP only gets a brief opportunity to quiz the minister and the minister always gets the final say. But at a select committee it is the members, and the chair in particular, who are in charge and they will ask ministers a series of in-depth questions, keeping him or her there for as long as they wish. Whilst new ministers might tell you that their appearances at the dispatch box are pretty terrifying, most experienced ministers will say that appearing before a select committee is a rather more taxing experience. It is for these reasons that many suggest select committees to be a rather more effective way of Parliament holding the government to account than most other methods that it has at its disposal. This is all relative of course; select committees don't exercise the same sort of powers as their counterparts for example on Capitol Hill in Washington DC. But relative to other aspects of the parliamentary process, the select committee system can be quite an effective way of holding ministers and others to account.

Other Select Committee Work

Most of a select committee's time will be taken up with inquiries, as just described. They do however work in other ways too. We explained earlier how select committees can be involved with legislation if the government chooses to publish a bill in draft prior to presenting the actual bill to Parliament. When this happens, the draft bill will be scrutinised either by the Commons select committee which carries out the day-to-day scrutiny of the department in which the draft bill has been drafted or, by a special joint committee of both Houses set up for the purpose.[280] Either way, the committee will carry out an inquiry into the draft bill similar to how it carries out regular inquiries as described above.

Select committees also carry out what might be described as 'non-inquiry' sessions. These would be small pieces of work carried out by the committee that don't necessarily result in a report. Included in these would be the regular hearings that committees hold with the Secretary of State and/or the Permanent Secretary of the department whose work the committee scrutinises.[281]

Finally, another important role played by select committees is the holding of pre-appointment hearings. Since the 2007/8 parliamentary session, select committees have been allowed to take evidence from candidates for certain key public appointments before they are appointed. The Coalition Government then specifically introduced legislation to give the Treasury Select Committee the statutory power of veto over appointments to its new Office of Budget Responsibility (OBR). But this power remains unique, with all other select committees having fairly limited influence over ministerial appointments.

The Public Accounts Committee

One select committee of the House of Commons is regarded by many as the most important select committee of all and that is the Public Accounts Committee (PAC). The PAC, which dates

---

[280] An example of a joint committee set up to scrutinise a draft bill would be the 'Joint Committee on the Draft Domestic Abuse Bill' whose 2019 report can be found here:

https://publications.parliament.uk/pa/jt201719/jtselect/jtddab/2075/2075.pdf

[281] For example, in October 2020 the Foreign Secretary Dominic Raab, gave evidence to the Foreign Affairs Committee on 'The Work of the Foreign, Commonwealth and Development Office'.

https://committees.parliament.uk/event/2268/formal-meeting-oral-evidence-session/

back to the middle of the 19th century, is not a departmental select committee. Rather, it scrutinises how public money has been spent across government. Has it been spent as Parliament originally voted for it to be spent? And has it been spent in a way that meets the rules concerning regularity, propriety and value for money?[282]

The PAC is always chaired by an MP from the Official Opposition and preferably one with ministerial experience at the Treasury. After the 2015 election Meg Hillier was elected as the PAC's chair and was re-elected after both the 2017 and 2019 elections. It generally holds one-off hearings on matters that are brought to its attention via reports from the National Audit Office (NAO). These reports are written by auditors who report through their head, the Comptroller and Auditor General, to the PAC. NAO staff are therefore not civil servants but servants of Parliament.

The Civil Service heads of all government departments (Permanent Secretaries), and their counterparts in other public bodies, are each designated by the Treasury as the Accounting Officer for their organisation. When Accounting Officers appear before the PAC they are not appearing on behalf of ministers but in their own right. In this role they are directly and personally accountable to the PAC for how public money is spent. Accounting Officers are seldom invited before the PAC to be told what a wonderful job they are doing. They are usually called there because something has gone wrong. For example, there may have been a major IT procurement exercise in a government department that heavily overspent its budget or did not work properly. Where things have gone wrong and public money has been wasted, the Permanent Secretary and other senior officials of the department concerned have to appear before the PAC to explain. PAC hearings can be, and often are, extremely difficult occasions for senior civil servants, who make sure that they are fully briefed on all aspects of the issue before they appear to give evidence.

---

[282] Treasury rules for spending public money are set down in Managing Public Money. https://www.gov.uk/government/publications/managing-public-money

In more recent times, and in particular after Margaret Hodge became the chair of the PAC after the 2010 general election, the PAC has rather widened its role to look more generally at how government collects and spends money. Its scrutiny in 2012 of tax avoidance by large multinational companies – Google, Starbucks and Amazon in particular – considerably raised the profile of this issue. The grilling that senior executives from these three companies received from Margaret Hodge and her colleagues on the PAC received a lot of coverage in the media and did much to put pressure on both the companies and on government to close some apparent loopholes in the tax collection system.

So it's not just senior public servants who may be required to appear before the PAC, but senior executives from the private sector too. This is particularly true of those who work for the large outsourcing companies such as Capita, G4S, Serco, Sodexo etc, which receive large amounts of public money to carry out services on behalf of the government. When they fail to deliver value for money in the services they deliver, it's not just the senior civil servants managing the contract who will be given a hard time by the PAC, but the senior executives of the companies too.

Ministerial Directions

Whilst the Accounting Officer may be personally and directly accountable to the PAC, sometimes a minister may want to spend money on a project that may not, for example, offer value for money. When this happens, the Permanent Secretary will discuss the matter with the minister. If they cannot agree, the Permanent Secretary will ask the minister for a 'ministerial direction' instructing the Permanent Secretary to release the money.[283] Ministerial directions are not given that often, but there have been many more in recent years than in earlier times. According to the Institute for Government, whilst 14 were given in the two years prior to the 2010 election, there were none during the

---

[283] Often, the simple act of a Permanent Secretary asking for a direction is enough to persuade a minister to change his or her mind.

Coalition Government until the three just before the 2015 election. In the three years 2018-2020 however, 32 ministerial directions were given by ministers in the governments of Theresa May and Boris Johnson. Of the 20 that occurred in 2020, 14 were due to the extraordinary levels of government expenditure that followed the outbreak of the Coronavirus pandemic.[284]

Whilst 'breaking' the normal rules of public expenditure might be understandable during a pandemic, other examples have not been viewed as so acceptable. In some cases, the fact that such expenditure has been made public due to the demand of the Permanent Secretary for a ministerial direction, has led to some criticism of the minister involved. A high profile example going back to the Blair Government occurred in 2002 when the then Secretary of State for Transport, Stephen Byers, wanted his Permanent Secretary, Sir Richard Mottram, to authorise additional expenditure of £8m to accelerate the construction of the Silverstone by-pass so that it would be ready in time for that year's Formula One British Grand Prix. While Sir Richard said that this expenditure couldn't be justified on transport grounds, the Secretary of State maintained that it was justified in the wider national interest. Sir Richard therefore requested a written ministerial direction. A copy of that direction would then have been sent to the Treasury and to the National Audit Office, leaving the Permanent Secretary essentially in the clear, unlike the Secretary of State, who suffered critical media coverage as a result.[285]

An example from David Cameron's time as Prime Minister concerned a charity called 'Kids Company'. When it ran into financial difficulties in 2015, ministers in the Cabinet Office

---

[284] https://www.instituteforgovernment.org.uk/explainers/ministerial-directions

[285] This was particularly embarrassing for the government given the negative criticism it had previously received following the donation given to the Labour Party by Formula 1 boss Bernie Ecclestone which had been linked to the government's decision not to ban tobacco advertising at Formula 1 events.

wished to provide financial support, against the advice of their senior civil servants. Two Cabinet Office ministers, Oliver Letwin and Matt Hancock, gave a direction to the Permanent Secretary of the department, instructing him to provide £3m of additional funding to the charity. Despite this public funding being given, just a few weeks later the charity went bust and there's been no sign since of the public money being recovered. Under the ministerial direction process, both the letter from the Permanent Secretary asking for a direction, and the ministers' reply giving it, became public documents which caused some embarrassment to the two ministers and to the government as a whole.

The Liaison Committee

Occasionally all the chairs of the Commons select committees meet together as the Liaison Committee. Its role is to consider the overall work of select committees, promote effective scrutiny of Government and choose committee reports for debates. It questions the Prime Minister about policy, usually three times a year.[286]

Although all of these roles are important, it's the latter which has given the Liaison Committee a much higher profile in recent years. One problem with the departmental select committee system is that there is no committee that specifically scrutinises the work of the Prime Minister and No 10. For this reason, in 2002 Tony Blair agreed to give evidence to the Liaison Committee, thereby becoming the first Prime Minister since Neville Chamberlain to give evidence to a select committee. He initially did this twice a year and thereby set a precedent for his successors to follow, although more recently Prime Ministers have usually agreed to appear three times a year.

There is also a Liaison Committee of the House of Lords which plays a similar role in the Upper House, except that it doesn't take evidence from the Prime Minister.

---

[286] https://committees.parliament.uk/committee/103/liaison-committee-commons/

Select Committee Witnesses

When witnesses give oral evidence to a select committee they sit at the open end of the horseshoe-shaped table around which the MPs sit. There could be up to six people giving evidence at any one time but usually it will be fewer. Select committees usually take oral evidence from people outside of government first, with ministers and civil servants giving evidence towards the end of an inquiry. When ministers attend, at least one civil servant will often attend with them to help with points of detail that may arise. Behind the witnesses sit people who are there to support them. There are also rows of seats where members of the public can sit, because virtually all select committee hearings are open to the public. When civil servants give evidence, the convention is that they speak on behalf of their ministers, except, as mentioned above, when they are appearing as Accounting Officers at the Public Accounts Committee. Civil Servants are there to explain, not to justify, and they are expected by their ministers to keep their personal views to themselves. The 'rules' governing civil servants' appearances before select committees are contained in guidance provided by the Cabinet Office.[287] (Within government, these rules are often known as the 'Osmotherly Rules' after the name of the civil servant who originally drew them up.) It's important to understand however that this guidance is a government document which has no parliamentary standing or approval. This sometimes causes tensions between government and Parliament. It can be quite challenging for civil servants appearing before a select committee. They are required to be truthful and to be as open and as helpful as possible. But they are also there to speak on behalf of their minister. Sometimes it won't easy to be doing all those things at the same time.

Ministers do consider that they have the right to refuse to allow a civil servant to appear before a select committee, even when a specific official has been asked by a committee to give

---

[287] The guidance can be found here: www.cabinetoffice.gov.uk/resource-library/guidance-departmental-evidence-and-response-select-committees.

evidence. (See for example Michael Gove's refusal to allow the former head of ethics at the Cabinet Office, Sue Gray, to give evidence to the Public Administration and Constitutional Affairs Select Committee when it was inquiring into the 'Greensill Affair' in July 2021.[288]) Not all committee chairs would accept that ministers have this right but it's difficult to deny that they do, given that ministers are ultimately accountable for all that goes on in their departments.

As mentioned, it can be a particular challenge for senior public servants when appearing before the Public Accounts Committee and in 2012 there was a rather public spat between the then chair of the PAC, Margaret Hodge, and the outgoing Head of the Civil Service Sir Gus (now Lord) O'Donnell. Sir Gus strongly criticised the way civil servants were sometimes treated by select committees. His criticisms, which included a description of some select committee hearings as *a theatrical exercise in public humiliation*[289], had been prompted in particular by Margaret Hodge requiring the most senior lawyer in HM Revenue & Customs to give evidence on oath during a hearing in November 2011.[290] Hodge made a robust defence of her committee to these criticisms in a speech to the Policy Exchange think-tank in March 2012. It's worth quoting this extract as it raises some very important issues about the accountability of ministers and civil servants:

> *[Senior civil servants] think we contravened the constitutional 'principle' that to maintain impartiality, civil servants should not be accountable to Parliament but should be accountable to ministers, who in turn are accountable to Parliament for all the policy and all the*

---

[288] https://committees.parliament.uk/committee/327/public-administration-and-constitutional-affairs-committee/news/156535/gove-blocks-greensill-ethics-supremo-committee-appearance/

[289] 'Parliament and the Law' p.117 Edited by Alexander Horne and Gavin Drewry. Bloomsbury Publishing 2018

[290] www.publications.parliament.uk/pa/cm201012/cmselect/cmpubacc/1531/11110701.htm

actions of the government.... Is that really a 'principle' of the British constitution, or a convenient view from a group who want to resist proper openness and accountability? Call it a convention or a principle – if it does not change, more taxpayers' money will be wasted, public services will continue all too often to provide poor value, and transparency and accountability will become a charade....

We live in an age of payment by results and performance management yet ministers are prevented from themselves appointing, promoting or sacking the senior civil servants for whom they are said to be accountable, on the grounds that this would politicise the civil service. You begin to wonder whether the whole doctrine of ministerial accountability is not constructed on a lie. How can anybody be held accountable for the actions of people they can't hire or fire? So civil servants escape external accountability because they are protected by the convention of ministerial responsibility, and they escape internal accountability because ministers are powerless to hold them to account in any meaningful way.[291]

Although Margaret Hodge's retirement in 2015 from the role of PAC chair relieved the tensions a little between select committees and senior civil servants, the debate concerning civil servants' accountability to Parliament continues to be a live one.

During the Covid pandemic, a lot of select committee evidence sessions were held virtually. Sometimes a few of the members of the committee might be in the select committee room, and possibly some of the witnesses too. At other times, everyone will have been participating virtually. As with many others aspects of life during the pandemic where people were forced to operate on a virtual basis, some advantages of using these new ways of working became apparent.

---

[291] Margaret Hodge. 'Accountability in Today's Public Service'. Speech at Policy Exchange, 15 March 2012

Thus select committees have continued to use virtual participation, in particular by witnesses. Fairly obviously, it makes it rather easier to take evidence from people who are many miles away from Westminster. It also facilitates having more diverse groups of witnesses appearing. The lack of diversity of witnesses is something that committee chairs have complained about in the past with, for example, the latest data showing that only just over a third of select committee witnesses are women.[292]

Appearing before Select Committees

Under the standing orders of the House of Commons, select committees have the power to send for *persons, papers and records*.[293] In other words, a select committee can in theory demand to see whomever and whatever it wants. The reality, however, is a little different. Tussles between government departments and select committees on the latter's access to official papers are not that unusual. For example, in 2017 there was a well-publicised dispute between Theresa May's government and the Select Committee on Exiting the European Union regarding the committee's access to the 'sectoral impact assessments' that the government had drawn up in respect of Brexit. The committee wished to see them but the government didn't want to hand them over. It was only when the House of Commons passed a resolution in November of that year, requiring the assessments to be shown to the select committee, that the government did finally release them.

People asked to appear before a select committee are obliged to attend (although, as we have seen, it is normally accepted in government that ministers can decline to send civil servants along to select committees if they wish to do so, even if not all MPs necessarily share that view.) But it is an interesting constitutional

---

[292] https://publications.parliament.uk/pa/cm201719/cmselect/cmliaisn/1860/186007.htm

[293] Standing Order of the House of Commons No 152 https://publications.parliament.uk/pa/cm201919/cmstords/341/so_341_05 1119_web.pdf

point as to what in practice Parliament's actual powers are to force a reluctant witness to attend. In 2012 the former Prime Minister Tony Blair refused to give evidence to the House of Commons Justice Committee's inquiry into the workings of the Freedom of Information Act. Blair was strongly criticised by the committee's chair, Sir Alan Beith, but no further action was taken. What a committee chair can do to persuade a reluctant witness to appear before their committee is to issue a summons. In recent years a summons has been issued to a number of people that a committee has wished to see including the media mogul Rupert Murdoch and his son James, and the boss of Sports Direct Mike Ashley. In these two cases the witnesses did finally appear before the committee after receiving the summons.

Perhaps rather more high profile examples of people refusing to appear as select committee witnesses concerned the 2019 Digital, Culture, Media and Sport (DCMS) Select Committee inquiry into 'Disinformation and Fake News'. As part of this inquiry they wished to take evidence from the boss of Facebook, Mark Zuckerberg and also from the former head of the Vote Leave campaign, Dominic Cummings. Both of these high profile individuals refused to give evidence to the committee. Zuckerberg was three times invited to attend and each time he declined, eventually doing no more than posting some comments on his Facebook page. (One wonders whether he might have been prepared to give evidence if there had been the option to give it virtually from his office in California.) Zuckerberg did send along Richard Allan, Facebook's 'Vice-President of Policy Solutions', to a hearing of the committee's to which parliamentarians from a number of other countries were invited to participate, but that did little to calm the ire of the DCMS committee and its chair, Damian Collins. (It also seemed a little odd that Allan not only was a senior executive of Facebook, he was also a Liberal Democrat member of the House of Lords. Whilst many members of the Lords have jobs outside of Parliament, few perhaps have them in the 21st century world of social media). In its report the committee said that Zuckerberg had *shown contempt towards… the UK Parliament.*[294]

Dominic Cummings also refused to give evidence to the same inquiry. Cummings of course went on to become Boris Johnson's chief adviser but the reason why the DCMS committee wished to see him concerned his former role in the Vote Leave campaign. This refusal was despite Cummings being summoned by the committee. The committee was so annoyed by Cummings' behaviour that in June 2018 it published a special report concerning his conduct which concluded that his failure to attend *in our view … constitutes a serious interference with the ability of this Committee to discharge the task assigned to it by the House.*[295]

The issue was then referred to the whole House of Commons for consideration. This was the first time since 1920 that such a debate had taken place in the House of Commons. The motion debated and passed by the Commons ordered that *Mr Dominic Cummings give an undertaking to the Committee, no later than 6pm on 11 June 2018, to appear before that Committee at a time on or before 20 June 2018.*[296]

But still Cummings failed to comply, so the matter was referred to the Commons' Committee of Privileges. This committee found that Cummings had committed a *contempt of Parliament* by refusing to appear before the DCMS Select Committee. It noted however that it would *not recommend that the House exercise any power of committal to prison in the matter of privilege referred to it.*[297]

---

[294] https://publications.parliament.uk/pa/cm201719/cmselect/cmcumeds/1791/1791.pdf

[295] https://publications.parliament.uk/pa/cm201719/cmselect/cmcumeds/1115/1115.pdf

[296] https://hansard.parliament.uk/Commons/2018-06-07/debates/3689394A-A303-4BE0-8D45-8A27E2D89CDA/Privilege

[297] https://www.parliament.uk/documents/commons-committees/Privileges-Committee/Resolution.pdf

This reference to the potential locking up of Cummings relates to the ancient powers of the 'High Court of Parliament'. About a third of the way up what is now known as the Elizabeth Tower, at the top of which is Big Ben, there is a little prison cell. Up until the middle of the 19th century, people found in contempt of Parliament could be taken to this cell where they would be left to rot until they agreed to do whatever was necessary to remove themselves from their contempt. There was never any serious question of this happening to Dominic Cummings – or indeed anyone else these days. Apart from anything else, we now have a Human Rights Act to protect people from such summary justice. Nevertheless, Cummings was held in contempt of Parliament and that was a serious offence.

Short of locking Cummings up, the House could in theory have summoned him to appear at the 'Bar of the House' (the white line across the floor at the entrance to the Commons) for a dressing down. But the Commons have not forced anyone to do this since 1957 when the editor of 'The Sunday Express', John Junor, wrote an article condemning a Government scheme that gave MPs special petrol allowances for their constituency work whilst, he claimed, the rest of the country was suffering severe fuel rationing as a result of the Suez Crisis. When his article was deemed to be in contempt of Parliament, Junor was hauled before the Speaker of the House, William Morrison, by the Serjeant-at-Arms. Junor apologised for what he wrote though defended himself by claiming that the fuel allowances were *a proper and, indeed, an inescapable subject of comment in a free Press.*[298] It is hard to imagine such an event happening now though – if only because with the Commons these days being televised, there would be real concerns as to how person held in contempt might behave.

What the DCMS Select Committee was able to secure, however, as part of its inquiry into 'fake news' were a number of

---

[298] https://api.parliament.uk/historic-hansard/commons/1957/jan/24/privilege-attendance-of-mr-john-junor

Facebook documents which were seized from an American businessman who happened to be on a trip to London. As the committee thought that the documents in his possession were vital to its inquiry, it despatched the Commons' Serjeant-at-Arms to the businessman's hotel to demand he hand over the papers. When he failed to do so he was escorted to Parliament where, threatened with fines and imprisonment, he released the papers. This was quite an extraordinary event and one has to wonder what would have actually happened if the businessman had continued to refuse to hand over the documents. Locking him up in the Elizabeth Tower seems an unlikely outcome.

This whole saga demonstrates very clearly that the powers of select committees to force people to give evidence are rather limited. As noted above, unlike in the legislatures of Scotland, Wales and Northern Ireland, it's not a criminal offence to refuse to appear before a committee at Westminster. This is because the 1689 Bill of Rights, which we discussed earlier, doesn't allow it: *the freedom of speech and debates or proceedings in Parliament ought not to be impeached or questioned in any court or place out of Parliament.*

But the Bill of Rights could be amended, and in 2011 the Coalition Government did say that it would bring forward draft legislation to make refusing to appear before a select committee a criminal offence.[299] But when a Joint Committee on Parliamentary Privilege, which had been specifically set up to consider this issue, rejected this idea, the government accepted this rejection in its response to the committee's report: [300]

> *The Government recognises the difficulties associated with criminalising contempt or legislating to confirm Parliament's penal powers, and agrees that neither is the*

---

[299] https://hansard.parliament.uk/commons/2011-07-14/debates/11071464000007/BusinessOfTheHouse

[300] www.publications.parliament.uk/pa/jt201314/jtselect/jtprivi/30/3002.htm

right approach.[301]

In May 2019 however, the Committee on Privileges returned to this issue once again, prompted to a large degree by the 'Cummings Affair', by launching an inquiry on 'Select Committees and Contempts'. In its report of May 2021 it recommended the introduction of *new legislation to provide a statutory basis for existing select committee powers to summon witnesses and compel attendance and provision of information*, adding that it wished to *hold a public consultation* on this recommendation.[302] The biggest issue that would arise if Parliament did legislate in this way is that it would give the courts a degree of jurisdiction over parliamentary proceedings which they are currently not allowed under the Bill of Rights. As the Clerk of the House of Commons said in his written evidence to the committee's inquiry: *it might be the thin end of a wedge; that somehow legitimate examination in one area might encourage what Parliament would consider to be illegitimate inquiry in another.*[303]

House of Lords Select Committees

The House of Lords does not have the same departmental select committees as the House of Commons. Instead it has a number of 'sessional' select committees (effectively permanent committees though they do need to be re-established each session), with others set up on an ad hoc basis, including, currently, one on Covid-19. Like in the House of Commons there are also select committees that look at domestic matters concerned with the running of the House and committees that scrutinise secondary legislation.[304]

The structure of Lords select committees was changed in

---

[301] www.official-documents.gov.uk/document/cm87/8771/8771.pdf

[302] https://publications.parliament.uk/pa/cm5801/cmselect/cmprivi/350/35003.htm#_idTextAnchor000

[303] https://committees.parliament.uk/writtenevidence/6148/pdf/

[304] A complete list of Lords committees from April 2021 can be found here: https://publications.parliament.uk/pa/ld5801/ldselect/ldliaison/193/19309.htm

April 2021 following the UK's departure from the European Union. For many years the most well-known Lords select committees had been the European Union Select Committee, including the various sub-committees that operated under it. This has now been replaced by a 'European Affairs Committee' which has just one sub-committee, on the Northern Irish Protocol. Not having departmental committees in the Lords limits the amount of overlap between the work of committees in the two Houses but if, say, the International Relations and Defence Committee of the Lords wishes to look at an issue similar to one being considered by the Commons' Foreign Affairs or Defence Committees, it is perfectly entitled to do so.

How select committees operate in the House of Lords is in many respects similar to those in the House of Commons. They sit around the same horseshoe-shaped tables but the party balance is different because the party balance in the House of Lords as a whole is different to that in the Commons. Most select committees in the Lords have no formal number of members nor political balance. (Such issues in the Lords are decided through the 'usual channels'.) However, at the moment, the majority have 12 members consisting of four Conservatives, three Crossbenchers, three Labour and two Liberal Democrats. There is, however, a 'rotation rule' on most committees, whereby members who have been appointed for four successive sessions may not be reappointed in the following session.

Perhaps the most striking difference between Lords select committees and those in the Commons is the degree of expertise amongst the members of a Lords select committee. The House of Lords contains many more experts in particular fields. It is therefore not at all unusual but considerably unnerving for witnesses who appear before a Lords select committee to find themselves facing some very well informed inquisitors.

Other Committees of Parliament

Before leaving this discussion, it's worth mentioning that there are a number of other types of parliamentary committee that are not select committees. We discussed public bill committees earlier. These are the committees that carry out the detailed scrutiny of most bills as they go through the Commons and are quite distinct from select committees. There are also numerous committees that operate wholly within a particular party in Parliament. The Labour Party has a number of backbench 'departmental committees' that keep an eye on the work of Shadow Cabinet members whereas the Conservative Party has the 1922 Committee to represent its backbenchers.[305] But these aren't select committees either since they are single-party and are not set up under the standing orders of Parliament. One parliamentary committee that looks rather like a select committee, and can easily be confused as one, is the Intelligence and Security Committee (ISC). If select committees scrutinise the work of individual government departments, the ISC carries out a similar function in its scrutiny of the work of the intelligence agencies – MI5, MI6 and GCHQ.[306] The ISC however isn't a select committee. Rather, it is a statutory committee, operating according to powers given to it by the Intelligence Services Act 1994 and the Justice & Security Act 2013. Its members are appointed by the two Houses of Parliament having been formally nominated by the Prime Minister in consultation with the Leader of the Opposition. Most of its meetings take place in private but the committee does occasionally take evidence from the heads of the three

---

[305] There is a widely held view that the 1922 Committee (or the '22' as many call it) gets its name from a meeting of Conservative MPs in 1922 which demanded that the party withdraw from the coalition government of David Lloyd George. Actually it was at a meeting of the Carlton Club in October 1922 where this demand was successfully made. The '22' was actually set up in 1923, following an initiative by newly elected Conservative MPs to facilitate cooperation within the party.

[306] MI5 is also known as the Security Service and MI6 as the Secret Intelligence Service.

agencies in public.[307]

Finally, in Parliament there are literally hundreds of 'All-Party Parliamentary Groups' (APPGs). These are informal groups of parliamentarians that operate in a way rather like select committees but without the latter's formal powers. There are number of both 'country groups' and 'subject groups'. Of the former, there is one for almost any country in the world and of the latter, there is vast range covering topics such as beer, cats, football, the Peak District and human rights.[308] They are open to all MPs and Peers but they must have at least one officer from the governing party and one from the official opposition party. Like select committees they will hold inquiries and publish reports, but no-one, ministers included, is obliged to attend their meetings or respond to their reports. The fact that APPGs are often externally supported and funded is, for some, controversial. For example, the APPG on the British Offshore Oil and Gas Industry has a secretariat run by the industry's trade association, Oil and Gas UK.[309] Whilst APPGs are subject to the rules and scrutiny of the Parliamentary Commissioner for Standards, there have been concerns that some of the secretariats that run a few of them are in effect lobbyists who are using their role with the APPG to bypass the rules on lobbying and that the financing of many APPGs by industry may give the latter undue influence over policy making.[310]

---

[307] https://isc.independent.gov.uk/. Note that the committee has a government web address rather than a parliamentary one. Because of the nature of its work it operates out of the Cabinet Office and is supported by civil servants.

[308] The full list is here:

https://publications.parliament.uk/pa/cm/cmallparty/210310/contents.htm

[309] https://publications.parliament.uk/pa/cm/cmallparty/210310/britiish-offshore-oil-and-gas-industry.htm

[310] See for example 'A hidden web of policy influence: The pharmaceutical industry's engagement with UK's All-Party Parliamentary Groups'. Emily Rickard and Piotr Ozieranski.

Before finally leaving this discussion of committees perhaps, for absolute clarity, we should also emphasise the distinction between, in particular, select committees and Cabinet committees. We discussed the latter in the chapter on 'Cabinet and Cabinet Committees'. Cabinet committees are committees of government, made up of government ministers and supported by civil servants. You would therefore only find politicians from the governing party, or parties, on them. Select committees, on the other hand, are cross-party committees of Parliament which hold those ministers to account.

What can cause confusion is that Cabinet committees and select committees sometimes have very similar names: for example, until a few years ago, there was a Home Affairs Cabinet Committee and a Home Affairs Select Committee. Both were often referred to as the 'Home Affairs Committee'.

https://journals.plos.org/plosone/article?id=10.1371/journal.pone.0252551

7

The 2017-19 Parliament

The 2017-2019 Parliament was an extraordinary one, the like of which we are unlikely to see again for some time. What allowed it to be so extraordinary were two linked events: the Brexit referendum of 2016 and the loss of Theresa May's government's majority at the 2017 general election. To these might be added the willingness of the Speaker of the House of Commons, John Bercow, to interpret the standing orders of the House of Commons in sufficiently creative ways to genuinely, and highly unusually, give the Commons a degree of control over the government that it hadn't exercised for many years.

Theresa May called an early poll in June 2017 by using the provision in the Fixed-term Parliaments Act for an early election to be triggered if two-thirds of all MPs voted it for it. At that election, to most people's surprise, she managed to lose the slender majority she had inherited from David Cameron a year earlier, forcing her to enter into a 'supply and confidence' arrangement with the DUP which we discussed in chapter one. This gave May's government protection from losing a vote of no confidence and from having its budget voted down. But it gave her little protection on the key issue of the Parliament - Brexit - because her party was so divided on the issue. Conservative MPs who had supported 'leave' in the referendum would often feel that May's government was pursuing a Brexit that was too soft, whereas the 'remain' element of her party felt it was too hard. Thus for differing reasons, MPs from both wings of the party often found themselves in the opposite voting lobby to May and her supporters.

In September 2017 the House of Commons debated the May Government's 'European Union (Withdrawal) Bill'. This was the key piece of legislation that would repeal the European Communities Act 1972 which had originally taken the UK into the EU. Because of its importance, the second reading of the Withdrawal Bill was taken over two days, at the end of which the Commons passed it by a majority of 17, with the DUP supporting it and just one Conservative MP – Ken Clarke – voting against. Where Theresa May ran into real difficulties was at the next stage of the bill which was, because of its constitutional importance, taken in Committee of the Whole House. The Committee of the Whole House considered the bill over six sitting days in November and December 2017. While it was in committee, the Conservative MP and former Attorney General, Dominic Grieve, tabled an amendment to the bill that required any withdrawal agreement that the government reached with the EU, and the associated 'framework on the future relationship', to be approved by a resolution of the House of Commons before it could be ratified. This is what became known as the 'meaningful vote'. (One might think that it is axiomatic that a treaty of such importance would have to be agreed by Parliament before it could be ratified but the right to agree and ratify treaties form part of the 'prerogative powers' that ministers enjoy which we discussed earlier.) The Commons considered the Grieve amendment on 13 December 2017. Although the DUP supported the government in its opposition to the amendment, as did two pro-Brexit Labour rebels, Kate Hoey and Frank Field, the amendment was supported by 12 'Remainer' Conservative MPs and was therefore passed by a majority of four. This was the first of many defeats that Theresa May suffered on the floor of the House of Commons.

The EU (Withdrawal) Bill finally received Royal Assent in June 2018, having been passed at third reading in the Commons with no

Conservative MPs rebelling and at both second and third reading in the Lords 'on the nod'. But significant damage had been done to the government's position on Brexit by Dominic Grieve's amendment.

In November 2018, Theresa May successfully completed a Withdrawal Agreement with the European Union although not before both her Secretary of State for Exiting the European Union, David Davis and her Foreign Secretary, Boris Johnson, had resigned from her government. She now needed to get her Withdrawal Agreement accepted by the House of Commons when they cast their 'meaningful vote'.

Before however the government was able to table the meaningful vote motion, it found itself held in contempt of Parliament. MPs on all sides of the House had passed a motion demanding to see the legal advice of the Attorney General concerning the Withdrawal Agreement that May had reached with the EU. The government refused to publish it, quoting the precedence of such legal advice not being made public. However the view of many MPs was that their motion superseded any such precedence and it therefore had to be respected. When the government again refused to publish the advice, the House passed a motion holding the government in contempt. Thus Theresa May's government became the first ever to be held in contempt of Parliament, although with no sanction attached to the contempt motion, the government was able to brush it aside.

The meaningful vote was originally scheduled to take place on 11 December 2018, but faced with an obvious defeat, the government pulled the vote at 24 hours' notice, despite four days of debate on the motion already having taken place. Speaker John Bercow has described the move as *deeply discourteous*.[311] It also caused intense frustration, not only on the opposition benches but amongst many on the Conservative benches too – so much so that a number of Conservative MPs forced a vote of no confidence in Theresa May as party leader. (This shouldn't be confused with a

---

[311] Ibid. John Bercow p.318

vote of no confidence that the whole House might pass in the Prime Minister and government.) Whilst Theresa May saw off that vote, she was clearly very damaged in the eyes of many in her party.[312]

Theresa May nevertheless retabled the meaningful vote motion on 15 January 2019 but when it was voted on it was defeated by 432 votes to 202. This was the biggest defeat for a government in the House of Commons ever, with 118 Conservatives rebelling.[313] After such a cataclysmic defeat on a vitally important issue, one might have expected the Prime Minister to resign, but she didn't. The Leader of the Opposition, Jeremy Corbyn, did table a vote of no confidence in the government but this was defeated by 325 votes to 306.

In mid-February, a new anti-Brexit political party appeared in the House of Commons known as 'The Independent Group for Change' (also known as 'Change UK'). Seven Labour MPs defected from their party to join the new grouping, followed by three Conservatives, which further shifted the political arithmetic in the Commons against Theresa May's government. (This very short-lived party itself split after failing to win any seats at the elections to the European Parliament in May 2019. Some of their MPs then joined the Liberal Democrats and others restyled themselves as 'The Independent Group for Change'. All the breakaway MPs who stood for re-election at the 2019 general election, whether as Independent Group candidates or as Liberal Democrats, lost their seats and a week after the election, the party was wound up.)

On 12 March 2019, Theresa May made a second attempt to get her Withdrawal Agreement passed by the House of Commons. She fared slightly better this time: whereas the defeat on the first meaningful vote had been the biggest ever for a government in the

---

[312] 117 Conservative MPs voted in favour of the no confidence motion.

[313] Note, this wasn't however the biggest ever rebellion by MPs of a governing party. That remains the rebellion in 2003 by Labour MPs over going to war in Iraq.

Commons, this time it was only the fourth biggest ever, by 391 votes to 242. Following this defeat, under the terms of a motion passed by the Commons a couple of weeks previously, the government was now required by the Commons to bring forward a motion which ruled out a no-deal departure from the EU. This amendment was passed by 312 votes to 308.

With the date of departure from the EU of 29 March 2019 looming, and with a no-deal exit for the meantime being ruled out, Theresa May agreed to ask the EU for a delay to the UK's departure until 30 June, but only if the Commons passed the meaningful vote at the third time of asking, adding the threat of a much longer delay if the Commons voted no. But before this vote could be held, Theresa May faced an additional hurdle when the Speaker ruled that he would not allow the government to table the same motion on which it had been defeated on 12 March; in other words, a third meaningful vote could not just be a rerun of the second one. In justifying his decision, he quoted a precedent from 1602 which appeared in Erskine May that: *a motion or an amendment which is the same, in substance, as a question which has been decided during a session [of Parliament] may not be brought forward again during that same session.*[314] So, in other words, the government couldn't retable the same motion again any time during the current session of Parliament. In the end, the government got around this problem by holding a meaningful vote only on the Withdrawal Agreement itself rather than on the Withdrawal Agreement *and* the Future Partnership Declaration which the earlier meaningful votes had been on. It would be therefore technically wrong to call the vote that took place on 29 March as 'meaningful vote number three' but, whatever its description, it was defeated by 344 votes to 286. The sizes of the defeats were getting smaller, but this was still yet another huge defeat for the government. The date of this third vote was significant as it occurred on the day that the UK was supposed to leave the EU.

What happened next was one of the more extraordinary events in the 2017-19 Parliament so far: the 'seizing of the order

---

[314] Ibid. John Bercow p.328

paper' by backbench MPs. As we discussed earlier, a government is largely in control of the agenda of the House of Commons so long as it has a majority on the floor of the House. But Theresa May's government, of course, didn't have a majority and so a cross-party coalition of MPs, led by the Conservative MP Sir Oliver Letwin and the Labour MP Yvette Cooper was able to gain the support of MPs to suspend Standing Order 14. This is the standing order of the Commons which states that government business has precedence at every sitting of the House. By suspending this standing order, MPs were able to take control of the agenda of the House of Commons. Government ministers were outraged that John Bercow had allowed this motion to be debated. In their view there was a well-established principle in the Commons that the government's business took precedence:

> *The Government have consistently said that we do not support the unprecedented removal of Government control of the Order Paper, no matter the circumstances. For many years, the convention has been that it is for the Government, as elected by the people and with the confidence of the House, to set out the business. It is for Parliament to scrutinise, amend and reject or approve. The Government will listen carefully to Parliament today, but, as I have explained, the approach to today's business sets an extremely concerning precedent for our democracy, and we will therefore oppose the business motion.*[315]

It may be that there is a convention that it is *for the government…to set out the business.* But it might be reasonable to assume that this convention only applies when the government has a majority of the seats in the Commons. This seemed to be the view of John Bercow:

> *Government control of the Order Paper has certainly*

---

[315] Andrea Leadsom, Leader of the House of Commons. https://hansard.parliament.uk/Commons/2019-04-01/debates/D77EE515-9BCC-4137-A596-B1BBA91ADDEF/BusinessOfTheHouse

> been the norm since the early twentieth century but, before then, it certainly was not. Standing Orders of the House are not the property of the government but, rather, as the title implies, that of the House. It can keep them, amend them or scrap and replace them wholesale as it wishes. The Clerks shared my view that if colleagues from different parties in the House wished to propose a suspension or disapplication of a Standing Order, they should be free to put such a proposition to the House.[316]

Thus the proposition to suspend Standing Order 14 was put to the House and passed. This was crucial because it allowed backbench MPs to introduce a Private Members' Bill (specifically, a Presentation Bill) that would stop the UK leaving the EU with no deal without the approval of Parliament and would delay the UK's departure from the EU to the end of June 2019. (Although Theresa May had already effectively agreed to the extension, this would make the asking for it a statutory requirement.) As we discussed in the section on legislation, Private Members' Bills are usually only considered on sitting Fridays and one of the reasons why few of them become acts (and, in particular, very few Presentation Bills become acts) is because so little time is allocated to their consideration. But on this occasion, with the control of the Commons' agenda having been wrested away from the government, there was time for the 'Cooper Bill' (as it became known after one of its main sponsors) to become law. The bill passed all its stages in the House of Commons in one day and received Royal Assent on 8 April, just five days after it was first introduced in the Commons. During the course of this very short process there were some dramatically tight votes in the House of Commons with the bill passing at second reading by five votes and at third reading by just one vote. On the other hand, when the government tabled an amendment to the bill at its committee stage to limit the length of the Brexit extension, this was defeated by 180 votes. The government had

---

[316] Ibid. John Bercow p.332

already suffered the biggest ever and fourth biggest ever defeats in the Commons and with this latest one, it had now suffered the second biggest ever. A day after the bill received Royal Assent, a motion was laid under the act that required the Prime Minister to seek an extension to the UK's departure from the EU to 30 June 2019. This was overwhelmingly passed in the Commons by 420 votes to 110. Theresa May then sought and received from the EU an extension of the UK's departure to that date.

On the same day that this bill was completing all its stages in the House of Commons, a very rare event took place that had last occurred in July 1993: the Speaker exercised a casting vote. This was on a motion tabled by the Labour MP Hilary Benn for indicative votes to be held on the various Brexit options (ranging from remaining in the Single Market through to a hard Brexit.) The vote on this motion was 310 ayes and 310 noes. The Speaker then cast his vote against the motion, explaining that

> *In accordance with precedent, and on the principle that important decisions should not be taken except by a majority, I cast my vote with the noes, so the noes have it. By casting vote, it is 311 to 310. That is the proper way in which to proceed.*[317]

A few days later, the EU actually granted an extension to the UK's departure though to 31 October 2019. It also said, however, that the UK would have to leave on 1 June 2019 if the UK didn't participate in the May elections to the European Parliament. This was something that the UK Government had been exceedingly reluctant to do but it now had no alternative. Theresa May and her government were in an almost impossible situation. They considered having yet another attempt to get the Commons to pass the meaningful vote but in the end decided to introduce the legislation that would give effect to the Withdrawal Agreement, without the meaningful vote having been passed. There was

---

[317] https://hansard.parliament.uk/Commons/2019-04-03/debates/8AAF1B EF-0694-4960-ACB8-F74CE53A3B94/BusinessOfTheHouse

considerable hostility across the House to this idea and, had Theresa May actually got as far as introducing the legislation in the Commons, it seems highly likely that the bill would have been defeated (and would have become the first government bill to be defeated on the floor of the House of Commons since Margaret Thatcher's Shops Bill in 1986.) But it the event the bill was never introduced – the outright hostility to it within her own party forcing May to announce that she would be resigning as Prime Minister as soon as a new Conservative Party leader had been chosen.

Before the new Prime Minister took office, all sorts of constitutional questions arose. The new Prime Minister would, of course, face exactly the same parliamentary arithmetic as had his predecessor. There was therefore speculation that if the new Conservative leader was not in a position to command a majority on the floor of the House of Commons, might Theresa May not recommend to the Queen that the new leader become Prime Minister? Would someone else perhaps be in a better position in respect of Brexit to command a majority in the House? And how far would some anti-Brexit Conservative MPs go to stop a new Prime Minister pursuing a no-deal Brexit? Would they, for example, support a vote of no confidence in the new Prime Minister as soon as he'd been appointed?

None of this, in the end, got in the way of the Queen appointing Boris Johnson as Prime Minister on 24 July 2019. But no sooner was he appointed, further questions were asked. Would, for example, Johnson start the summer recess early simply to stop a motion of no confidence taking place? And looking ahead to the date of departure from the EU which was now set at 31 October, might the new Prime Minister even prorogue Parliament for a long period of time to avoid it legislating to stop the UK leaving on that date if no deal had been secured? In the end, the former didn't happen but the latter did – even if what turned out to be the unlawful prorogation ultimately failed to stop a further delay to the Brexit date. Those words of William Gladstone about the British Constitution relying on *more boldly* than any other the good sense and the good faith of those who work it and those of Peter Hennessy about the need for people in government to behave like *good chaps* came to the forefront of some people's minds at this time.

Boris Johnson was clearly more prepared for the UK to leave the EU without a deal than his predecessor had been. And he was prepared to take steps – including one that was ultimately deemed by the Supreme Court to be unlawful – to ensure that the UK did leave the EU by 31 October. Thus the opponents of a no-deal outcome realised that they might again have to resort to some unusual parliamentary practices to stop it. Once again MPs successfully 'seized the order paper' to create time in Parliament for another Private Members' Bill to be passed that would delay the date of Brexit if the government hadn't negotiated an acceptable deal with the EU. Their method of taking control of the agenda however was, this time, a little different.

Under Standing Order 24 of the House of Commons an MP can apply to the Speaker for an emergency debate to take place on the floor of the House. If the MP is given leave to do so by the Speaker, he or she has three minutes to make a speech about why the issue is of such importance. The Speaker then decides whether the MP's application should be submitted to the House. The usual way for MPs to show their support for the application is to stand up. If, in the eyes of the Speaker a sufficient number of MPs show their support he may agree for the emergency debate to take place, usually on the following sitting day. Usually the motion on the order paper of the day will simply be 'that the House has considered the matter of ....' In other words, MPs aren't taking a decision. (Or, to use more formal parliamentary language, there is no substantive motion on which the House votes.)

On 3 September 2019, the Conservative MP and former minister, Sir Oliver Letwin, made an application under SO24 for an emergency debate to take place on Brexit. This received the support of many MPs in the House and was therefore granted by the Speaker. But, in a highly controversial move, John Bercow accepted a *substantive* motion for debate: not only did the motion say 'that this House has considered the matter of the need to take all necessary steps to ensure that the United Kingdom does not leave the European Union on 31 October 2019 without a withdrawal agreement'; it then went on to say that on the following day, Standing Order 14 which, as we have seen, provides that government business take precedence on any sitting day, be disapplied. To have a vote on a substantive motion in an emergency date was, according to the Institute for Government *completely unprecedented*.[318] Government ministers were outraged that John Bercow was prepared to interpret the parliamentary rules so flexibly so as to allow this to happen. But once he'd accepted the substantive motion, there was little that Boris Johnson and his ministers could do about it.

So the debate on the substantive motion was debated and then passed by 328 votes to 301. Once again, MPs had wrested control of the agenda of the Commons from the government. They then used this on the following day, 4 September, to pass all the stages of a Presentation (Private Members') Bill that was very similar to the 'Cooper Bill' of May 2019 which had put back the date of Brexit to 30 June. This bill became known as the 'Benn Bill' after the Labour MP Hilary Benn who introduced it. Having been passed by the Commons, the Lords examined the bill for a couple of days before it received Royal Assent on 9 September. Under the terms of the act, the government would be forced to ask for a further extension to the departure date unless MPs had, by 19 October, approved the UK's departure from the EU (in effect, another 'meaningful vote'). This was something that Boris Johnson had expressly said he would not let happen, declaring that he would *rather be dead in a ditch* than postpone Brexit beyond 31 October.[319] It was this desire to stop Parliament from further delaying Brexit that prompted the unlawful prorogation of Parliament. However, the order given by the Queen had set a date

---

[318] https://www.euronews.com/2019/09/02/what-is-standing-order-24-euronews-answers

[319] https://www.theguardian.com/politics/2019/sep/05/boris-johnson-rather-be-dead-in-ditch-than-agree-brexit-extension

for prorogation to start on 9 September which, as it transpired, was the very day that the Queen gave Royal Assent to the Benn Bill. So it is, as previously suggested, somewhat ironic that the prorogation, even if it hadn't been deemed by the Supreme Court to be unlawful, wouldn't have stopped the passing of the Benn Bill.

The day after the Supreme Court had found against the government, Parliament returned. Just a couple of weeks later though, on 8 October, the government did lawfully prorogue Parliament and the very long 2017-19 session came to an end. The new session started with the Queen's Speech on 14 October. In contrast to the previous session, this session turned out to be an extremely short one. Three days after the start of the new session, Boris Johnson managed to secure a new Withdrawal Agreement with the EU, having renegotiated the 'Northern Ireland Protocol.' If, however, the UK was to leave with this agreement on 31 October, the deal would have to be agreed by the House of Commons. As mentioned, the Benn Bill required this agreement to be given by 19 October. Because 19 October was going to be reached without the Withdrawal Agreement being passed, the government ordered the Commons to sit on that day, despite it being a Saturday. The government hoped that on that special Saturday sitting MPs would vote in favour of its Withdrawal Agreement. But instead, MPs passed an amendment to the government motion, by 322 votes to 306, which refused to approve the deal until the legislation that would implement it had been passed. The reason why MPs did this was because they were concerned that if they approved the deal, but the implementing legislation wasn't then passed by 31 October, the UK would still end up leaving the EU with no deal.

Three days later the government introduced that implementing legislation. It was passed at second reading by 329 votes to 299 but MPs then rejected the bill's programme motion by 322 votes to 308.[320] The government, realising that it wouldn't

---

[320] As mentioned in chapter six, a programme motion sets out a timetable for a bill going through the House of Commons. Without a programme

be able to get its legislation passed in time, became obliged to seek a further extension to the date of the UK's departure from the EU – something that Boris Johnson had expressly said wouldn't happen – which the EU granted on 28 October, putting the date back to 31 January 2020. Prior to the vote on the programme motion, Boris Johnson had stated that if it were lost, he would abandon attempts to get his deal approved and would instead seek a general election. This is what he duly tried to do and, as was explained earlier, he finally succeeded in getting an election only by introducing a bill that allowed for an election to take place, notwithstanding the requirements of the Fixed-term Parliaments Act. And as we saw, once the Liberal Democrats and the SNP gave their support to the bill, Johnson's wish for a general election was granted, with Parliament being dissolved on 6 November in advance of the general election on 12 December. Following the Conservative Party's substantial victory at that election, the government tried again with its implementing legislation, with the bill itself removing the need for any separate meaningful vote to take place. This time the EU Withdrawal Agreement Bill was passed comfortably by the Parliament, thereby facilitating the UK's eventual departure from the EU at the end of January 2020.

---

motion in place there is a danger that a bill might be 'talked out' or 'filibustered' by its opponents.

8

Devolution

When Labour came to power in 1997 it was committed to a wide-ranging programme of constitutional reform, which included establishing devolved governments in Scotland and Wales and a city-wide administration for London. Labour was also committed to implementing its Conservative predecessor's proposals for a legislative assembly in Northern Ireland. The creation of devolved institutions in Northern Ireland was part of the wider 'Good Friday' or 'Belfast' Agreement which was crucial in bringing peace to the province. In Scotland and Wales however devolution was perhaps more of a process, the end of which wasn't necessarily clear. What Tony Blair and his colleagues almost certainly didn't envisage however was that devolution, in particular to Scotland, might actually eventually facilitate the break-up of the United Kingdom. Devolving significant powers to the new Scottish Parliament at Holyrood was seen by Blair's government as a means of putting a dampener on the Scottish independence movement. Simply, if significant powers were devolved to Scotland, then fewer Scots would desire independence. But if that was the thinking in the late 1990s, it was perhaps misguided. Rather, Scottish devolution has led to significantly increased support for the Scottish National Party (whose raison d'être is to secure independence for Scotland) particularly since the 2014 independence referendum. And the forcing of Scotland to leave the EU against the wishes of a majority of its citizens following the Brexit referendum gave a further substantial boost to the cause of Scottish independence. Back in 2014 those Scots advocating independence had said that the referendum that year was a 'once in a generation' opportunity to gain it. But just a few years later, Brexit has possibly provided an opportunity for supporters of Scottish independence to try again.

The Creation and Development of Devolved Government in the UK

Before 1999, ministers in the British Government generally treated Scotland, Northern Ireland and Wales in a similar way to other parts of the United Kingdom. They consulted the Secretaries of State for Scotland, Northern Ireland and Wales on how UK policies might affect those nations, but most policies were applied evenly across the United Kingdom. From Westminster the view of Cardiff was little different from that of Worcester. In the third decade of the 21st century it looks very different, with significant powers being exercised by the devolved governments in Scotland, Wales and Northern Ireland. And if the exercise of these powers had for a long time been largely unnoticed by many people living in England, the Covid pandemic showed starkly the extent to which these governments were able to apply policies different to each other's and to those of the UK Government who were largely taking decisions for England alone.

Before legislation was passed at Westminster to set up the new devolved administrations in Scotland, Wales and Northern Ireland, the people of these countries were asked whether they wanted devolved government in their particular part of the UK. This was done by holding referenda in 1997 in Scotland and Wales, and in 1998 in Northern Ireland. In Scotland the people had two votes: one to decide whether they wanted to have a Scottish Parliament and a second to decide whether such a Parliament should have tax-varying powers. The referenda in Scotland and Northern Ireland produced comfortable majorities for 'yes' (to both questions in Scotland), but in Wales it was much closer, with only 50.3% voting in favour and 49.7% voting against. In fact the result of the referendum in Wales was in the balance right up to the result from the last set of ballot papers to be counted in Carmarthenshire. And half the voters in Wales didn't vote at all.

In 1998, three acts were passed at Westminster that allowed for devolved government to be created in Scotland, Wales and Northern Ireland. These were the Scotland Act, the Government of Wales Act and the Northern Ireland Act. Each defined the powers and responsibilities of the devolved legislature and administration. Because they are acts of the Westminster Parliament, only Westminster can amend or repeal them.

Devolution in the United Kingdom is asymmetrical. In other words, government is different in the various nations that make up the UK because different amounts of power have been devolved to each. This asymmetry reflects the different sizes, histories and aspirations of the different parts of the UK. One size clearly does not fit all.

England

Most striking in this asymmetry is the position of England, where there is no legislative devolution at all, beyond that given to local government. So no tiers of government between local authorities and central government in England have any power to make laws specific to their part of the country. And of course there is no English Government or Parliament. So on matters that only affect England, it is the UK Government and the Westminster Parliament that make and implement law.

Whilst no new tiers of government with legislative powers have been set up in England, the degree of what one might call 'executive devolution' has, since the late 1990s, been quite significant. Since 2000, for example, London has had a mayor and a Greater London Assembly (GLA) to which the mayor is accountable. Whilst the GLA has no legislative power, it does have substantial budgetary powers and powers over policies on transport, planning and policing (among others).

The Blair Government did plan further devolution within

England, putting forward proposals in 2002 for elected regional assemblies. A referendum on the issue was held in one region of England, the North East, where the government felt that the creation of an elected regional assembly might be popular. But the result of the referendum in 2004 was a 78% to 22% vote against the idea of setting up an assembly. Following this result there were no further moves to establish regional assemblies in England.

The main development in English devolution after Labour lost power in 2010 was the creation of metro mayors. This created an additional tier of government, between Whitehall and the traditional local authorities, to take over responsibilities deemed to be too large for individual councils to deal with. Metro mayors are directly elected leaders of city regions spanning a number of local council areas. The mayors chair a 'mayoral combined authority' (MCA) that is made up of the leaders of all the councils in the region.[321] The powers granted to mayors and MCAs vary from region to region but, generally speaking, they hold powers over issues such as planning, transport, training, business support services and economic development.

The first city region to have a metro mayor was Greater Manchester, with Andy Burnham elected in 2017. Eight more regions followed: the Liverpool City Region, the West Midlands, Tees Valley, the West of England (including the Bristol urban area), Cambridgeshire and Peterborough, the Sheffield City Region, North of Tyne and West Yorkshire. The last of these, West Yorkshire, elected its first mayor in May 2021.

Some elected metro mayors have significant profiles, not just in their English regions but also nationally - in particular the metro mayors of Greater Manchester and the Liverpool City Region, Andy Burnham and Steve Rotheram. These two former Labour MPs both played high profile roles in support of their

---

[321] Metro mayors are not to be confused with local authority mayors who are directly elected leaders of individual councils. These have existed in many parts of England since 2002

regions during the Covid pandemic.

Scotland, Wales and Northern Ireland

The devolved legislatures of Scotland, Wales and Northern Ireland function quite differently from the Westminster Parliament. Because all three legislatures are elected by systems of proportional representation, majority single party governments are less common than they are at the UK level. They are also all unicameral: single chambers with no House of Lords equivalent. The lack of a second chamber means that their committees play a larger role than those at Westminster in the scrutiny of legislation. Initially, the legislatures of each of the devolved administrations served fixed terms of four years but they now all have five year terms to limit clashes with UK general elections.

Scotland

The new devolved government in Scotland was initially known as the Scottish Executive until the passing of the Scotland Act 2012 (see below), although the term 'Scottish Government' had been widely used for some time. The legislature is the Scottish Parliament. Until the 2007 Scottish parliamentary elections, Scotland had been ruled by a Labour-Liberal Democrat coalition administration. Following those elections however, a minority Scottish National Party (SNP) administration, led by Alex Salmond, took power. This government successfully survived four years of minority rule and went on to win an outright majority in the elections of 2011. In 2016 the SNP government was once again re-elected, albeit as a minority government and with Nicola Sturgeon now as First Minister. Following the 2021 elections the SNP remained in power, once again as a minority administration, having fallen one seat short of winning a majority.

The current Scottish Government has a First Minister and eleven other Cabinet ministers (known as Cabinet Secretaries). It also has sixteen other ministers, including the two law officers:

the Lord Advocate and the Solicitor-General for Scotland.

The Scottish Parliament has a total of 129 members who are called Members of the Scottish Parliament (MSPs). They are elected in two groups. There are 73 constituencies in Scotland that each elect a member to the Parliament.[322] Scotland is then divided into eight regions that each elect seven members to the Parliament. Candidates are taken from party lists in each region so that the overall number of MSPs elected from each party in a region is as proportional as possible to the votes cast for that party in the region.[323] This brings the total to 129 MSPs.

Powers of the Scottish Government and Parliament

The Scottish Parliament has the power to make primary legislation ('Acts of the Scottish Parliament') in all areas that are not reserved to Westminster.[324] The original list of reserved matters can be found in Schedule 5 of the Scotland Act 1998. Anything not on this list was within the competency of the Scottish Parliament, which means it can pass primary legislation in these areas.

Under the 1998 Scotland Act, the Scottish Parliament had been given the power to vary the UK standard rate of income tax by plus or minus 3%. This power had never actually been used by the time a new Scotland Act, in 2012, gave the Scottish

---

[322] These are the constituencies represented in the Scottish Parliament. There are only 59 Scottish seats at Westminster, reducing to 57 under Boundary Commission proposals published in June 2021.

[323] This system is one of a variety known as 'Additional Member Systems' of election.

[324] A particularly pernickety lawyer might say that, strictly speaking, acts passed by the devolved legislatures are not primary legislation since the power to make them derives from acts passed at Westminster, which in effect makes such legislation secondary not primary. In their scope however they are similar to acts of the Westminster Parliament, though, unlike Westminster Acts, it is possible for them to be struck down in the courts.

Parliament the power to levy its own Scottish income tax. Using this tax the Scottish Government could now raise about 35% of the money it had previously been given by the UK Government. The remaining 65% would continue to come from the UK Government as before. The 2012 Act also gave the Scottish Government borrowing powers for the first time as well as devolving to Scotland some other taxes (stamp duty and landfill tax) and some new policy areas including control over speed limits and drink-driving laws. (Following their transfer, the Scottish Government almost immediately announced plans to lower drink-drive limits in Scotland.) The act, as noted above, also formally renamed the Scottish Executive as the Scottish Government.

However, before most of these new powers were actually transferred, the Scottish Government decided that it wished to hold a referendum on whether Scotland should have independence from the UK. Under the existing Westminster legislation, the Scottish Government had no power to hold such a referendum but, under pressure to allow one to take place, the UK Prime Minister David Cameron agreed for the power to hold a referendum to be transferred to the Scottish administration. This was done via what's known as a 'Section 30 Order' – section 30 of the 1998 Scotland Act being that part of the legislation that allows additional powers to be transferred from Westminster to Edinburgh. It's important to understand however that this was done on a 'once-only' basis, which is why the current Scottish Government would once again need the permission of the UK Government to hold a legal second independence referendum.

Shortly before the independence referendum was held in September 2014, an opinion poll suggested that the Scottish electorate might vote for independence. This sufficiently spooked David Cameron and the leaders of the other major UK parties into offering a commission to look at further new powers that could be given to Scotland if the Scottish people voted no to independence. Following the 'no' vote in the referendum the Smith Commission was duly set up with its report forming the basis of a new

Scotland Act that was passed in 2016. This act went someway beyond what the Scotland Act 2012 had provided for, with the Scottish Government being given the power to set all rates and bands of income tax with the exception of the personal allowance. It was also now able to keep all income tax receipts and half of VAT receipts. The 2016 Act also substantially increased the powers of the Scottish Parliament over welfare policy.

Northern Ireland

The government in Northern Ireland is known as the Northern Ireland Executive and the legislature is the Northern Ireland Assembly. The Northern Ireland Executive is unusual in that it is based on an enforced system of power sharing. The coalition government is made up of the five largest parties, namely the Democratic Unionist Party, Sinn Féin, the Ulster Unionist Party, the Social Democratic and Labour Party and the Alliance Party. The first four are the two biggest parties from each side of the sectarian divide in Northern Ireland. The Alliance party is a non-sectarian party, allied to the Liberal Democrat party in Great Britain.

The 1999 Northern Ireland Act requires the largest parties to work together. In the 2021 Northern Ireland Executive, the First Minister, Paul Givan of the Democratic Unionist Party, and the deputy First Minister, Michelle O'Neill of Sinn Féin, have to operate, in effect, as 'one person'.[325] Neither can act without the other's consent. (This is why the small "d" in 'deputy' is important – the two in effect have equal power.) A further eight ministers are drawn from the five parties in the coalition, and two junior ministers support the First and deputy First Ministers. Due to difficulties between the parties that make up the Executive,

---

[325] When Arlene Foster resigned as leader of the DUP in April 2021 she was replaced by Edwin Poots MLA. Poots was himself replaced, shortly after, by Sir Jeffrey Donaldson MP. Neither Poots nor Donaldson however became First Minister. Poots nominated Paul Givan MLA as his party's candidate for First Minister who was then confirmed in the position by the Northern Ireland Assembly.

there have been two long periods since 1999 when the Executive was suspended (2002-2007 and 2017-2020) during which 'direct rule' from Westminster was reintroduced. (Direct rule had been in place from the collapse of the previous Northern Irish institutions in 1972 through to the implementation of the 1998 Act.)

The Northern Ireland Assembly has 90 'Members of the Legislative Assembly' (MLAs). It had previously had a membership of 108 but this was reduced in 2016. Elections to the Assembly are based on the eighteen Westminster constituencies, with each constituency electing five members via the single transferable vote system of election. This system allows voters to list the candidates in order of preference and, like the Scottish and Welsh systems, is broadly proportional in outcome. At the 2017 election the DUP once again won the most seats, although only one more than Sinn Féin; thus Arlene Foster remained as First Minister (until her resignation in April 2021) with Michelle O'Neill staying on as deputy First Minister. The next elections to the Northern Ireland Assembly will take place in May 2022.

Powers of the Northern Ireland Executive and Assembly

The legislative model in Northern Ireland is similar to the Scottish model in that the Assembly can pass acts in all areas that are not retained by Westminster under the Northern Ireland Act 1998. However, in Northern Ireland there are two categories of such matters – those that are 'Excepted' and those that are 'Reserved'. Excepted Matters are listed in Schedule 2 of the Northern Ireland Act. These are areas retained by Westminster, with no prospect of their being devolved in the future. Reserved Matters are listed in Schedule 3 of the Northern Ireland Act. These are areas that, with the consent of the Secretary of State, may be transferred to the Assembly at a later date. For example, policing and criminal justice matters were a reserved matter until they were devolved to the Northern Ireland Assembly in April 2010. All devolved matters in Northern Ireland are referred to as 'Transferred Matters'.

Of the three original devolution settlements of the late 1990s, the Northern Irish one has changed the least so, unlike the devolved administrations in Cardiff and Edinburgh, the Northern Ireland Executive continues to have no power to make changes to income tax rates.

Wales

In Wales the executive is known as the Welsh Government (formerly Welsh Assembly Government). Prior to the Assembly elections of 2007 the administration had consisted of the Labour Party ruling either alone or in coalition with the Liberal Democrats. After those elections however, the Welsh Government consisted of a coalition between the Labour Party and Plaid Cymru with the Labour leader Carwyn Jones as First Minister and the leader of Plaid Cymru, Ieuan Wyn Jones, as Deputy First Minister. However, at the 2011 Assembly elections, Labour won exactly half of the seats in the Assembly and went on to form a single party administration with Carwyn Jones continuing as First Minister. At the 2016 Assembly elections the Labour Party lost one seat, and formed a coalition administration with the Liberal Democrats. In 2018 Carwyn Jones stepped down as First Minister to be replaced by Mark Drakeford. At the 2021 elections, the Labour Party again won exactly half the seats and therefore continued in government, although no longer in coalition with the Liberal Democrats who won just one seat.

In the Welsh Government there are nine Cabinet ministers, including the First Minister and five deputy ministers.

When it first came into being, the legislature in Wales was known as the National Assembly for Wales (and commonly referred to as the Welsh Assembly). In 2020 its name was changed to the Welsh Parliament or, in Welsh, the Senedd. The Senedd has 60 Members (MSs), who, like Scotland's MSPs, are elected through a combination of constituencies and regional lists.

There are 40 constituencies in Wales that each elect an MS.[326] Wales is then further divided into five regions, each of which returns four members to the Senedd. As in Scotland this produces a result where the number of seats won by any party is broadly proportional to the number of votes that party has won.

Powers of the Welsh Government and Senedd

The Welsh model of devolution was originally quite different from that of Scotland and Northern Ireland. The National Assembly for Wales (now Senedd) has been able to make primary legislation only since the Government of Wales Act 2006 came into effect. Before then, it had the power only to make secondary legislation using powers given to it by Westminster Acts. But the 2006 Act only allowed the Assembly to pass primary legislation in detailed areas specifically transferred to it by Westminster. The act however did allow for a referendum to be held on whether the Assembly should be given full primary legislative powers in certain policy areas. This referendum was held in March 2011 with the people of Wales voting in favour of these powers being granted. This whetted the appetite of many in Wales for yet further devolved power, resulting in the UK Government setting up a Commission (the "Silk Commission") to review the operation of devolution in Wales.

In 2014 the Coalition Government introduced a Wales Bill to give legislative effect to many of the Silk Commission's proposals, particularly in respect of the fiscal powers of the Assembly. Stamp duty, business rates and landfill tax were devolved, with the Assembly able to replace them with new taxes specific to Wales. The Assembly was also given limited powers to vary income tax rates. The Silk Commission had also proposed that Wales should move to a model of devolution similar to that of the Scottish Parliament and the Northern Ireland Assembly

---

[326] These are the constituencies represented in the Senedd. There are also 40 Welsh seats at Westminster, reducing to 32 under Boundary Commission proposals published in June 2021.

whereby specific matters would be reserved to Westminster with all other matters being devolved to Cardiff. This change came into effect with the passing of the Wales Act 2017. The reserved matters are specified in schedule 7a of the act. By not appearing in this schedule, a number of additional policy areas were thereby devolved to Wales, including aspects of water policy, marine affairs, energy and rail franchising.

In 2019, the Welsh Government first used its new powers over income tax. The rates of the three tax bands set by the UK Government were each reduced in Wales by 10p in the pound, with Welsh ministers having the power to decide what Welsh rates they should add to these new lower UK rates. So far the Welsh Government has decided to keep the total tax rates paid by Welsh taxpayers the same as those paid by taxpayers in England and Northern Ireland.

The Law Making Powers of the Devolved Administrations

The devolved administrations can make both primary and secondary legislation. Their power to make primary legislation derives from the acts that originally set up them up.[327] Their power to make secondary legislation however derives from two sources. Any act passed by one of the devolved legislatures may confer powers on ministers in that nation to make secondary legislation. But secondary legislation can also be made under acts in devolved areas that were passed at Westminster prior to devolution. An example of the latter would be the Food Safety Act 1990, which allows ministers in Scotland, Wales and Northern Ireland to make secondary legislation using powers which, prior to devolution, were used by ministers in the UK Government to make legislation across the UK.

Although the devolved legislatures are able to make primary legislation, there are limitations on this competence. As we have

---

[327] And, in the case of the Senedd, the 2006 Government of Wales Act.

seen, the legislatures in all three nations can legislate only in areas not retained by Westminster. There is, however, another consideration affecting legislative competence: all legislation of the devolved legislatures must comply with the European Convention on Human Rights.

The devolved administrations in Scotland, Wales and Northern Ireland have been set up under a statutory framework which means their actions and their legislation can be challenged in the courts on these and other grounds. Until 2009 the highest court of appeal on devolution matters was the Judicial Committee of the Privy Council but, since then, this function has been the responsibility of the Supreme Court.[328] On a number of occasions the UK Government has referred to the Supreme Court a bill passed by one of the devolved legislatures, prior to the bill receiving Royal Assent. A particularly high profile case related to Brexit. As the Scottish Government was unhappy with the provisions made by Westminster to ensure legal continuity following the UK's departure from the EU, it introduced its own 'UK Withdrawal from the European Union (Legal Continuity) (Scotland) Bill' to make separate provisions for legal continuity in Scotland. When this bill was passed by the Scottish Parliament in March 2021, the Attorney General and Advocate General in the UK Government challenged the bill in the Supreme Court, arguing that it was outside the competence of the Scottish Parliament to pass such legislation.[329] In this case the Supreme Court found against the UK Government, ruling that the Scottish Parliament did have the competence to pass such legislation, except in respect of one section of the bill which the judges deemed was attempting to amend the Scotland Act 1998 which

---

[328] The JCPC, whose membership is often identical to that of the Supreme Court, is the highest court of appeal for a number of Commonwealth countries, in particular those of the West Indies. Although no devolution case ever went to the JCPC, in 2002 the right of the Scottish Parliament to pass an act banning fox hunting was challenged, unsuccessfully, in the Scottish courts on Human Rights grounds.

[329] The Advocate General is the UK Law Officer who advises the UK Government on matters concerning Scots law.

the Scottish Parliament didn't have the power to do.[330]

The reason why primary legislation passed by the devolved legislatures can be challenged in the courts in this way is because these legislatures aren't sovereign in the way the Westminster Parliament is. We discussed in chapter one the doctrine of parliamentary sovereignty in respect of Westminster and saw how this meant that it wasn't possible to have legislation passed by the UK Parliament struck down in the courts. But the three devolved legislatures are statutory bodies i.e. they operate according to acts passed by Westminster. So if they appear to step outside the constraints set on them by these acts, they can be challenged in the courts.

This ability to challenge in the courts primary legislation passed by the devolved legislatures could be crucial to any attempt by Nicola Sturgeon's Scottish Government to bring forward legislation in respect of another independence referendum. As we have seen, under existing legislation the Scottish Parliament doesn't have the power to legislate on such matters; these are reserved to Westminster and were only transferred to Scotland in respect of the 2014 referendum on a 'one-off' basis. Whilst David Cameron was prepared to allow the Scottish Parliament to legislate for the referendum to take place in 2014, Boris Johnson has been clear that he opposes a second independence referendum. This doesn't necessarily stop the Scottish Government introducing such legislation in the Scottish Parliament, but if the Parliament passed such legislation it seems highly likely that it would be subject to legal challenge. The UK government would have four weeks to decide whether to challenge the bill in the Supreme Court, with the challenge probably being made in the name of the Attorney General and

---

[330] https://www.supremecourt.uk/cases/docs/uksc-2018-0080-press-summary.pdf. The Supreme Court judgment refers to 'section 17' of the bill, as opposed to 'clause 17'. This is because Scottish Parliament bills and acts are both divided up into sections. As we saw earlier, bills at Westminster are divided up into clauses which become sections only when the bill becomes an act.

Advocate General. Even if the UK Government was however reluctant for any reason to go down this path, it seems inevitable that a private individual would challenge the legislation, initially in the Court of Session in Edinburgh.

However, for the referendum bill even to be introduced in the Scottish Parliament, it would first have to be agreed as *intra vires* (i.e. within the powers of the Scottish Parliament to legislate on such matters) by both the Lord Advocate, who is the senior law officer of the Scottish Government, and by the Presiding Officer of the Scottish Parliament. This could prove to be a significant hurdle for the Scottish Government to overcome even before the legality of the ensuing bill was challenged in the courts. The Lord Advocate's role in the Scottish Government is similar to that of the Attorney General's in the UK Government although, perhaps importantly, she isn't an elected politician from the governing party in the way that the Attorney General is.[331] The Presiding Officer of the Scottish Parliament, elected after the May 2021 Scottish parliamentary elections, is Alison Johnstone MSP. Before the election she had been a Scottish Green MSP. As Presiding Officer, like the Speaker of the House of Commons, she has to act with rigid impartiality. But if she is asked to make a judgement on whether any referendum bill is within the powers of the Scottish Parliament to consider, would her former membership of the pro-independence Scottish Green Party be relevant?

What Has and Hasn't Been Devolved to Scotland, Wales and Northern Ireland?

Substantial legislative powers have now been devolved to Scotland, Wales and Northern Ireland in major areas of domestic policy such as health, education and training, local government, housing, local economic development, agriculture, fisheries, many aspects of transport, the environment, tourism, sport and heritage.

---

[331] The current Lord Advocate is Dorothy Bain. UK Attorney General is Suella Braverman who is also the Conservative MP for Fareham.

This devolution of responsibility for particular areas of public policy has led to a substantial divergence in approach across the United Kingdom: examples include tuition fees for higher education, prescription charges, long-term care for elderly people and the management of the Covid pandemic. But there are still a number of very important areas of policy that remain undevolved. These include the constitution (including the devolution acts themselves), foreign affairs, defence and national security, and some areas of macro-economic, fiscal and monetary policy.

In other important areas of policy, powers have been devolved to some nations but not to others. As we have seen, the ability of the three devolved administrations to set their own rates of income tax varies considerably. Additionally, some aspects of social security are devolved matters in Northern Ireland but not in Scotland and Wales whilst law and order matters (policing, prisons, probation, the courts etc.) are devolved in Scotland and Northern Ireland but not in Wales.

The reason for the different approaches in respect of law and order are largely historical. When Scotland became part of the United Kingdom in 1707 it kept its own separate legal and criminal justice systems. So for nearly 300 years prior to devolution, Scotland had had a judicial system separate to that of England and Wales. It would therefore have been perverse if law and order matters had not been devolved to the Scottish Parliament in 1999. Wales, on the other hand, had been part of a unified legal jurisdiction with England since the 16th century; so for hundreds of years Wales hadn't had its own judicial system. Thus such matters weren't devolved to Wales in 1999. However, since then, a substantial body of Welsh law has come into being, leading to calls for the devolution of justice powers to Wales and the creation of a separate Welsh legal system. Northern Ireland is different again. When Ireland was partitioned in 1921 a new legal system was set up for Northern Ireland. Prior to its suspension in 1972, the management of the Northern Irish judicial system was the responsibility of the old Stormont Parliament. After 1972 these powers, along with all other powers of the Stormont

Parliament, were transferred to Westminster while direct rule was exercised over Northern Ireland. In 1999, logically, law and order matters would have been devolved to the new Northern Ireland Assembly as they were to the Scottish Parliament, but due to the political sensitivity of policy areas such as policing, prisons and the courts, the UK government decided to delay devolution of these matters to the Assembly until 2010.

One area that is devolved in Northern Ireland but not in Scotland and Wales is the Civil Service. Civil servants who work for the Scottish and Welsh Governments are part of the same Civil Service as those who work for the UK Government. The Northern Ireland Civil Service has, however, been a separate organisation since the creation of Northern Ireland in 1921.

How Devolved Government is Financed

Whatever legislative powers are enjoyed by the devolved administrations, a key factor in their ability to exercise real power is the extent to which they control their own income. This is an area where the power of the devolved administrations had been, until recently, very limited.

The UK Government allocates money to the various UK Government departments through the spending review process. It then allocates block grants to the devolved administrations of Scotland, Wales and Northern Ireland based on the 'Barnett Formula'. This formula was created when Joel Barnett was the Chief Secretary to the Treasury in the 1970s and therefore pre-dates devolution.

To explain how these block grants are calculated: the UK Government determines the total amount of money to be spent on any particular area of government in England. The Barnett formula, which is essentially constructed on the relative populations of Scotland, Wales and Northern Ireland and the proportion of any particular area of government that is devolved in each country, is then applied to these amounts to produce specific pots of money to be allocated to the devolved administrations. Before devolution, these precise amounts would be spent by the UK Government on those areas of policy in Scotland, Wales and Northern Ireland. The devolved administrations, however, can spend the block grant - which is made up of all the individual amounts - however they wish. Thus they have considerable freedom to choose how to spend their pot of cash. What they couldn't do until recently however was to change the size of the pot. But the Scottish and Welsh Governments can now do this by levying different tax rates in their countries compared to the rest of the UK.

An interesting recent example of the Barnett formula in action concerns the substantial increase in spending by the UK Government during the Covid pandemic. Quite a lot of this extra expenditure was on matters that are devolved to Scotland, Wales and Northern Ireland – health being the obvious example. Because this extra money allocated by the UK Government was for England only, substantial additional sums, under the Barnett formula, were allocated to the devolved governments in Belfast, Cardiff and Edinburgh.

Since in recent years there has been some devolution to Scotland and Wales of power over tax, with some tax revenues now accruing directly to the devolved governments there, some adjustments have had to be made to how the Barnett formula works. Essentially, the block grants that the Scottish and Welsh Governments now receive are reduced by an amount that the UK Government would have expected to raise had the taxes not been devolved. The devolved governments then compensate for this reduction in their revenues using the taxes that have been devolved to them. The total revenue that they then have at their disposal could be more or less than what they would have received prior to the tax devolution, depending on the tax rates that they levy.

The Barnett formula has always been quite controversial. Despite its huge importance to the devolved administrations, the way it operates has never been set in stone. So there was controversy, for example, as to whether the substantial expenditure on the 2012 Olympic Games should be classified as 'England only' expenditure, given that almost all the money was being spent in England and that sport was a devolved matter in Scotland, Wales and Northern Ireland. Were the expenditure classified so, under the Barnett Formula substantial extra grants (known as 'Barnett Consequentials') would have been paid to the devolved administrations. The UK Government, therefore, not surprisingly decided to classify the expenditure on the Olympics largely as 'UK-wide'. There was also controversy over the £1bn funding package for Northern Ireland that was negotiated as part of the Conservative-DUP agreement after the 2017 general election. When the UK Government stated that this money would fall wholly outside the Barnett process it led to complaints from the Scottish and Welsh Governments who would otherwise have received more funding as a result of the grant to Northern Ireland. But because the Barnett Formula has no legal underpinning there was no way by which the decision could be challenged.

What is perhaps the most controversial aspect of the Barnett Formula is that it leads to the amounts of public expenditure per capita across the four nations of the UK being significantly different. This is because what the formula calculates each year is the amounts to be given to the devolved administrations based on the *additional* expenditure that the UK Government has agreed for England. The formula therefore preserves the differences in expenditure across the four nations which in the past have been significant. Thus, for example in 2018/19, public expenditure per capita was 25% higher in Northern Ireland, 21% higher in Scotland, and 15% higher in Wales than it was in England.[332]

Devolution and Westminster

Westminster remains the sovereign parliament of the UK, being able to legislate on any matter across the UK. MPs from Scotland, Wales and Northern Ireland continue to sit in the House of Commons to represent their constituents on matters that are not devolved. Although in theory the Westminster Parliament still has the power to legislate in any area across the whole of the UK, in practice it normally

---

[332] https://www.instituteforgovernment.org.uk/explainers/barnett-formula

doesn't. Even when it does, this is usually done only with the consent of the devolved legislature. This is due to the 'Sewell Convention', named after Lord Sewell who was the Scottish Office Minister in the House of Lords during the passage of the Scotland Bill in 1997-8.

The Sewell Convention

If the Westminster Parliament wishes to legislate for Scotland, Northern Ireland or Wales on a devolved matter, according to the Sewell Convention, a 'legislative consent motion' should be passed in the relevant devolved legislature before the Westminster Bill passes the last stage at which it can be amended.[333] If the devolved legislature's consent is withheld, it is then up to the UK Parliament to decide whether to amend the legislation or to pass it as it stands.

Although the Sewell convention is mentioned in both the Scotland Act 2016 and the Wales Act 2017, it isn't legally binding and therefore the convention doesn't place any statutory limits on the power of Westminster to legislate on all matters across the UK if it wishes to do so. Legislative consent motions have been passed hundreds of times across the three devolved legislatures since 1999 and, in the vast majority of cases, this has happened without any controversy. But during the passage of Brexit legislation at Westminster, real disputes arose between the UK Government and the devolved administrations in this area.

The UK's relations with the EU were clearly always an area reserved to Westminster by the devolution acts. However, many of the policy areas over which the devolved legislatures had competence were also areas where much of the legislation was made at the EU level, rather than by national parliaments. Thus much of the legislation passed at Westminster to implement Brexit was bound to impact on the competences of the devolved legislatures and would therefore, under the Sewell convention,

---

[333] In Scotland, legislative consent motions are commonly known as 'Sewell motions'.

require their consent. Despite this however, both the EU Withdrawal Bill and the European Union Withdrawal Agreement Bill were passed at Westminster without the consent of at least one of the devolved legislatures due to disagreements between the UK Government and the devolved administrations over certain aspects of the bills. When this happened to the EU Withdrawal Bill in 2018 it was the first time that Westminster had ever legislated in a devolved area without the consent of the Scottish Parliament.

In the case of the European Union Withdrawal Agreement Bill, all three devolved legislatures withheld their consent, but the UK Parliament in any case passed the bill in January 2020. And later that year both the Scottish Parliament and the Senedd also voted to withhold consent to another key piece of Brexit-related legislation, the UK Internal Market Bill. The UK Government's position on this legislation was that it simply replaced EU internal market rules with similar rules for the UK, following the UK's exit from the EU single market. The view of the Scottish and Welsh administrations, however, was that the process through which EU single market rules were developed was fundamentally different to how the UK Government was proposing to make rules for the UK single market. Whereas the EU sought to find agreement between member states, the view of the Scottish and Welsh Governments was that the UK Internal Market Bill unilaterally imposed regulations on the devolved institutions. Thus their parliaments withheld their consent to the bill. This did not, however, stop Westminster passing the legislation.

The West Lothian Question

What has always loomed large during the development of devolution in the UK is the issue of England and, in particular, what is commonly described as the 'West Lothian Question' (so called as it was raised in its modern form in the 1970s by the MP for West Lothian, Tam Dalyell, when devolution was mooted by the then Labour Government). As there is no English Parliament, any legislation specific to England is made by the House of Commons and the House of Lords, which have members not only from England but from Scotland, Wales and Northern Ireland too. This means, for example, that Scottish MPs at Westminster have a say over education matters in England but English MPs have no say over education in Scotland, where education is devolved to the Scottish Parliament. One solution might be to create an English Parliament or regional assemblies with powers similar to the Scottish Parliament, but there is no appetite for this at the moment.

It has been quite easy to paint this issue as being 'unfair to the English', particularly when combined with the way that the Barnett Formula leads to greater public expenditure per head in the non-English parts of the UK. Whilst it wasn't totally surprising that Prime Minister David Cameron flagged up the idea of 'English votes for English laws' (EVEL) after the 2014 Scottish independence referendum, his timing may not have been entirely advisable, since raising the issue only hours after the referendum result was announced caused much irritation in Scotland and provided a boost to the fortunes of the SNP and the independence cause more generally.

EVEL, the operation and discontinuation of which we discussed in chapter six, only partially dealt with the West Lothian Question. For one thing, EVEL ignored the House of Lords whose members cannot be defined by nationality. And furthermore, even though some bills, or parts of bills, had been classified as 'wholly English' since EVEL was introduced, the system ignored the working of the Barnett formula. A piece of legislation going through Westminster may be 'England only' but, due to the way Barnett works, it might still have a knock-on effect on public expenditure in Scotland, Northern Ireland and Wales in which MPs from those nations have a legitimate interest. It is interesting how reports in mid-2021 of EVEL's imminent demise were couched in terms of its abolition giving Scottish MPs 'the right to vote down English legislation'.[334] This was of course true, but EVEL's eventual abolition only represented a reversion to the pre-2015 position.

The Future of Devolution and the United Kingdom

Tony Blair's first Secretary of State for Wales once said that devolution was *a process, not an event*.[335] And so it has proved to be. But in the late 1990s, few people if anyone would have believed that the setting up of devolved administrations in Cardiff, Belfast and Edinburgh might, one day, facilitate the break-up of the United Kingdom.

As we have seen, devolution within England has been quite limited, though the creation of new metro mayors continues. Devolution to regional assemblies as once considered by the Blair Government continues however to be off the agenda. Even further off the agenda is the creation of an English Parliament, given that the benefits of devolving power to a body representing over 80 per cent of the UK population are not obvious to most people. It would also raise a number of practical issues, not least being the problems that would arise if a party had a majority amongst UK but not English MPs. Thus this idea developed no further than the short-lived introduction of 'English Votes for English Laws' in the House of Commons.

In Northern Ireland, the exercise of devolved powers in the province by locally elected politicians continues to be an implicit part of the continuing peace process. However, just as Northern Ireland marks the centenary of its creation, there are serious

---

[334] For example, this article in 'The Times'
https://www.thetimes.co.uk/article/scottish-mps-could-vote-down-english-laws-in-michael-goves-attempt-to-save-union-s5mkpgrtd

[335] Rt Hon Ron Davies MP
https://hansard.parliament.uk/Commons/1998-01-21/debates/4acb236e-1500-4eef-b6d4-9018e591dc5d/GovernmentOfWalesBill

questions now being raised about its future constitutional status. For the first time in Northern Ireland's history, there are more of its people who would classify themselves as catholic than protestant. That doesn't mean that a reunification of Ireland is likely any time soon, but the probability of it happening has clearly been increased by the fall-out from Brexit. Well before the Brexit referendum was held, it was abundantly clear that there would be significant problems for the island of Ireland were the UK to leave the EU. It would either lead to some sort of customs border being reimposed between Northern Ireland and the Republic or one being created between Northern Ireland and the rest of the UK. Either option was bound to have a damaging effect on the peace process in Northern Ireland which is always fragile and, with Boris Johnson's government having gone for the latter option, it's the unionist community that is the most upset. With tensions running higher in the province than they have for many years it may be that, in the not too distant future, a British Government will allow a referendum to be held in Northern Ireland on the issue of reunification. Reunification would also of course have to be accepted by the people of the Republic of Ireland but were both sides to agree to it, Northern Ireland's secession from the UK would very likely follow.

In Wales, as we have seen, significant new powers have been given to the Senedd and its National Assembly predecessor since the first Government of Wales Act was passed in 1998. Perhaps of all the non-English parts of the UK, the future of Wales as part of the union is the least uncertain. However, even though the pro-union Labour Party did well in the 2021 elections to the Senedd, with Plaid Cymru falling back a little, it's probably fair to say that independence for Wales was a bigger issue at those elections than it had ever been before, following an opinion poll in March 2021 showing 39% support for independence.[336]

But it's in Scotland where there is perhaps the biggest threat

---

[336] https://nation.cymru/news/poll-shows-highest-support-for-welsh-independence-ever-recorded/

to the future of the United Kingdom. Since the original devolution settlement for Scotland, substantial new powers, as we have seen, have been devolved, particularly over matters such as taxation and welfare. But these powers still fall a long way short of satisfying the desire of many in Scotland to run their own affairs. Crucial matters such as defence and foreign policy remain matters for the UK Government: thus Scotland could be taken out of the EU against its wishes and continues to host the British nuclear deterrent on the Clyde against the wishes of many Scottish people and certainly against the wishes of the current Scottish Government.

It is perhaps not appreciated by many that the degree to which Scotland is 'governed by Westminster' is still substantially greater than the extent to which the UK was ever 'governed by Brussels' when it was a member of the EU. Yet it was a desire not to be governed by Brussels that was instrumental in persuading a majority of British voters in 2016 to favour leaving the EU. Boris Johnson may well have set his face against the idea of a second independence referendum but with the Scottish people electing a pro-independence majority at the Scottish parliamentary elections of May 2021 this may be an increasingly difficult line to hold.[337]

Whether the UK Government eventually allows a second independence referendum to be held remains to be seen. And if a referendum is held, it's impossible to know how the Scottish people would then vote. But it's hard to argue against the view that the future of the United Kingdom looks less secure now than it ever has.

---

[337] Although the SNP didn't win a majority at those elections, their seats combined with those won by the pro-independence Scottish Green Party did create a majority of MSPs favouring independence.

Concluding Thoughts

As William Gladstone said in 1879, *the British constitution presumes more boldly than any other the good sense and good faith of those who work it.*[338] It is, as we have seen, what Peter Hennessy has for many years described as the 'good chap' theory: that the British system of government relies to a considerable degree on the good behaviour of those who work within it. It may be a description that uses language which is a bit dated these days but it's one that has stuck with me ever since I first heard Hennessy use it in the early 1990s.

So what is a 'good chap' in respect of the British system of government? Perhaps it's best described by the 'Nolan Principles' which were drawn up in 1995 by the Committee on Standards in Public Life under its first Chair, Lord Nolan. The Committee had been set up by the then Prime Minister John Major in response to concerns about the unethical behaviour of certain politicians, most notably including the 'cash for questions affair' in which two Conservative MPs had been accused of taking cash in return for asking parliamentary questions on behalf of the owner of Harrods, Mohamed Al-Fayed. I think the seven Nolan Principles are worth spelling out in full here.[339]

---

[338] Ibid. William Gladstone

[339] https://www.gov.uk/government/publications/the-7-principles-of-public-life

The Seven Principles of Public Life

Selflessness
Holders of public office should act solely in terms of the public interest.

Integrity
Holders of public office must avoid placing themselves under any obligation to people or organisations that might try inappropriately to influence them in their work. They should not act or take decisions in order to gain financial or other material benefits for themselves, their family, or their friends. They must declare and resolve any interests and relationships.

Objectivity
Holders of public office must act and take decisions impartially, fairly and on merit, using the best evidence and without discrimination or bias.

Accountability
Holders of public office are accountable to the public for their decisions and actions and must submit themselves to the scrutiny necessary to ensure this.

Openness
Holders of public office should act and take decisions in an open and transparent manner. Information should not be withheld from the public unless there are clear and lawful reasons for so doing.

Honesty
Holders of public office should be truthful.

Leadership
Holders of public office should exhibit these principles in their own behaviour. They should actively promote and robustly support the principles and be willing to challenge poor behaviour wherever it occurs.

Figure 13

Readers can judge for themselves the extent to which ministers in the current UK Government, or indeed in any other UK Government, meet these standards, but there have been a number of events in recent years that might lead one at least to ask some questions.

The Brexit referendum, whatever one thinks of its outcome, seriously affected the operation of the British system of government. In the responses of the May and Johnson Governments to the result, one could be forgiven for thinking that the view of the British people expressed in this single vote overrode any other aspects of the principles on which the UK system operates – parliamentary sovereignty being perhaps the most obvious one but also other principles such as the Sewell Convention by which the governments of Scotland, Wales and Northern Ireland expect to be properly consulted by the UK Government on matters that affect their competences. Most notably, the 'will of the people' as expressed in the EU referendum justified, in the eyes of Boris Johnson and his ministers, the unlawful prorogation that drew the monarchy into party political controversy and was so strongly and unanimously condemned by the justices of the Supreme Court. No-one should underestimate the importance of the view of the people as expressed in a referendum and I have never been one to sign up to the notion that the referendum was 'only advisory'. Technically, in a system with a sovereign Parliament, referendums are advisory, but that doesn't mean that they can be ignored. But nor does a referendum result allow a government to ride roughshod over key constitutional principles by trying to suspend Parliament (the unlawful prorogation) because they feared it was about to do something they didn't like (i.e. delay the date of Brexit).

Nor does it allow the government to threaten to ignore laws passed by Parliament because they conflict with the 'will of the people'. But this is exactly what Boris Johnson's government seemed to be threatening to do when the Benn Act was passed in September 2019. Parliament had legislated to allow Brexit to be delayed in certain circumstances. That was now law. But the government's response to the act being passed was to state *we must respect the referendum result and the UK will be leaving the EU on 31 October whatever the circumstances.*[340] So was the government suggesting that it might simply ignore the law? (It

---

[340] https://petition.parliament.uk/archived/petitions/269157

won't have escaped anyone's notice of course that the UK didn't actually leave the EU on 31 October 2019.)

To the above we could add: (i) Boris Johnson's refusal to take action when his Home Secretary was found to have broken the Ministerial Code (see chapter two); (ii) his government's readiness to break international law and renege on the commitments it gave to the EU in respect of the position of Northern Ireland post-Brexit;[341] (iii) the number of times his ministers have been found by the courts to have acted unlawfully;[342] (iv) the almost casual willingness of ministers, and the Prime Minister in particular, to mislead Parliament;[343] and (v) the events surrounding the resignation of Matt Hancock as Health Secretary in June 2021 which raised serious questions about his hiring of an intimate friend who had family connections in the healthcare business as an adviser and non-executive director. (To be clear, the concerns around Hancock's behaviour weren't just about infidelity and hypocrisy.)

There are also concerns about what is happening to my former employer, the Civil Service. One of the great strengths of the UK system of government has always been, in my view, that we have officials working in it who are permanent. Not only does this mean we avoid the hiatuses experienced when governments

---

[341] https://www.bbc.co.uk/news/uk-politics-54097320

[342] As examples: the Court of Appeal ruling in November 2020 that the Education Secretary Gavin Williamson had acted unlawfully by removing safeguards for children in care at the start of the pandemic without consulting children's rights organisations; the High Court finding in February 2021 that the then Health Secretary Matt Hancock had acted unlawfully by failing to publish Covid-19 contracts worth billions of pounds within the legal 30-day period; and in June 2021 when the Cabinet Office Minister Michael Gove was found by the High Court to have unlawfully awarded a contract to a communications company which was run by associates of himself and his former adviser Dominic Cummings.

[343] https://www.huffingtonpost.co.uk/entry/boris-johnson-new-rules-to-correct-lies-to-parliament-speaker-hoyle_uk_60896f80e4b02e74d2223224

change in countries like the United States but also that officials can 'speak truth to power' – in other words, advise ministers with objectivity and impartiality. This in my view is hugely beneficial to the governance of the country. As anyone who's ever worked in any kind of organisation knows, people always like to bring their bosses good news. But that's exactly what we don't want in government. What we want are officials who will give their minister the unvarnished truth, be it good or bad. And because in the British system the minister isn't the civil servant's boss, officials ought to be able to do just that. But can we any longer be absolutely certain that today's Civil Service is adhering to those 19th century Northcote-Trevelyan principles? Finding senior officials in today's Civil Service who are also on the payroll of a bank is extremely worrying.[344] Seeing very senior civil servants leaving office for reasons that are far from normal is even more so – in particular the resignation in February 2020 of the most senior civil servant at the Home Office, alleging he had become the target of a *vicious and orchestrated* briefing campaign after trying to persuade the Home Secretary, Priti Patel, to change her behaviour.[345] (The subsequent case he took to an employment tribunal eventually cost the British taxpayer £340,000 plus legal costs.)

Most worrying of all though is the fact that civil servants in recent times seem more ready to break the rule that's clearly set out in the Civil Service Code about *not knowingly misleading Parliament or others.*[346] In chapter three I referenced some recent instances highlighted by the Institute for Government where civil servants had been less than 100% accurate in their public communications. More shocking than those was to hear a senior select committee chair in July 2021 say that the most senior civil servant in the Home Office had recently given evidence to her committee that was *simply not true* and that it *really troubled* her when *civil servants are reinforcing the things that ministers are*

---

[344] https://www.bbc.co.uk/news/uk-politics-56733465

[345] https://www.bbc.co.uk/news/uk-politics-56281781

[346] Ibid. Civil Service Code

saying that are just wrong. Civil Servants do have a duty to impartiality and a responsibility to be accurate about the facts. It's obviously a big concern for me that the Home Secretary is not telling us the accurate situation, but it troubles me in terms of the civil servant situation as well. [347]

It would be all too easy to dismiss these comments as partial, coming as they did from the Labour chair of the Home Affairs Select Committee. But that would, in my view, be wrong. This was the first time I had ever heard a select committee chair clearly suggest that civil servants had knowingly given evidence to a committee which they knew to be inaccurate.

Because of the importance of the 'good chap' theory to the way the UK is governed, it concerns me when the person who coined that phrase (Peter Hennessy) expresses in late 2019 his concern that *general standards of good behaviour among senior UK politicians can no longer be taken for granted.*[348] He and his co-author Andrew Blick speculate as to why this is the case:

> *It may be that changed circumstances, in particular the Brexit turbulence, have made it difficult for those who wish to behave properly to ascertain correct courses of action. Much of the present difficulties might reflect a Prime Minister who, for all his gifts, is tone deaf on the melodies of the constitution. Perhaps, more widely, the current political environment has tended to elevate*

---

[347] Yvette Cooper, chair of the Home Affairs Select Committee, speaking on the 'Commons People' (Huff Post) podcast of 23 July 2021. She was discussing the recent appearance before her committee of the Home Secretary and her Permanent Secretary to discuss 'The Work of the Home Secretary'. The evidence session can be watched here: https://parliamentlive.tv/event/index/d2ede615-9b6f-4e87-93fd-58b5e1d4a65c. The transcript of the evidence session can be read here: https://committees.parliament.uk/oralevidence/2602/html/

[348] Andrew Blick and Peter Hennessy 'Good Chaps No More? Safeguarding the Constitution in Stressful Times'. https://consoc.org.uk/wp-content/uploads/2019/11/FINAL-Blick-Hennessy-Good-Chaps-No-More.pdf

'chaps' who are less inclined to be 'good'. The supply of well-intentioned candidates might have diminished, as could the general level of respect accorded to previously understood rules, possibly in society as a whole. It could, moreover, be that the 'good chap' system was always flawed, that it was neither desirable nor as effective as was imagined, and that any success that it appeared to attain owes much to a measure of fortune, that has now expired, exposing its fragility.[349]

And they conclude that:

recent events suggest it is worth considering the implications of a decline in the viability of the 'good chap' system in this country. And that the system by its normal standards has experienced a genuine shock, not confined to but exemplified by the great prorogation stand-off. It needs urgent attention.... If general standards of good behaviour among senior UK politicians can no longer be taken for granted, then neither can the sustenance of key constitutional principles.[350]

As more recent events further strengthen these concerns then perhaps it is now time to consider whether the UK should have a set of rules that clearly prescribe the core principles and procedures of its system of government and that are enforceable in the courts. And if that is thought to be too fanciful or too difficult, then at least some piecemeal changes could be made. For example, as the Institute for Government has recently suggested, the Ministerial Code could be strengthened, with the Independent Adviser being able to launch investigations into its potential breach without needing to be invited to do so by the Prime Minister and by giving the Code some legal

---

[349] Ibid. Blick and Hennessy

[350] Ibid. Blick and Hennessy

underpinning in a similar way to the Civil Service Code.[351]

Of course, simply writing down the rules doesn't necessarily provide a solution. One only has to look at recent events in the United States to realise that written constitutions aren't the answer to all of a country's problems. But the consideration of one for the UK might at least prompt people to think a little more about the system that we now have. Are we actually comfortable with a system of government where so many of the rules are unwritten and, even where the rules are written down, they can easily be changed by simple majorities in a Parliament over which the government has considerable control? And beyond this overarching question, are we comfortable having an unelected Head of State? Have we devolved powers to Scotland, Wales and Northern Ireland that are sufficient to avoid the break-up of the United Kingdom? Are we happy with a House of Commons that lacks real potency when the government has a large majority and with a House of Lords whose members are largely appointed by the Prime Minister, has senior clerics from one branch of one religion guaranteed seats in it and is hamstrung due to its total lack of legitimacy? And are we comfortable with a UK electoral system that so distorts the views of the British people as expressed at the ballot box?

The ultimate test of any constitution is the fairness, order, peace and stability it creates in the society it serves. Viewed historically and comparatively on this measure, the British system may be thought to have scored well. But it has long contained within it inherent characteristics that bring both benefits and concerns. At one time I might have concluded that it brought those benefits and concerns in equal measure. But following the events since the Brexit referendum of June 2016, I'm less sure.

As I mentioned in the preface to this book, I worked for the governments of Thatcher, Major, Blair, Brown and Cameron with

---

[351] https://www.instituteforgovernment.org.uk/publications/updating-ministerial-code

little difficulty. Of course I didn't agree with all that each of them did – that would have been an impossibility. But I did understand that they had been democratically elected to run the country and that it was my job as a civil servant to help them do that as efficiently and effectively as possible. I also understood however that, in return, the ministers I served would play the game too, following not only the laws of the land but also its codes, conventions and unwritten rules. If we can no longer take this for granted, perhaps it's time to consider whether our 'make-it-up-as-we-go-along' constitution, with its lack of checks and balances and its hugely powerful executive, is one with which we wish to continue.

About the Author

Paul Grant was a civil servant in the UK Government from 1986-2012. For 20 years of that time he worked as a senior lecturer in Policy and Government at the National School of Government (NSG). He now works freelance, providing consultancy and training on the UK system of government.

At the NSG Paul designed and ran a range of training courses on various aspects of the UK system of government. A particular focus of his training was to provide new fast stream entrants to the Civil Service a thorough understanding of their new working environment.

Paul has a particular interest in constitutional and parliamentary matters. He has run training programmes in the UK and across the world for organisations both inside and outside of government.

Printed in Great Britain
by Amazon